Life in *limbo*

My battle with depression, infertility and mental illness

Some people seem to breeze through life and everything falls into place easily... but for others life can be a constant struggle. Matt's book offers an honest, intimate and heartfelt insight into the reality of infertility and mental illness, and gives hope to those who may be dealing with similar issues.

I understand from experience the journey to have a family is not always easy. I admire people like Matt and Ali, who have the courage and strength to take on the challenges and not only grow from them, but share their experience in the hope it will help others.

Mark Richards
1 x World Surfing Champion, 1 x World Masters Surfing Champion

I suffered from depression and I think that everybody has someone close to them that has suffered from it too. Everyday is a new day and the book, 'Life in Limbo' is a great read and shows just how easy it is to get depressed but there's always light at the end of the tunnel even though you don't know it at the time.

Mark Occhilupo
1 x World Surfing Champion

Life
in
limbo

My battle with depression, infertility and mental illness

BIG SKY PUBLISHING
www.bigskypublishing.com.au

Matt Barwick

Big Sky Publishing Pty Ltd
PO Box 303, Newport, NSW 2106, Australia
Phone: 1300 364 611
Fax: (61 2) 9918 2396
Email: info@bigskypublishing.com.au
Web: www.bigskypublishing.com.au

Cover design and typesetting: Think Productions
Author's Photo: Andrew Haynes

National Library of Australia Cataloguing-in-Publication entry (pbk)
Author: Barwick, Matt.
Title: Life in limbo : my battle with depression, infertility and mental illness / by Matt Barwick.
ISBN: 9781921941924 (pbk.)
Subjects: Barwick, Matt.
            Depression in men--Australia--Biography.
            Infertility, Male--Australia--Biography.
            Mental illness--Australia--Biography.
Dewey Number: 616.8527

National Library of Australia Cataloguing-in-Publication entry (ebook)
Author: Barwick, Matt.
Title: Life in limbo : my battle with depression, infertility and mental illness / by Matt Barwick.
ISBN: 9781921941931 (ebook : pdf)
Subjects: Barwick, Matt.
            Depression in men--Australia--Biography.
            Infertility, Male--Australia--Biography.
            Mental illness--Australia--Biography.
Dewey Number: 616.8527
Printed in China through Bookbuilders

If I keep holding out, will the light shine through?
Pearl Jam

For Ali, Ollie and Isobel
And for Steve

Contents

Chapter 1
Something's missing

So there I was, alongside my old schoolmate Anthony on his wedding day, sitting as groomsman at the bridal table. It should have been a happy occasion, yet I found myself sitting there, mulling over my life. Why do weddings cause such introspection? At 28 I was a fortunate guy—don't get me wrong—I had a lovely wife, challenging career, supportive friends and comfortable home. But I felt a lack of something. Was it kids? Sure, I have always adored mucking around with kids and found I could easily relate to them. But I wasn't ready for my own—something was holding me back.

Scanning the room, I caught a glimpse of a woman whose elegance and beauty instantly attracted my attention. But what I found most appealing was that she didn't appear to be pretentious, like many women of such natural beauty. Instead she seemed reserved, almost shy.

I tried not to stare as I unconvincingly surveyed other parts of the room, momentarily indulging in one of my favourite hobbies: people watching. There was much to absorb, as Italians approach everything with gusto—weddings in particular are a celebratory affair of sensory overload; you are expected to eat your body weight in pasta, dance and sing until your feet ache and lungs burn. There is no question they know how to put on a monumental party with all their extended family acknowledging a newfound union. Regardless of the generation all were enthusiastically involved, from the ageing grandfather showing style and confidence on the dance floor, to the energetic youngsters running amok, chasing one another playfully in, around and under the beautifully adorned tables. This joyous pandemonium was intriguing to observe, particularly for me being one of the few privileged non-Italian guests.

But my attention was pulled back to the woman across the room. I kept glancing at her throughout the evening, until at last I decided it was now or never. I stood up nervously and walked across the dance floor towards her, dodging frenetic dancers.

'I've been watching you all night', I said, trying to sound like those men in movies that have far more charisma than me.

'Really?' she replied blankly.

'You're stunning. Has anyone ever told you that?'

'Yes actually,' she said raising one eyebrow, 'my husband.'

'He's a lucky man. I wouldn't leave a woman as ravishing as you alone for a minute. Where is he, if you don't mind me asking?'

'Never you mind', she responded with a flirtatious smile which I took as an invitation to pursue her further. So without hesitation I gently drew her close, then kissed her long and sensually. It was just as I had imagined it would be. Perfect.

'You're so silly Matt,' said Ali, 'are you drunk?'

'Hardly, I've barely drunk a thing, I'm the designated driver—remember. We agreed it was your turn to have a few. I hope you're making the most of it!'

'It's not fair that I'm left at this table full of people I don't know, while you're up there on the *fancy* table.'

'I'm sorry babe but there's not much I can do about it—is there?'

'It's not the most fun way to spend our first wedding anniversary', she said, turning her head away in protest, preventing me from going in for another smooch.

'I know, but the night's still young babe—would you like to dance?'

'No, you know I hate dancing. How about we go outside for some fresh air instead?'

'Sounds good', I said with a wink, hopeful of some prolonged canoodling.

The night air was so cold that our breath hung like smoke and the back of our throats tingled. We contentedly nestled in each other's arms.

'What a great wedding', Ali said. 'It's so nice seeing all the different generations together—so many families.'

'Those Italians know how to breed better than most, that's for sure.'

'I know', Ali said. 'Did you hear Anthony mention in his speech that they're going to start trying for kids straight away?'

I looked away, sensing this was a loaded question. 'Yeah—talk about not wasting any time.'

'I've been wondering whether maybe we should start thinking about having kids soon.'

'How soon is soon?'

'Like now…'

Those two words hung in the air for a moment, as Ali tried to make eye contact to gauge my reaction, knowing full well I was hopeless at hiding my true feelings.

'I thought we'd agreed to wait till we were in our thirties', I said. 'I'm not sure I'm ready to be a dad yet.'

'It's not like you have a child straight away—it can take a while—and in the meantime we can get used to the idea.'

'You mean it doesn't happen overnight?' I responded, rolling my eyes.

'What are we waiting for—really—we're married, have a lovely home, good jobs, have done some travelling. There'll never be the *perfect* time. I think the time is right now.'

'I guess…'

Ali did have a point, I doubt whether there was ever going to be the perfect time. I have always wanted to be a father but I just felt I had so much more growing up to do myself before I was ready. Dads know stuff. Vital manly stuff like how to tie knots and fix things— they impart worldly knowledge. As I thought this through it dawned on me that by the time my child was pressing for the answers to all life's difficult questions, I would be several years older, well into my thirties, by which time I was bound to be more knowledgeable—failing that I could always revert to Google for advice, or whatever had taken its place by then. Besides, I knew I'd been wondering about kids myself recently—Ali had just beaten me to the punch.

'OK, let's do it!' I found myself saying.

'Are you serious?' Ali said. 'You want to start trying for a baby?'

'Yep, let's have a baby', I said, kissing Ali until her smile broke through the kiss.

So just like that we decided. Once the decision was made it was startling how comfortable I was with it. It was fitting that we agreed to embark on the next meaningful phase of our life together on the night of our first wedding anniversary. We returned to the reception and my eyes were immediately drawn to the young children playing without a care in the world. Watching the kids, I soon realised that the prospect of impending fatherhood was more exciting than daunting.

I was eager to leave the reception early as I had organised an anniversary surprise for Ali. We were to spend the night at the most exclusive five-star hotel in Canberra. I had already packed an overnight bag full of Ali's essentials (that her mother had kindly dropped off at the reception hall earlier in the day). I was convinced Ali didn't have any idea. But we were drawn into the celebrations and didn't leave until midnight. As we commenced the drive Ali noticed, even in her inebriated state, that we weren't taking the normal route home.

'Where are you going?' she quizzed.

'You'll see.'

Once we arrived at the hotel Ali was suitably impressed with both my gesture and the opulent surrounds. We ran ourselves a spa, lay back and let the warm bubbles massage our bodies. After the cleansing spa we retired to bed and made love. Afterwards, in the post-coital glow, it dawned on me with delight that our familiar companion of many years—Mr Contraception—would no longer be necessary. Good times were ahead.

This was definitely something that was going to take getting used to. Ali and I had been together since university, over ten years now. During our entire relationship we had been ultra-careful when it came to contraception. Even when utterly inebriated after a night out drinking I never ventured near the nether regions without the suitable attire. I treated my sperm as a highly volatile toxic substance that must be given no opportunity to journey towards its desired target. Ali was on the pill, which by itself is said to be 99.9 per cent effective, but we weren't taking any chances, because at that stage in our lives neither of us wanted a little dependant running around. Using two forms of contraception would put most people at ease. Not me. I recall one time we had a pregnancy scare, when the hardware failed. It wasn't a pleasant experience for either of us as we waited in trepidation for several weeks, but luckily the back-up did its job and we were in the clear. I remember our overwhelming relief. Every month I was relieved when Ali mentioned that our 'friend' had arrived: our code for her period—because you hear stories of couples who use condoms and the pill yet miraculously get one past the keeper. Things were definitely going to be different from now on.

The hotel suite appeared even more palatial in the soft spring morning light. We spent the morning taking photos and then having tea on one of the balconies that overlooked the croquet lawns while we leisurely watched the players below. All in all, it was the perfect morning—definitely a story for the grandkids.

That afternoon we had planned to have lunch at a café at the National Library, our wedding venue. It was our first time back since our wedding and, upon entering, fond memories came flooding back. None more so than our wedding dance to 'Better Together' by the Hawaiian artist Jack Johnson that was sung live by some local musicians who did a splendid rendition. They masterfully captured the laid-back essence of the melody that typified our relationship; the lyrics too resonated strongly with us:

Love is the answer
At least for most of the questions in my heart,
Like why are we here? And where do we go?
And how come it's so hard?
It's not always easy,
And sometimes life can be deceiving,
I'll tell you one thing, its always better when we're together.

We firmly held the view that it was indeed better when we were together, so we decided to have 'Better Together 8/10/05' engraved on the underside of our wedding bands to symbolise the fundamental spirit of our relationship. Undeniably, our union has always felt just right, as if we were soulmates, destined to be together forever.

The same cannot be said for other aspects of my life. From an early age I have always wished that I was one of those astonishingly gifted individuals who had oodles of talent in some particular pursuit and knew instinctively which direction to take. Was I meant to be doing something in particular which would enrich the lives of others and make a difference? What if what I was meant to be doing was never realised for lack of trying? How awful—a life wasted. I didn't covet fame or wealth, I just yearned for a more meaningful life beyond the ordinary— something *more*—but what exactly, I had no idea.

One thing is for certain: I have always found music mesmerising. I couldn't live without it. There can be a connection made between the artist and the audience and a common appreciation and understanding. Jack Johnson's 'Better Together' holds this significance for both Ali and me; it's *so* much more than just a song.

I was soon snapped back to the present by Ali who was eager to get back onto the topic of starting a family. I could see she was elated by the idea as she had barely touched her lunch, while I was busy devouring mine. Never one to really yell or raise her voice, she leaned expectantly towards me from across the table to improve her chances of being heard over the bustling lunch-time patrons.

'You're still cool about last night—about having kids and stuff?'

'Yep', I replied with my focus still on my plate.

'Well there are a few things we have to sort out.'

I casually put down my cutlery and looked up, sensing she wanted my undivided attention. 'Like what?' I said. 'I just assumed we'd have heaps of unprotected sex—which is fine by me.'

'Well there's that…' she said, shooting me a provocative grin. 'But I've gotta go off the pill and then I think they say you should wait three months before trying.'

'They—who're they? I want names…three months—you've got to be kidding!'

'That's what I've heard, I'll check with Ava though.'

Ava was a pint-sized Iranian, with a penchant for techno beats and anything purple, and her striking eyelashes were envied by all—even some of the boys. But beneath her beauty was a fiercely passionate individual, who always let her feelings be known. Ali and Ava were introduced at university around the time Ava met her future husband Niklas. On first impression, Niklas appeared to fit the stereotypical German mould: serious, polite and precise. But a closer inspection revealed a wittier and more carefree character—evidenced by his untamed mane and series of tattoos that likely symbolised rebellion against his strict German roots. Together they were an affable and spirited couple. Their good-natured and humorous outlook was contagious and we all soon became wonderful friends.

Ava and Niklas were the parenthood pioneers. They held the auspicious title of being the first of our friends to have a baby; beautiful Tara. I remember visiting them in hospital with Ali, days before I was due to embark on a boys-only ski trip to Canada. At the time our lives couldn't have been going in more different directions.

I was amazed at the transformation I witnessed. It was so apparent how this new arrival had instantly changed our friends. Suddenly there was a dependant who required constant attention and dictated that they become selflessly responsible for her health and wellbeing. But they didn't seem overly fazed by the prospect of this ongoing, round-the-clock commitment that I considered daunting. Sometimes you see footage of new parents looking shell-shocked—dumbfounded even—as if they have no clue what to do next. Not Ava and Niklas, they were naturals from day one it seemed, or at least well practised. During the months leading up to the birth Niklas, like any modern-day metro-sexual, took immense pleasure in practising nappy changing and attending breastfeeding classes. What exactly he learnt about breastfeeding that could be practically applied, I'm not entirely sure. Personally, I wouldn't dare interject and offer words of advice if my wife were having difficulties breast-feeding.

Despite being perfect parental prototypes from the outset, initially Ava showed some overly protective motherly instincts. I recall, during our first visit to the hospital, her barking at me, 'Matt, have you washed your hands?' before I even approached to touch the baby—which easily scared me into politely forgoing a hold. Not that I was overly eager for one in the first place, because, to be honest, newborns have always freaked me out more than a little. They look so helpless and fragile. When holding them there seemed to be a definite technique involved that eluded me. Supposedly, you have to provide constant support to the head. Some people are naturals at this and make it look so easy. I, on the other hand, tense and begin to cramp up after only a few minutes, even though I'm only holding something that weighs around three kilos. Eventually my unease is visible, with anguish written all over my face, and I'm relieved to be rescued by a more willing and capable onlooker.

At the time of Tara's birth, the sight of both Ava and Niklas seamlessly taking on their new roles with confidence and enthusiasm made it apparent to me that I was in *no way* ready to have a child. But now, some seven months later, I was well and truly warming to the prospect—which made me wonder whether men have a much less publicised biological clock of their own. Maybe the male population has been secretly keeping this valuable knowledge guarded for fear that our female companions may use it to their advantage and put the hard word on us.

As the months progressed the Richter family flourished—Ava and Niklas were role-model parents—no question. So obviously I was fine with Ali's suggestion to check with Ava on ideal 'baby baking' technicalities for our future bub in the oven. After all, there's nothing worse than getting the ingredients wrong when baking—the result can be disastrous.

I knew for certain that my mum was going to be overjoyed to learn that Ali and I were trying to have kids—because, at this point in time, she was still not a grandmother, much to her disappointment. She had given up dropping subtle hints to my older brother and only sibling Steve and me, realising that she wasn't getting any younger and if she was going to be able to enjoy her grandchildren her useless sons needed to get a move on. So instead she resorted to playing the martyr, unusual behaviour for such a stoic French lady. Her favourite saying had become: 'By the time I'm a grandmother I'll be too decrepit to help, you'll be pushing me around in a wheelchair!' And she no longer referred to 'them' as grandchildren, instead she preferred to use the term 'hypotheticals'.

Which she felt better encapsulated their likelihood. Steve and I were pretty competitive—like most bothers—we even joked how we virtually raced to get married. Fortunately, I won, marrying Ali five months before Steve and Nicole got hitched. But we never entered into a contest to see who could impregnate first—why? I'm not sure. Dad, however, was much less vocal about wanting grandchildren, probably because he had enough on his mind, having recently made the big move down the coast when he and mum separated after more than 30 years together.

When we told Ava and Niklas they were beyond excited.

'Excellent, a playmate for Tara!' Ava declared.

Sure enough, Ava had all the details. Ali was right, doctors did suggest that women wait three months after going off the pill because they needed to take folate during this time and ensure that sufficient quantities were in their system to prevent certain birth defects such as cystic fibrosis. Ava was also quick to point out that we needed to get private hospital health cover straight away because only after 12 months insurance cover were you eligible for a rebate on a hospital stay, which was another incentive to wait three months before trying. Oh the technicalities—I had no inkling!

I did, however, find it rather amusing that we couldn't just go about falling pregnant the old-fashioned way. After all, it appeared to work fine for our parents and grandparents. Ali's suggestion was obviously the modern-day approach, taking into consideration findings from the latest scientific studies on the topic. Or maybe this approach had more to do with Ali's Virgo nature, where things had to be planned, lists drawn up, a road map formulated, which could then be followed through religiously. In many respects this modus operandi suited me fine too, as I'm also a Virgo—the two 'Virgins' aspiring to have a child together. If our astrological signs had any say in the matter we were going to have no chance.

So we took Ava's advice. Ali went off the pill and started taking folate. Ali was also adamant that we not try to fall pregnant in those first three months, so she convinced me to still use a condom—I reluctantly agreed. On more than one occasion during that period I thought modern science has a lot to answer for. Nevertheless, our pursuit of 'hypotheticals' had begun.

Chapter 2
Up the duff in no time

The self-imposed three-month waiting period went swiftly as we busied ourselves with home renovations—our little piece of Oz that we pretended we owned, when in reality we were slaves to the mortgage monster like most of our generation. The place needed work as it was devoid of any architectural benefits. In summer we would sit in our sweltering lounge room of an evening and peel ourselves off the couch every so often to refill the ineffectual air-conditioner. By winter, the nation's capital would live up to its icy reputation and it was not uncommon for us to wake of a morning and see the warmth of our breath condense before our eyes. Despite its failings we were committed to making DIY improvements as best we could.

Our view was that we were both fit and healthy individuals. Neither of us smoked or drank alcohol excessively—so when the boom-gate was lifted (so to speak) it would only be a matter of months before Ali was up the duff. So we focused on trying to make our home hospitable for a new arrival. We were definitely in intensive 'nesting mode' and we knew that once the baby came we wouldn't have the time, money or energy for renovations.

I honestly expected that Ali would fall pregnant within the first few months, rendering her unable to assist, so that I would be left forging ahead with the baby deadline looming. But this was not the case. Every unsuccessful month that our 'friend' arrived there was a small sting of disappointment. But neither of us was overly concerned as we had only been trying for six months—surely this was just a slight detour before reaching parenthood. I would often joke with Ali and suggest that she not buy any feminine hygiene products in advance because this was sending her body mixed messages—tantamount to getting the inflatable mattress out before the unwanted 'friend' has even shown up.

Our problem may have been simple. Maybe, in hindsight, we just weren't shagging enough, because mostly we were both too tired from our DIY exploits. Perhaps the two Virgos were busy making sure every other part of our lives was in order and we overlooked putting the 'Bonk often' on the To-do list.

Even though we were only in the early stages of trying for children, we couldn't resist telling Charlie and Jen, or C&J as we fondly called them, who were our dearest friends. I met Charlie while working in a cinema, around the same time Ali and I got together. The part-time job was tolerable and the extra cash got me through university. Charlie was a projectionist and together we would spend many late-night shifts chatting about movies and music. Charlie was always entertaining to work with, particularly when he would endeavour to identify the exact time in a movie that nude scenes occurred and relay this crucial information to the male ushers so that they could coordinate their cinema checks to coincide with these opportune moments. He was not shy to admit he enjoyed the female form. Not surprisingly, Charlie was also somewhat of a lady's man—gradually making his way through the female staff while working his undeniable charm. That was until he met Jen, the only woman capable of taming him with her intellect, allure and compassion.

Jen is one of those rare effervescent individuals you feel blessed and privileged to call a friend. She brings positivity to almost all situations and simply thinking about her brightens your mood and makes you smile. In a world where it seems we are increasingly bombarded by bad people, doing atrocious acts, Jen is truly a Good Egg. She selflessly puts others before herself time and time again. If you have a problem, Jen has a problem. Even if you haven't disclosed your problem, she has the uncanny ability to sense when things aren't right and will tirelessly press, persist and persuade until you open up. She is relentless (but only with the best of intentions); her heart is always well and truly in the right place. But she won't nag you on Facebook, she's not interested in using social media to keep in touch with loved ones, preferring more organic, personal interaction. If it sounds like I'm her biggest fan, there are undoubtedly many more vocal supporters.

C&J married within a year of Ali and me, and the four of us have been tight ever since. So Ali and I saw telling them as a big step. We knew we couldn't keep it a secret from them because they knew us both too well. They would have been onto us as soon as our behaviour changed even slightly, particularly Ali not drinking alcohol. When we did break the news, Jen was her usual vocal self.

'What, I thought we had a pact?' insisted Jen. Referring to a supposed deal whereby Ali and Jen had previously agreed to fall pregnant around the same time. This strategy was seen to lessen the impact on the friendship and reduce any potential isolation or alienation brought on by the bub—one in, all in, type mentality. I could see the logic. I too would prefer being able to hang with Charlie if I had busted my leg and couldn't work for a year—if he could join me that would be ideal.

But Ali's response was swift and resolute.

'No, I never made a pact, you just assumed I did. Besides, you have years before you're thirty. I'm thirty next year! There's no way I'm waiting for you, I'll probably be all dried up and barren if I wait much longer!'

Despite our initial misfortune, those around us had more success. Ali's eldest sister, Rebecca, and her husband, Mark, had their first child, 'Stone'. Well that's what he was called while in utero, after Olivia, Ali's eloquent, petite middle sister, became fed up with dull nicknames like 'The Bump', so instead hatched 'Stone'—considered to be suitably rock inspired—after Rebecca, heavily pregnant, saw U2 in concert. Not a bad introduction to the live music experience for little 'Stone'. When the beautiful boy was born, 'Stone' remained his name for some time, much to our surprise. Both parents are exceptionally intelligent career professionals, Rebecca a doctor and Mark an IT specialist, yet together they appeared to genuinely struggle to come up with a suitable name for their son, despite being given ample warning of the deadline—nine months in fact. I suspect Mark was to blame given his addiction to research: he loves nothing more than getting the best deal possible.

Which I can understand when he's buying a toaster or mobile phone, but how can you really compare names—they're subjective. No amount of research can give you an answer. There is no answer—it's not like one name comes with more features than another, or has a better warranty or after sales service. Instead there is an abundance of choice, which I suspect was the cause of the delay.

Initially, Ali and I, together with other friends and family, were sent photos of 'Stone' over the internet. Childbirth is a wondrous feat but I'm not convinced that those first few shots of the baby ripe from the womb are all that necessary. Babies, seconds old, often look akin to a grotesque creature from the *Alien* movies—not the most flattering of images of mother or child. Yes, these photos are a record for posterity of this momentous event, but they can be excessively graphic in nature. And with the advent of digital cameras there is no limit to the number and resolution of photos that are taken at this time.

Mark, being a self-confessed techno-boffin, delighted in taking and distributing umpteen shots of a couple's truly private moment. Some of these shots showed exhausted Rebecca looking the worse for wear and still in a somewhat drug-induced haze which made me question whether these photos had been vetted by Rebecca prior to widespread publication over the web. Once cast into cyberspace who knows where they could end up. By the time Ali and I came to Sydney to visit several days later the name 'Luke' was finally chosen and seemed to fit quite well. Luke looked decidedly cuter than those first few images which was a huge relief. As I said before, my experience with newborns was limited, but I was officially now an uncle for the first time, and I'm not sure what I would have said or done had Luke turned out to be an ugly baby. Don't deny it—it does happen. Let's be honest, not all babies are cute. Some have facial features that are already way out of proportion, like a massive nose or huge ears. The worst case, however, in my opinion, is when the infant already resembles physical characteristics of an elderly person. Sure when confronted with a less than attractive baby everyone still coos and says the appropriately predictable remarks like 'he's *so* cute'. The problem is I'm not that good an actor and more often than not my facial expressions betray my best effort at being polite and civil.

I can be performing suitable commentary while my eyes are bulging out of my head and my jaw has dropped to the floor—aghast at the ghastly creation before me. No such problem with Luke, he was an adorable bundle—thank goodness, otherwise I may have been labelled the 'nasty' uncle from the outset.

Ali and I both took turns at holding Luke and he was wonderfully accommodating, not showing any signs of distress. At the time I couldn't help but indulge my imagination and pretend, just for an instant, that this was our child, which filled me with an immense sense of adoration, achievement and pride. I could see in Ali's eyes that she desperately wanted this—to be in this position. I really wanted this too. It absolutely did feel like the greatest symbol of a couple's love.

The second success story was that of Anthony and Isla, who welcomed their first son, Thomas, into the world around nine months after their honeymoon, by our calculations. Anthony was the man with the Golden Gun: one shot, one kid. A real Deadeye Dick. We knew they were going to start trying after the wedding but this was ridiculously efficient—which did make me feel a little inadequate, given that by this stage Ali and I had been trying for around seven months, to no avail. We were yet to break the dreaded one-year milestone of trying, so I refused to consider the notion that there was a possibility that we couldn't have kids and how we would cope in such an event. Later, watching Ali hold Thomas, the image again sat very comfortably with me. I prayed that our time would come soon. Ali was undoubtedly ready. Simply observing how affectionate, caring and compassionate she was with these babies made it clear she would make an outstanding mother—I just hoped it was going to be soon.

Chapter 3
Pregnant?

Then something remarkable happened.

'Our *friend*'s late', Ali announced one evening after work as we casually cooked dinner.

'Seriously?'

'Yep…'

'But our *friend* is never late.'

'I know.'

In fact our 'friend' is renowned for being exceptionally punctual—like a German train. Come to think of it Ali is part-German; maybe she had inherited some of this German precision and timing. I stopped chopping the vegies and put the knife down, concerned that the conversation might distract me enough to lose a digit.

'How late is late?' I asked, not wanting to sound too excited.

'A couple of days I think.'

'Really…' I said, trying to hide the smile that was already creeping across my face. 'Should we get a test done?' I suggested, again trying not to get our hopes up.

'I suppose it couldn't hurt, but let's wait a few days first.'

'OK.'

The next few days were a torturous wait. Despite my best attempts to be nonchalant and wait patiently in the hope that by some miracle (or more accurately a heap of intercourse) our 'friend' had decided to go on a nine-month hiatus, I started to indulge in the idea of being a dad and slowly release the emotional handbrake that had been holding back such thoughts. Suddenly, I possessed an altered perspective on life.

Stressful issues at work became trivial and nothing could faze me. It all seemed like insignificant gumf compared to the possibility of being a father—life had a new meaning and purpose.

Finally the agreed 'test day' arrived, still with no sign of our unwanted 'friend'. The anticipation was palpable. I had a fitful night's sleep contemplating the joyous outcome—having to seriously rein in my excited mind that was restlessly contemplating all the pleasant deeds that would have to be done once we were pregnant: ultrasounds, nursery decorating, buying baby paraphernalia, telling family and friends. The list was endless but I considered each item to be a privilege.

That day, Ali turned to me in bed. 'Should I do it now?' she asked, the excitement evident in her voice, like a child aching to unwrap presents at Christmas.

'Now's as good a time as any', I replied. 'Do you want me to come with you?'

'To the toilet…? No! I'm just peeing on a stick.'

'Gee, sorry for asking. I figured you might need moral support.'

'It takes a while to get a result. Once I've done *the business,* I'll come back.'

'And what are we hoping for again?' I asked.

Ali looked at me sideways, trying to gauge whether my question was an honest one, or whether I was playing the fool.

'To be pregnant…' she shot back with a fake grimace.

'I know *that*, but what indicates we're pregnant on the stick thing?'

'Oh…red's positive, blue's negative—I think', replied Ali, as she fumbled to retrieve and re-read the instructions.

'Can we make sure we're clear on that.'

'Yep, it says here: red positive, blue negative.'

'And just to confirm, positive means "pregnant" yes?'

'Of course!' Ali said. 'Stop being silly, what else could it mean?'

'Well it depends on the circumstance', I replied. 'If someone didn't want to be pregnant, then a positive outcome for them would be a negative result.'

'Stop trying to confuse me, can we just do this—*please.*'

'Sorry, I'll stop muckin' around. Good luck', I said, giving her a kiss before she leapt out of bed and bound eagerly down the cold corridor.

Ali came back minutes later holding the pen-like pregnancy tester. We sat together on the bed staring at the indicator panel, not daring to blink for fear of missing the result. Time seemed to stand still as we waited expectantly. *A watched pot never boils,* I felt like saying but thought better of it considering Ali had clearly grown tired of my comedic routine. The seconds passed excruciatingly slowly, then the minutes. Then, without warning, the tester changed colour. Blue. Not an indecisive pale blue or better still a reddy-blue. No, this was an unmistakable dark blue. There was no denying the results were in: we were categorically, certifiably, not pregnant.

As the unwelcome result sunk in we both looked visibly deflated and held one another for some time. Ali was clearly withholding tears and I tried to find the appropriate response to console her but found I was lost for words, overcome by complete shock and disbelief. Ali finally broke the silence.

'We should get ready for work, otherwise we'll be late.'

She made her way to the shower and I was left alone on the bed staring at the blue stick, slowly shaking my head.

'Fuck…', I murmured.

Which was the best I could come up with.

Eventually, I too got up and started dressing for work. As I retrieved my shoes from the bottom of the wardrobe I spotted a small A4-size box that I hadn't noticed before. Intrigued, I picked up the box that was yellow with a pattern of white polka-dots. Without thinking I opened it and was confronted by something that snapped at my heartstrings. It was a book titled *My Baby Book* with a charming caricature of a mother hen and two chicks encircled by a love heart. I carefully flicked through the pages and each one caused another unwelcome twang on my already reverberating heart. Obviously the book was intended for parents to document the significant stages of their newborn's life. Pages with titles like: *we are having a baby!; put your ultrasound pic here; the day you were born; the first time you …* etc. I was both mesmerised and saddened by this unexpected find. Had I discovered this book several weeks earlier it probably wouldn't have affected me so profoundly, but given the emotional roller-coaster of the past few days it served as a timely and harsh reminder of how close we'd imagined we'd come to starting this journey.

I was interrupted from these thoughts by Ali's fragrant scent as she scampered past me naked from her shower and began to dress.

'What's this?' I said, trying to sound nonchalant.

'Nothing, just a book I bought for if we get pregnant', she said.

Ali continued to dress, seemingly unperturbed by my finding. She turned her back, opened the wardrobe, then hesitated, as if unsure of what to wear. Then I heard the faintest sob from the other side of the door and I hurried to console her in my arms. Eventually the tears eased and she spoke.

'I saw it at the shops and I couldn't resist', she said, her voice breaking. 'Rebecca has a similar one for Luke and it's so cute, did you see...?'

'Yes, I saw how ridiculously cute it is.'

'If we don't have kids we can just give it to someone as a present', Ali said. 'I don't want you to think I've become some crazed pregnancy-obsessed freak!'

'Look babe, it's important we remain positive—our time will come—I promise.'

'OK.'

But this discovery had disturbed me. I didn't think it was a good idea to purchase such items. What next, baby clothes, toys etc? It highlighted the potential for an unhealthy habit to form. I was already thinking that maybe Ali was starting to show signs of becoming fixated on having a baby. What worried me most about this was that I'm a firm believer in the theory that your state of mind plays a considerable role in your health and wellbeing. If Ali was uptight and stressed about falling pregnant this could further inhibit our chances. It could easily become a vicious cycle. If our attempts (and subsequent failures) became more protracted, Ali's behaviour might spiral into dogged determination, particularly if she were fast approaching 40—the age many women wanting children find horrifying, as their eggs are down to seriously low numbers.

This scenario was reminiscent of a TV documentary Ali and I had once stumbled on. It was about a group of women who couldn't orgasm despite their committed efforts. Many of these women had tried all types of assistance from countless sexual aids, aromatherapies, acupuncture, tantric techniques, pills, potions and porn. You name it, they had tried it, but to no avail. The documentary was trialling a new form of experimental therapy that shot tiny pulses of electricity through electrodes into the women's vaginas to stimulate orgasm.

What we found to be most confronting and downright hilarious, at the time, was how focused and intent these women were on reaching orgasm. One woman was adamant that she felt that she wasn't truly a woman without having experienced an orgasm—that she hadn't truly lived and her life was devoid of satisfaction. She spoke with such conviction of her fierce dissatisfaction. All the while her husband was sitting beside her, with shame and inadequacy written all over his browbeaten face. Another participant spoke of how she was constantly plagued by the longing to orgasm. She said she often found herself scowling at random women in the street and was filled with jealousy and rage at the prospect of all the powerful, mind-blowing orgasms everyone else was enjoying.

In the end, the invasive procedure worked for some women and they experienced the fabled heights of sexual rapture—if only momentarily. Others had no such release, no fire-works, no pins and needles. Nothing. These women were left feeling more inferior, isolated and dejected than before.

Now I was left wondering whether Ali was gradually heading down a similar road? Would she start to stare at pregnant women, ogle newborns and glare enviously at their mothers? Would she turn over the channel every time a baby food commercial was on TV? Would she become increasingly angry and frustrated at our inability to conceive to the point of breakdown, suffering a severe case of baby-rabies? Would I be a pitiful husband like the ones in the TV documentary, incapable of giving his wife what she so desperately wanted? Was that possible, or was I reading too much into the situation? After all, it was only a baby book and I too had something that I had been hiding from her.

I had been given a plastic toolset from my work colleagues as a secret-Santa present some years ago. I had held onto it all these years because I dreamt that one day it would be a perfect plaything for our own child. Was this behaviour much different to Ali's? Granted, I hadn't bought the toy, it had been given to me, but I still held onto it and was hopeful that *my* child would be its recipient rather than someone else's.

A couple of nights later, after the disappointment had dissipated somewhat, we both lay in bed together, quietly reading our respective books, when I decided to bring up my 'orgasm women' concerns, just for my peace of mind.

'Babe, can I ask you something?'

'Sure', she replied.

'How are you coping with all this … pregnancy … stuff?'

'How'd you mean?' she replied, without even lifting her head from between the pages.

'I'm just worried …'

'Why?'

'The baby book …' I said, motioning towards its hiding place in the wardrobe.

'I know how it must look, but I just thought it'd be nice—that's all', she said, lifting her eyes. 'Is there really anything wrong with that?'

'No. I just don't want you to get like those "orgasm women" from that documentary we saw that time—remember?'

'Please … I'm nothing like *those* women, they were batty', Ali asserted defiantly.

'We must try and maintain a positive frame of mind. It's very important—promise.'

'I promise.'

Chapter 4
'If' we get pregnant, not 'when'

We decided it was time to forget our pregnancy preoccupation for a bit and spend a week in sunny Queensland—the perfect escape from the last of the icy Canberra winter. But I had an ulterior motive. I remembered Anthony's father dispensing sage conception advice to the groomsmen during pre-wedding rituals: *Relax* was the crux of his message and he was speaking from experience as Anthony had taken some time to be conceived. At the time I recall being indifferent to his counsel as I had figured my plunge into parenthood would be some time off. How wrong I was, as that evening marked the beginning of this quest. Now, given his wise recommendation, I found myself trying to monitor my stress levels in case they were somehow messing up the quality of my baby gravy. I didn't feel particularly tense but sometimes it's hard to tell. Actually, come to think of it, in many ways I was living every adolescent boy's dream: enjoying copious amounts of copulation with a stunning woman. Needless to say I was hopeful that having a break by the sea, free from work pressures, would do the trick and we would finally fall pregnant.

The vacation was fantastic—rejuvenating beyond expectation but unfortunately we had no luck on the pregnancy front. Despite our best efforts to remain positive and upbeat about our pregnancy prospects, after the eighth unsuccessful month the seed of doubt regarding infertility was planted in our minds where it began to flourish. The usual tone of optimism that accompanied any reference to children started to change too. We found ourselves both more reservedly saying '*If* we have kids…' where previously we had spoken with resounding enthusiasm and confidence '*When* we have kids…' Arguably a minor difference, easily overlooked by some, but for us it was the beginning of a monumental shift in mindset.

We started to briefly discuss what our options might be if it turned out we were barren.

IVF: Both of us were against the idea from the outset. All the hormone drugs, egg collecting, and cryogenically freezing of embryos made it sound more like a sci-fi experiment than the creation of human life. We considered the rigmarole too invasive and unnatural a process—not to mention costly.

Sperm or egg donor: Ali was quite open to the notion of receiving either sperm or an egg from someone else, depending on where the problem was. Ali's take was that at least the child would be created by one of us. This alternative did not sit well with me because, from my perspective, the child wouldn't have any biological link whatsoever to one of us—not showing any resemblance to either its supposed father or mother. I personally would feel like the third wheel, the non-contributing bystander, if my lousy, languid sperm was the culprit and I was relegated to watching from the sidelines.

Surrogate pregnancy: We both agreed that the many underlying complexities relating to surrogacy—finding a willing surrogate, legal custody arrangements, adoption rights—were all too daunting and potentially problematic. Not that our opinion was based on any prior knowledge of the surrogacy laws in Australia; rather, our biased view came from having seen too many American TV shows on surrogacy complications.

Adoption: Ali was opposed to the thought of adoption because she had worked in family policy and had heard too many gloomy stories about the difficulties of adoption and I tended to agree with her.

No children: This was a saddening prospect but one that seemed increasingly possible given recent failures. So we tried to put a positive spin on being eternal DINKS (Dual Income No Kids). Obviously there would be some financial benefits to being childless. But really I had no idea how substantial, until we sat down and did the maths. I was astonished to discover that today in Australia it's commonly accepted that a single child will cost around $250,000 from birth to early adulthood, when they are expected to leave the nest. Unless you're Italian that is, then that figure probably doubles given that some of my Italian mates happily stayed at home well into their thirties—much to the dismay of their parents who subsequently saw their retirement delayed indefinitely.

We toyed with the idea of how frivolous we could be with the surplus funds: buy a holiday house, frequent overseas trips, work part-time and volunteer more. We tried to convince ourselves that it was a viable—almost attractive—option. We could get two dogs, provided Sweep was accommodating. We would surround ourselves with our friends' and families' children—taking great pleasure in becoming known as the 'crazy' aunt and uncle renowned for spoiling all the nieces and nephews silly with lavish excursions and exorbitant gifts.

Deep down though we both knew that the DINKS option meant missing out on a whole lot—something that you can't simply put a price on—something that is rarely well articulated but commonly understood. These ruminations reminded me of a fine example that encapsulated the jubilance of being a parent. Many years ago at work, in my early twenties when the notion of having little tackers was a distant desire, I was given a congratulatory card to sign for a colleague who had just had her first child. Initially, I sat there for some time lost for the right words, as I had no actual appreciation for the enormity of this experience. I scanned the other comments of support and found that they mostly shared the same stale obligatory sentiment with little consideration given. Until I came across one written by a young mother herself which read: 'You will wonder how you ever lived before, enjoy!'

This simple statement resonated with me as it hinted at a more fulfilled life with children.

The final option was the most dire: *separation,* to allow the fertile member of the partnership the opportunity for a family elsewhere.

When I brought it up, Ali was quick to dismiss it.

'It doesn't work without you. *Better Together* remember!' she replied almost in tears.

I was comforted and reassured by the conviction of her response but not altogether convinced. Sure, if we were to discover that Ali was barren,

I personally would have been willing to concede that we couldn't have children and continue to live a charmed and fulfilled life together. No question it would be painful to come to terms with at first but over time I would have come to accept our fate. But I saw the opposite scenario, of me shooting blanks, as far more distressing. Increasingly, as my own unease regarding my possible infertility descended like a dark, ominous cloud of uncertainty, my fears that Ali may leave me escalated. Because even as a male I could recognise and appreciate the primordial urge to be a mother. This is an exceptional bond like no other. I had heard countless examples of women say that mothering a child is the greatest, most natural, perfect experience of their lives. And while I knew the love Ali and I share is amazing and special I didn't know how it compares to that unique implicit love fostered between a mother and child. There is no question that Ali would be an extraordinary mother and subsequently I wasn't sure that I could willingly let her forgo that experience simply to be with me. How could I deny her another chance at the most natural of gifts? How could I be so selfish? I adore and care for her too much to cause her any pain or anguish. *If you love someone, set them free …* isn't that how the saying goes? It would have broken my heart to see her leave but the alternative of living with the guilt would be too much to bear.

Moreover, a part of me feared that maybe she wasn't being truthful with herself when she voiced unwavering support for our relationship. What if she was subconsciously denying her true feelings, suppressing her innermost desire to be a mother? Then years, or decades later, when her eggs had well and truly dried up and there was no possible chance of her ever being a mum, she started to resent me for not being able to give her what she so badly wanted? Her resentment, being only slight at first, could burgeon with ferocity as the years progressed until eventually the relationship—which we assumed was unbreakable—was shattered beyond recognition and we separated. I'm not sure which would be worse: losing her now or losing her later. In desperation I began to ask for help from a higher being, not that I'm overly religious, but when all else fails a little divine intervention couldn't hurt. Not that I was requesting immaculate conception—I was still a more than willing participant.

Chapter 5
The child lottery: Tiger or terrific kid?

I love spending time with kids, I always have. They are heaps of fun. I envy their ability to keep it simple, to maintain an uncomplicated outlook on things, where enjoyment seems to take centre stage. This enjoyment doesn't necessarily have to come from overly contrived and complicated activities. Often the simpler pursuits are the most rewarding and fun. Like a swing or a game of hide-and-seek. The latter has pretty basic rules but in the right surroundings can provide hours of entertainment: the exhilaration of hiding and the anticipation of hunting down the prey. Games like this are the foundation of many a happy childhood.

I find that when I'm around kids a bit of their childish perspective rubs off on me, if only for a while, and for a moment I feel young at heart. Time becomes irrelevant. This is a welcome relief from my normal adult outlook where trivial daily pressures seem habitually to preoccupy my subconscious. In the company of children you can clown around, play the fool and observers just think you're being an enthusiastic and attentive minder. I love all that stuff: Easter egg hunts, water fights, pulling moronic faces, making funny noises, all of which can be unfairly frowned upon as juvenile by some, if children aren't present.

Most of all I adore how you can be downright silly in their company and they revel in your stupidity and are instant accomplices. Or how you can conjure up absurdly illogical games with the most unlikely of props and they will gladly play along, even when they aren't entirely sure what the purpose of the game is. They are willing contributors regardless. The essence being: what does it matter, as long as we're all having fun, right? If we could somehow bottle this attitude and call it 'the essence of youth' there would soon be a global shortage.

It was my eagerness to connect with my inner child that motivated me to introduce an activity at my work's annual Open Day. The Open Day showcases to the general public what the scientific organisation I work for does, and the activities are designed to encourage family participation. This year I decided to introduce a treasure-hunt game, where kids use a hand-held GPS (Global Positioning System) unit to navigate to hidden treasures around the expansive grounds of the work complex, while at the same time learning a little about mapping, which is what I do for a profession.

The treasure hunt was a real hit with the kids and parents alike. The little ones, in particular, quickly became accustomed to the GPS and were thrilled to run around after the treasure. I too had loads of fun, being mischievous and trying my best to lead them astray, not wanting them to find the treasure too easily. The children's energy and enthusiasm was infectious. At one point though I did begin to feel a little overwhelmed being surrounded by all these happy families. Part of me started to feel marginally jealous and glum at the possibility that there was a chance that I might miss out on being a dad and attending events like this. Then Tiger rocked up and changed all that.

You heard him before you saw him. He made terrible growling sounds in the distance like a pack of hungry dogs and the notion of volume control was lost on this child. He was relentlessly loud. The boy didn't walk. He raced everywhere and never stopped. Eventually, his mother literally grabbed him by the scruff of the neck and held him still. She had a glazed look of exhaustion on her face, as if she was operating on auto-pilot, trying desperately to conserve what little energy she had left. She almost seemed removed from reality, as if she had mentally gone off to some quiet, tranquil sanctuary far from this manic, unstoppable force.

'Hi guys', I said, trying to sound as inviting as possible. 'What's your name, mate?'

'Tiger!' he screamed, jumping up and down on the spot still in the grasp of his mother.

'Can I leave him with you?' Tiger's mother pleaded, shiny beads of sweat appearing on her forehead.

'No, sorry, all kids must be accompanied by an adult', I replied in the most authoritative tone I could muster—her disappointment evident. I quickly explained to the gathered crowd how the activity was going to operate. Then the instant I finished my spiel Tiger was off, like a greyhound that hadn't been exercised in months.

'Tiger commme baaaack, it's a treasure hunt ... not a race!' Tiger's mother yelled in a hoarse and broken voice.

But this did little to suppress his non-stop, bull-at-a-gate approach. Clearly he knew no other speed than flat out. He was indeed Tiger by name, Tiger by nature. I wondered if this had always been his name since birth, or whether this was just a nickname that had stuck for good reason. I considered asking his mother but thought better of it. While we were walking around the treasure-hunt course I summoned the courage to enquire about Tiger, as I had never experienced such terror first-hand and was honestly taken aback by his relentless behaviour.

'Gee, Tiger's got some energy...'

'You don't know the half of it', she responded, shaking her head knowingly.

'I see why they ban red cordial', I replied, trying to inject a little humour. But she was having none of it—nothing was funny about her circumstance.

'I wish it were that simple', she said, looking ahead to where her son ran rampant in the distance.

'Is he ... always ... like this?'

'Pretty much', she replied, looking like a defeated woman.

I was lost for words. I really felt for this hapless woman. Life can be blatantly cruel. Clearly Tiger had some behavioural disorder like ADHD and was a handful 24/7. What a nightmare. I'm not sure I could cope. Suddenly, as terrible as it sounds, I saw a potential upside to not being able to have children—there would be no chance of having a Tiger.

Later that afternoon I heard an announcement over the PA system. It was about Tiger or, more accurately, a call to Tiger's mother to come and collect him from reception. Somehow they had become separated.

I dare say she had knowingly gone AWOL for a period, in a last-ditch effort to get some much needed respite.

For the final scheduled treasure hunt of the day a friend and colleague, David, arrived with his wife, Erica, and their two children, a girl and boy, aged eight and three. I willingly chaperoned them around the course and they were a delight—so polite, sweet, smart and engaging— quietly determined to complete the treasure hunt. They were both a pleasure to be around, undeniably terrific. Within minutes of being in their company my aspiration to have children was reignited, even knowing the risks of having a Tiger. Who was I kidding; I still wanted to be a dad badly. Although the experience of having been around so many different kids throughout the day really made me see that having a child is a lottery, in that you have no inkling of the type of child you're going to get: a Tiger or a terrific kid.

The following day at work, David stopped by my desk with a gift. He explained how the previous evening, spontaneously and unprompted, both his kids wanted to make me a card as a thank you for taking them on the activity. The handmade cards were charming, decorated with a vibrant array of texta-colours but most of all it was the imperfections that were so endearing—how they were a funny non-symmetrical shape—yet the care and attention was evident. Inside each card was a personal message of thanks, which their parents must have helped with. I immediately pinned both these cards to my cubicle wall where they have remained ever since as a constant reminder of how enjoyable and adorable kids can be.

Chapter 6
The nephew drop

For someone with no previous experience of babies, I had certainly been receiving an unprecedented amount of baby exposure of late which showed no signs of abating when Rebecca brought Luke down from Sydney for an unexpected visit. I found it astonishing how much Luke had changed in the several months since we had first seen him at the hospital. He had so much more movement and control over his limbs. Rebecca even showed us how he had started doing baby push-ups—unbelievable! Although I realised that a baby constantly changes as soon as it's out of the oven I had no idea *what* happens *when*, such as when they typically start to crawl, walk, talk, feed themselves, abandon nappies, read, ride a bike, play chess, learn to drive—any of these milestones. I assumed there were countless reference books on the subject but I had never had a need to read them.

So when Rebecca asked if I would like a hold I had no sense of what to expect. The last time I held Luke he was immobile, all wrapped up in the cocoon of a blanket. All I had to do was support his head with my shoulder—although I even managed to find this difficult. Now she passed me something that looked much more like a miniature person, with arms and legs flailing around independently. I knelt down over the playrug that had been set up in our lounge room and held Luke with one arm around his waist and the other cushioning his bottom. He appeared quite content in this position, so I chatted to Rebecca who was sitting in the couch opposite.

'Gee, he's so squirmy, he moves heaps more since we last saw him', I said.

'They grow up pretty fast', replied Rebecca.

'He's got so much strength for a little tacker, particularly in his legs.'

'He sure does, we think he'll be a rugby player one day.'

'I can see why!'

In my peripheral vision I noticed Ali sidle up to the two of us. She knelt down and started making obligatory baby noises. I was distracted by the conversation with Rebecca but assumed Ali was coming in for a hold of Luke so I began to lessen my grip. But Ali wasn't expecting Luke at all. In an instant he fell face first onto the floor. *Thump!*

'Maaaaatt!' Ali yelled—and she never yells and hardly ever calls me Matt—so I knew I had messed up big-time—really dropped-the-ball (pardon the pun). She gave me a look of sheer disbelief. It was a scathing look that I had never seen before which clearly said *How could you?* without the need of a word being uttered. This was a real maternal look of disappointment. As if suddenly this shameful act cast doubt over our entire relationship and, more specifically, my suitability to raise progeny.

There was a moment's silence, then Luke let out an almighty howl. Ali scooped him up and passed him straight to Rebecca. Immediately I was struck by the god-awful thought that he had hurt himself badly. Had he broken something? Are babies that brittle? *Please let him be OK.* Several minutes elapsed and Rebecca consoled Luke like only a mother can and gradually his howling lessened to crying which eventually dissipated to infrequent sobs. All the while Ali stared at me and I had nowhere to hide from her fierce glare.

Rebecca didn't seem nearly as distressed by the whole sordid affair and was remarkably forgiving once she realised there was no permanent damage done. I, on the other hand, was a little harder to convince.

'He's fine', said Rebecca. 'Aren't you, little man? Just a little bit shocked … that's all. It's OK.'

'Are you sure he hasn't hurt himself?' I said. 'He hit the floor with a hell of a thump. Thank God I was kneeling down and not standing up.'

'Thank God for the cushioning of 1970s shag-pile carpet', Rebecca said with a laugh.

Luke eventually settled, at which point Ali and I engaged in a rather heated dispute as to how this occurred and who was at fault.

'What happened?' Ali asked, looking ashamed.

'I don't know … I just figured you were taking him, so I lessened my grip.'

'But what made you think that?'

'… Just that you were so close to me and talking to Luke.'

'That doesn't mean I'm automatically going to hold him!'

'You're right, it's all my fault—sorry—my mistake.'

'Mistake—you dropped our nephew!' Ali scolded. 'You have to be more careful next time.'

'Oh don't worry, there won't be a next time', I replied. 'I promise not to hold Luke until his 18th birthday.'

'Don't be silly.'

'I'm serious—Rebecca I'm so sorry.'

Despite my best effort to apportion blame elsewhere, it was futile—I had no real argument—it was baseless. The harsh reality was that I was solely to blame and I knew it. I had dropped my only nephew—plain and simple. Embarrassed Uncle Move #1: The Drop. Never before had I been so ashamed, embarrassed and sick in the pit of my guts.

Moreover, I became consumed by feelings of doubt regarding my abilities as a father. I had always taken great comfort in the expectation that I would be an excellent dad when the time came. I had nothing much to base this on other than people saying to me 'Oh you are so good with kids' but obviously this latest incident suggested otherwise. Sure I may be excellent at *playing* with children but whether I could actually look after them was another question altogether. Maybe this was a sign that I wasn't cut out to be a father after all. Maybe I lacked the essential parental instincts and was instead destined to forever be the crazy (and unpredictable) uncle (who sporadically dropped children).

Soon after the episode Ali was off to the gym leaving me with Rebecca and Luke. The first few minutes after Ali's departure were awkward to say the least. Luke, although no longer crying, still showed signs of distress. I found myself trying to break the silence by repeatedly apologising for my stupidity.

'Shit, I'm sooo sorry. Shit, I can't believe I dropped Luke. Shit, I'm sooo sorry.'

Eventually Rebecca changed the subject and we discussed various topics and I enquired about how she was finding being a mother—how reality compared to her expectations. After half an hour or so Luke looked as content as ever in his mother's arms and had calmed down completely. Maybe it wasn't the worst situation after all—no harm, no foul—I had certainly learnt my lesson that's for sure.

'Matt, would you like another hold of Luke?' Rebecca asked, much to my surprise.

'No, thanks, I'm fine. I reckon I've caused enough grief for one evening.'

'Are you sure?'

'Yep, anyway, he'd probably start to wail being anywhere near me— poor little guy.'

'Give it another go', she insisted.

'Seriously, you're willing to trust me again?'

'Sure', she said, with confidence happily passing Luke to me.

This time I was sitting on the floor cross-legged with Luke in my lap. I instantly put two hands firmly around his waist, possibly tighter than necessary, but I wasn't taking any risks—not this time. To my astonishment he didn't object at being held by his terrifying uncle. Instead he seemed quite relaxed and subdued, content to take in the surroundings with stern concentration. I began to relax, but not my grip. Rebecca and I started chatting again and I sensed my confidence returning. Then unexpectedly Luke launched himself clear out of my tight grasp with the commitment and assurance of a BASE jumper. I had no inkling he was capable of such a move. There were no warning signs, no initial squirming to forewarn of such an athletic feat. Luke went from stationary and calm to a projectile in an instant. I was consciously holding him in a way that prevented him from falling *forward* but not *up*. I had no idea he was capable of up! *I am such an amateur.*

He flew horizontally ahead of me for what seemed like an eternity, then landed heavily, face-first, spread-eagled, only centimetres from the unforgiving edge of a solid timber coffee table. Luke's previous outburst was nothing compared to the horrific distress he voiced, reaching unimaginable decibels. Rebecca quickly picked him up and assessed him for serious injury. He had a slight red nose but, apart from that, he looked to have again escaped relatively unscathed, but his screams didn't let up, even after a considerable time, which made Rebecca look visibly shaken and upset. The relentlessness of his anguish started to concern Rebecca, so she again inspected for damage, but found nothing. I was left to observe this horrendous scene that I had caused, in stunned silence—left to contemplate my arrant ineptitude and incompetence.

I couldn't believe what had just happened—*again*. I was being so careful. Thank God he didn't hit the coffee table; he could have done some serious damage. How would I live with myself if he had been permanently scarred by the experience? You can dismiss a once off, learn from it and move on. The first mistake is excusable to a degree, but the second is sheer stupidity. The Virgo in me was so disappointed in myself.

Rebecca insisted it was time to go and started to pack up Luke's things and I helped, where I could, and loaded the baby paraphernalia into the car. I again apologised profusely for my poor baby-handling skills but I sensed Rebecca was really itching to go—to be free of the uncoordinated uncle who had caused such mayhem. I waved goodbye then returned to the house.

Once inside I was alone—alone with my foolishness. I placed my hands over my face and yelled

'Fuck! ... Idiot ... Idiot ... Idiot ... Fuck!

I continued to berate myself over and over in this terribly inarticulate and ineloquent manner. Sometimes I find only a few choice words are needed to really encapsulate the moment. I couldn't fathom what had just happened. Dropping my nephew twice within half an hour, how blatantly inexcusable and shameful.

I then wondered what the protocol for such an unthinkable act was? Should I ring Mark the father and apologise in advance? How should I go about explaining such a sordid sequence of events? Should I contact the grandparents and apologise to them as well? Would I become the laughing stock of the entire extended family, forever ridiculed and forbidden from having contact with young children? Would my mishap be eternally to blame for any and all of Luke's future failings or transgressions no matter how minor—my name used in vain when the kid didn't do his homework or clean his bedroom later in life, skipped school or broke his curfew as a teenager?

I was lost as to what to do next. One thing was certain: I had to tell Ali. I couldn't possibly keep it from her—which I dreaded given her severe reaction to the first incident.

Ali came home from the gym and the instant she opened the door I was fessing up like a guilt-ridden Catholic at confession. I explained, in some detail, what happened and could hardly believe the words that were coming from my mouth.

'You did what … again … how!' she bellowed, her face aghast.

I tried in vain to somehow justify my ineptitude to her but there was no escape, no absolution. No comforting words of support or forgiveness from my wife. Not this time. Instead all I got was a look of complete disgust.

'Maybe it'll be a good thing if we don't have kids?' I said sarcastically with a shrug of the shoulders, trying to lighten the mood. But this poor shot at humour was met with an even harsher look.

'Just jokes …' I added quickly, trying to diffuse the situation, but it was too late, the damage was done.

Days later I still felt overwhelming guilt over the dual dropping drama. In an attempt to expunge the continuing shame and remorse from my mind, I recounted the harrowing story to C&J to gauge their reaction to the severity of these transgressions. They were both shocked but appeared equally baffled at how I repeated the accidental blunder. This time I refrained from trying to explain the bungle.

Then Charlie recounted a child-care story of his own, which involved a close friend of his brothers, who was out to dinner one night with his wife and their two young children, both under the age of 12 months. At the end of the evening the family made their way to the car, with the husband slightly inebriated and the wife the sober designated driver. Once at the car the father started to collapse the stroller to put it in the boot. But despite his concerted efforts he couldn't quite seem to make it fit as it usually did—his inability undoubtedly affected by his alcoholic stupor, and the dimly lit car-park making it difficult to diagnose the problem—yet he persisted in trying various angles, but became increasingly frustrated by his failure to make it fit, given this was something he had done successfully countless times before. Being a typical male he eventually resorted to the only remaining option: brute force, pushing hard against the pram in one final try—still no success. Then, in a moment of terrifying clarity, he realised what the problem was. Both of the kids were still *in* the collapsed pram. Astonishingly, both were still sound asleep and despite this forceful encounter neither suffered any lasting effects from the ordeal.

For a moment I was left speechless, wondering whether to laugh or cry at this story.

'See, don't worry about it mate', said Charlie. 'I'm sure Luke's fine—a little drop's nothing—besides you'd be amazed how flexible kids are!'

'That story is a shocker,' I replied, 'I don't feel quite as bad about what I did now.'

Several days later Ali and I were invited to the Richters' for dinner. Still not feeling completely absolved I was compelled to exorcise my demons further and again recount the dropping episodes.

'Matthew, how could you!' said Ava, her exotic Persian eyes boring an indelible hole in my conscience.

None of my friends ever call me Matthew, except Ava, when she scorns my behaviour. Niklas, however, was much more relaxed, as usual.

'Ah that's nothing', he said. 'Dude … don't stress. Kids are real bendy.'

'Says *you*, who dropped *our* beautiful daughter.'

Niklas scrunched his face as if the reminder caused him physical pain. 'Ahhh … yeahhhhh …'

'On concrete!' said Ava, shooting Niklas a searing scowl.

'Well … ahhh.'

'How did that happen?' I interjected.

'Tara was in her high-chair on the back porch, I turned around to get something, she jumped straight out and landed head-first on the cement.'

'Really, that's horrific.'

'Tell me about it,' said Ava, throwing her arms in the air. 'I leave her alone with Papa and look what happens. Men: they can't be trusted.'

'Actually, it was pretty bad', said Niklas. 'Poor Tara made a lot of noise—we were real worried—we ended up going to casualty.'

'And was she OK?'

'Yeah, turned out it was just a bad bruise', said Ava, with a look of concern that only a mother can give. 'But it was scary at the time, we thought she might have a fracture, or brain damage, or something.'

I was relieved that even my parenting idols could commit such a blunder. Maybe there was hope for me yet.

Chapter 7
Holidays: catalyst to conception?

Approaching the end of the year there was still no sign of a baby despite our partaking in a religious routine of lovemaking virtually every second day, the act of which was thoroughly enjoyable but the lack of result was disheartening. We had well and truly expected to have a bun in the oven by now and after 10 months of trying we were confronted with somewhat of a dilemma. We had promised some time ago that we would visit friends who were living and working in New York on a two-year secondment. With less than nine months remaining on their stay, we knew we had to start thinking about when we might schedule our visit. Increasingly, as their overseas experience was nearing the end, our friends had been repeatedly asking us for details of when they could expect us, because they had numerous other visitors whom they had to accommodate and they wanted to ensure no double bookings.

If only we could have been honest about our predicament then I'm adamant it wouldn't have been so difficult. Instead we had to be subtly non-committal whenever the topic was raised. This was extraordinarily difficult for a pair of Virgos like us, as we thrive on planning things down to the last detail and being clear about our future endeavours; being vague and carefree about such plans goes very much against the grain.

But we were in a quandary. How do you plan for a holiday when you are hoping to pop? The main problem, as we saw it, was avoiding any travel during the first trimester when plane travel is mildly discouraged as some studies suggest there is a greater risk of miscarriage. But we weren't pregnant. Our lives were on hold. We found it difficult to commit to an agreed date.

A colleague of Ali's had been in an identical situation and had booked flights to New York but fallen pregnant so was forced to cancel the holiday. We saw this as a bitter-sweet outcome, one which we would be jubilant to find ourselves in. So we decided to book our flights arriving in the west coast of USA in mid-March. This date gave us another four months of trying before departure.

Really, we wished that, like Ali's colleague, our commitment to the future would somehow be the catalyst to our conceiving. That somehow Ali's eggs and my sperm would sense that now, unlike in the many previous months, wouldn't be the most ideal time for the two to get together. Then, like a pair of rebellious lovers, they would become more enthusiastic about engaging in their tryst, just to prove a point more than anything. This thinking defied logic and was downright foolish—I know. However, loads of plain old shagging alone clearly wasn't working for us; we considered anything was worth a shot. If we could somehow trick ourselves into conception we would be ecstatic with the outcome.

Besides, we didn't really have a choice. We had to arrange some sort of vacation as the two of us had accrued oodles of leave, which our employers were pressuring us to use. I realise how ridiculous this sounds—how rarely the two words 'leave' and 'pressured' are uttered together. Normal people, those not waiting expectantly for an event that is ten months overdue (and counting), have active social lives and can't wait to go on holidays, and often find themselves with a leave balance in arrears—from having too much to do and not enough downtime in which to do it. Whereas Ali and I were the opposite, exhibiting the behaviour of expectant parents in waiting—willingly putting our urges to explore the globe on hold. Instead we saved our leave once we started trying for a baby, so that we would have the maximum amount of time off when it eventually came. Although neither of us anticipated our current childless position after such a long period.

Chapter 8
Avalanche of announcements

The New Year's holidays arrived and they were a welcome break from the monotony of work. We had organised a few relaxing days down the coast with C&J and the Richter family. On arrival at the family beach house Ali and I immediately went about resuscitating the place as it was dark, dank and briny from lack of occupants. Soon the sun and salty breeze filled the rooms. We had barely unpacked our things when the phone rang. It was Ava.

'I just wanted to check the food situation?'

'We've pretty much got everything', I replied.

'Are you sure, what's on the menu, is there any seafood?' I started to go through the list of assorted foods that we had decided upon earlier, including seafood, which I knew Ava loved.

'So there *is* seafood?' Ava confirmed, sounding worried. 'What about soft cheese?'

'We have plenty of Camembert and Blue Cheese—all your favourites—trust me, we have food covered.'

But Ava didn't seem satisfied by my response. Instead she still seemed disturbed about the culinary arrangements.

'There may be a problem on the food front.'

'Why, what's wrong?'

'Nothing's *wrong*, it's just that we have some news ...' There was a long pause, where I thought the phone might have gone dead.

'We're pregnant again!' In an instant all the questions regarding the food made sense. I tried to sound as blithe as possible.

'That's fantastic, congratulations!' Ali overheard me and jumped up screaming.

'Congratulations … for what?'

'Ava and Niklas are pregnant.'

'Seriously, wow, that's wonderful news', said Ali, as I passed her the phone to offer her own words of support.

Several hours later, when the Richter family arrived, they were immediately plied with questions from the girls about Ava's pregnancy. How far advanced was she? Was it planned? Who's the father? All the usual. They explained that Ava was around four months pregnant and how they desperately wanted to tell us earlier but were holding off in the hope that Ali and I would have a similar announcement around the same time. Alas that was not to be. My response was curt.

'Gee, if you're waiting for us, you may have been announcing it when the kid was two years old.'

As a joke I started calling Ava 'the Vessel'. My persistent dissing had the desired effect as she soon showed some mild objection towards such a derogatory title and defended her position with a barrage of quick-witted retorts.

Despite my banter, I was thrilled by the news and didn't begrudge them an ounce of happiness. If anything I felt a little guilty, hoping that Ali's and my failed attempts hadn't in some way taken the shine off this momentous and rare occasion. I hoped that Ava and Niklas hadn't been suppressing their feelings of excitement and joy on our behalf. Moreover, the last thing I wanted was their pity. I would be mortified if it ever came to a point where the mere topic of children wasn't discussed in our presence for fear it might upset the 'unstable' childless couple.

The New Year's Eve celebrations were full of revelry. Buoyed by this latest development everyone was in great spirits. The alcohol flowed freely and we indulged in a smorgasbord of seafood. All of us except Ava, of course, who had to avoid the food and alcohol she enjoys for obvious reasons but this did nothing to dull her mood because she was understandably elated by the presence of her precious cargo.

As usual Tara was enchanting and in no way cramped our style. Rather she was the life of the party and entertained us with her singing and dancing. She was brimming with confidence and now had a broad vocabulary at her disposal. I was astounded by how quickly she had grown up. The night was truly a family affair and the perfect illustration of how to raise a child, in my opinion. It showed how having a child shouldn't mean the end of social events with friends because such events don't fit in with the regimented child-rearing routine. Children should be allowed to adapt to their parents' lifestyle.

As the beginning of another year approached we bid farewell to Tara as she was put to bed without tantrum. The adults continued to party into the wee hours of the morning, drinking and playing cards—having a boisterous time. More than once I was compelled to ask Niklas whether we should keep it down for Tara who was sleeping in her room down the corridor.

'Dude, don't worry,' he said, 'she's used to it and sleeps through anything.'

I was left in awe of Ava and Niklas again exhibiting their relaxed and effortless perfect parenting style.

That night, after everyone had retired to their rooms, Ali and I were as committed as ever to maintain our frequency of fervent frivolity between the sheets. The only problem was the house had paper-thin walls and we were in serious danger of being overheard. We both knew too well that regular romps were of paramount importance, irrespective of the suitability of the location. We soon realised that the only way to successfully engage in this venture without detection was via stealth-mode and not our usual exuberant approach. So we decided to slow things down—a lot—like two snails getting it on with neither being hard-pressed for time. Not the raunchiest of images, I know, but you get the idea. We later termed this effective technique the 'lazy dirty'.

The following day we all emerged from slumber by late morning a little worse for wear. Except Ava, who was her usual sassy and effervescent self, having not abused her liver in welcoming the New Year, and was up early playing with an equally sprightly Tara.

Ali and I had a quick breakfast, then went off to visit other friends, David and Erica, holidaying in a beachfront bungalow nearby. When we arrived Erica invited us in from the blistering heat for a welcome cool drink on the couch. Then the kids, with Dad in tow, returned from a morning on the beach, gleefully encrusted with salt and sand, and in need of refreshment after dragging up from the water all sorts of beach paraphernalia: flippers, buckets, goggles, towels. Erica was nursing their other recent addition to the Anderson clan, who was less than a year old. The older kids were given ice-blocks, much to their delight, and with treat in hand they went off to play with some other children from the neighbouring bungalow.

'They're go, go, go aren't they', I commented.

'Always', said David.

'How do you keep up?' Ali asked.

'We don't half the time,' sighed Erica, 'luckily they entertain one another.'

'That's handy', I said. 'How was your New Year's celebrations?'

David poured me some more refreshing home-made lemonade. 'Quiet. We'd crashed well before midnight. But the kids were up at sparrows to drag me down to the beach with 'em. How about you?'

'We had a fantastic time,' I said, 'stayed up well past our bedtime having a good old laugh—drinking and playing games.'

'I remember those days, partying without kids', said David, looking seaward towards the distant horizon like an old seadog reminiscing over remarkable voyages from a lifetime ago.

'It wasn't a child-free zone,' said Ali, 'friends had their two-year-old with them.'

'That's impressive', said Erica. 'Actually … we have something to tell you guys … we're having another baby!'

For a moment I sat in stunned silence, my mouth closed, playing with ice using my tongue. The announcement wasn't shocking. After all, they were clearly a baby-making factory. It was just that it seemed that some couples were born to breed in serious quantities, while others struggled to bring one addition into their lives. It was as simple as that. Erica is one of those mothers who looks like she would be capable of caring for countless kids—an entire football team wouldn't faze her—the more, the merrier.

Ali soon piped up with the appropriate words of congratulation, realising that I was off in my own little world of contemplation and self-pity. I eventually followed with words of similar sentiment, but wondered whether my facial expression betrayed their insincerity—

again. We didn't stay much longer after that; we said our goodbyes and wished them an enjoyable remainder of their holiday.

We sat in the sweltering car, our faces instantly flushed by the oven-like conditions, the air-con rattling full-bore yet struggling to have any impact.

'You can't be serious!' I yelled over the racket.

'Some people have all the luck', Ali said, dejected. 'They've got three and one on the way. We just want *one*.'

The following day we bid the Richters farewell and headed up to Sydney with C&J. We planned to meet up for lunch with Pat, an old work colleague of mine whom we hadn't seen in many months. Ever since he moved to 'couple land' he had become particularly elusive. This was uncharted territory for Pat, who had a renowned reputation as very much the Casanova and who enjoyed spreading his wild oats. So I was intrigued to meet Jade, his newest partner, who appeared to have tamed the wild Pat.

On arrival Pat was sitting alone in the café taking in the picturesque outlook of the inlet where shimmering turquoise water snaked its way through the golden sand out into the ocean. 'Hey Pat, long time no see mate. Happy New Year's!' I said as we approached.

Pat stood up and we shook hands vigorously like Aussie blokes do. 'Same to you mate.'

'Where's Jade?'

'She's on her way.'

We spent the next while in animated conversation, eagerly catching up on things. Then, in walked a lady who stood expectantly at the end of our table. 'Guys, this is Jade', said Pat, leaning over to give her a kiss, clearly smitten. A doting look I had never witnessed before from the normally unflappable Mr Charisma.

'G'day everyone', said Jade, who looked overwhelmed at meeting so many of Pat's friends at once.

We all introduced ourselves and started to peruse the menu. When the time came to order Jade said that she wouldn't be joining us for lunch as she wasn't feeling well.

'Gee, your New Year's must've been massive—still recovering 48 hours later?' I commented.

Jade went silent and Pat looked sheepish, an all too familiar look. *Don't tell me … Not them as well? They've only been together for a few months. They couldn't possibly…*

'Jade and I are having a baby!'

Unbelievable!

Again the all too familiar pleasantries were exchanged. We gathered from the way they talked that this revelation was as much of a surprise to them as it was to us. Pat looked shell-shocked, making us think that they had only recently found out they were pregnant and neither had come to terms with it yet.

If the previous announcements over the past few days had affected me, this latest one had me positively stunned—three out of four. You've got to be kidding, give a guy a break. Was this Karma repaying me for some awful deed in a past life? Dropping Luke perhaps? Or was I involved in some secret social experiment to test my resolve and patience under such duress? To see how I would cope if everyone around me fell pregnant. Could I keep it together?

Lunch was necessarily brief as we had a considerable distance to travel before the day's end. We said farewell to Pat and wished him and Jade all the best for the coming months.

As soon as we returned to the confines of the car Jen, as usual, was quick to voice her support, always selfless and optimistic, there to shoulder others' problems. 'Guys, I'm so sorry. It must be hard hearing all your friends falling pregnant. Hang in there, your time will come. I know it.'

'Thanks Jen', Ali and I replied in unison still stunned.

'Well at least Charlie and I can categorically say that we are *not* pregnant, nor are we planning to be, any time soon—and that's a promise!'

Chapter 9
Technically infertile

January came and went and still no success. The disappointment was more pronounced as we had now surpassed the dreaded year since we began trying to fall pregnant. We were technically now classified as an 'infertile couple', according to Ali who had been doing some research on the topic. Just like that we had become a statistic, in a category I had never expected to find ourselves in, and I was not at all comfortable with the label. Not merely because of all the negative connotations but because it also heralded a watershed moment from which there was no turning back—we now had to seek medical intervention into why we hadn't fallen pregnant naturally.

This genuinely saddened me and, apart from dreading the thought that there was anything biologically wrong with either of us, I was upset because, from my perspective, we had missed out on a unique opportunity as our baby, if it ever did come, would be no longer simply a naturally formed genesis of our love for one another. Instead, from this point forward, the process was to be tainted by consultations to discuss clinical, scientific procedures. This was not how Mother Nature intended progeny to be conceived.

I began to feel immensely jealous, realising that we would never 'fall' pregnant like so many of those around us. I wondered how this commonly used term originated. We 'fall' over and hurt ourselves. The word implies an unexpected accident or mishap, which is odd in relation to pregnancy. As if 'oops' we didn't think *that* could happen—and indeed for some couples this is true, Pat and Jade being a case in point. But others, who may be trying their darnedest to have a baby will, when the time comes, inevitably announce that they too have 'fallen' pregnant.

I consciously avoided using the term because I got irritated every time I heard it, since for me it implies an element of ease and unexpectedness—neither of which encapsulates what the future held for Ali and me unfortunately. Our path to conception was likely to be more accurately defined by words such as 'induce', 'cajole', or 'meddle'.

At this unwelcome milestone, part of me, however, began to think that maybe we shouldn't intervene. That we shouldn't meddle and instead should just play the hand we had been dealt in life. People all have different hardships or disabilities thrust upon them in life. Maybe infertility was the cross that we had to bear. Maybe, genetically speaking, it was in our best interests not to have a child. But from our discussions over the many months of failure I knew Ali held the opposing view. She was open and enthusiastic to explore the other options modern medicine had to offer that would increase our chances of conception. So that was exactly what we were going to do because I didn't have the heart to disappoint her.

So Ali booked in with her GP to have some blood tests done. The results were positive—she was ovulating, which was a good start. But it turned the spotlight directly onto me and whether or not I was producing quality baby batter. Few things are as emasculating as the prospect of shooting blanks. Men joke about it constantly but that is probably because they realise that, genetically speaking, it is of the upmost importance and subsequently the topic is never far from our subconscious. I was hopeful, however, that my sperm was just fine, since I had always done my best to keep them happy—like wearing boxer shorts from an early age (once I found out that it helps to regulate the temperature of the testicles for ideal sperm production). Also, I have been fortunate enough to never have suffered any major testicular trauma. Unlike a dear friend of mine who, in his youth, slid down a tree truck, but got snagged by a protruding nail that sliced his scrotum open—leaving his testicles exposed, dangling like a pair of ripened cherries. Fortunately, my only minor mishaps in the nether region had been the infrequent knee to the groin from my older brother during adolescent fights.

Despite my optimism I still had to get a sperm-analysis test done, which obviously required me to provide a sample. Thankfully I was told I could do this in the privacy of my own home, which was a relief. I was given a small plastic container by my doc in which to do the business and was under strict instructions to deliver it to the clinic for testing within 15 minutes of collection. Otherwise there was a risk that the little swimmers would all stop swimming—which would require a re-sample—not the result I was hoping for.

The next morning my usual pre-work routine was well and truly disrupted. Just before leaving the house I adjourned to the bathroom. For a short period of time I was a little flummoxed as to how I was going to effectively get the required projectile fluid successfully into the small container, which was looking tinier and tinier by the minute. Quite frankly, at the point of climax such considerations are normally the furthest thing from my mind and I questioned whether I would have the fine motor skills at my readiness in which to achieve this collection. Heaven forbid if I were to miss the mark completely; I doubt whether there would be any point in trying to salvage the sample off the bathroom floor. Finding traces of dust or, worse still, microscopic organisms would surely have the clinic asking serious questions. What's worse was the fact that I couldn't exactly give it a practice shot. Well, I suppose I could, but there would be some delay between collections and I knew Ali was waiting. Furthermore, I suspected the second round of swimmers may be inferior to the first.

By this stage I had worked myself up into a bit of frenzy and really wasn't in the mood. But I knew there was a job to be done. So I did my best to imagine arousing scenarios and in due time produced the goods, miraculously hitting the target at the critical moment—although nearly dropping the container on the floor in the process. I observed the contents momentarily, wondering if this sample was really indicative of my best efforts—but I had no real way of knowing.

With my precious cargo wrapped up and kept warm in my pocket, as instructed, I hurriedly made my way in the car to the clinic, dropping Ali off to work on the way. The morning traffic was unusually hectic and I found myself frantically weaving between cars. As the time elapsed I began speeding in order to make the deadline—wondering how I would try and explain the reason behind my misdemeanour to the police were they to pull me over. Fortunately I arrived with no such encounter but with only a few minutes to spare. Flustered by the morning's ordeal, I had no time to gather myself. I had to deliver the goods immediately.

I made my way up to the entrance, towards a set of heavily tinted automatic doors which failed to open on approach. I looked at my watch: 8:02 am. *The clinic should have been open by now*. I stepped back from the doors as a lady stormed up beside me.

'Haven't the slackers opened yet?'

'Nope, I don't think so', I replied.

Irritated, she started banging on the glass door. 'Let us in guys!'

Suddenly the doors opened and she marched in like she was on a mission. I hung back momentarily, not wanting to look as pushy, then I noticed beside the door there was a crate of milk cartons, which I gathered must be their daily delivery. As a gentlemanly gesture I decided to carry the delivery into the clinic. Once inside I made my way to the reception desk and placed the crate on the counter. I waited patiently while overhearing the loud woman chat casually with several of the staff members who had congregated in and around the reception desk area. It appeared that this lady either worked here or was unusually familiar with the staff. Meanwhile, no-one paid me any attention for some time and I started to get concerned about my impending deadline and the viability of my cargo.

'Excuse me', I said politely interjecting.

'Yes', one of the ladies behind the reception responded.

'I've got a delivery.'

'Oh, that's great, just leave it there', she said and continued with her lively conversation full of colourful language I would expect to hear at a footy match and not at a medical facility. I was a little confused by her response, so I tried to clarify.

'Sorry, I mean ... I have a *sample* to deliver.'

There was a moment's silence while she took in my response.

'My apologies dear, I thought you were the milkman!' she replied, snapping into her professional demeanour. Upon hearing this distinct change in tone the remaining group quickly realised that I was a patient and started scattering like cockroaches to their respective posts. I handed over my sample and associated paperwork. Keen to make a quick exit I turned to go.

'Excuse me sir, there are some details you haven't filled out.' I turned back around as the lady motioned towards some blank sections on the label of the container. *Damn it!* I had been so preoccupied with successfully collecting the sample, then making sure I got it to the clinic on time, I had totally forgot about filling out the details on the container.

'Sorry, I completely forgot.'

'That's fine, I can fill it out now for you if you'd like', she said with pen poised.

'Sure, thanks', I said, less than excited.

'Your name sir?'

'Matt Barwick.'

'Date of birth?'

'6/9/77'

'Sample time?' she asked, with not even the slightest hesitation. I wasn't expecting this question and it stumped me a little. I looked at my watch and did the calculation.

' ... 7:50 am.' Then the lady mumbled something I couldn't quite make out.

'Pardon', I said.

'How long since you last had sex?' she said quietly, looking uncomfortable.

I hesitated for an age, my cheeks flushed with embarrassment. Umming and ahhing, to make it look like I was deep in thought, when in reality my brain had gone blank. I hate being put on the spot with questions, let alone ones of such a personal nature. I hadn't foreseen this question coming. *Shit!* I'm not sure of the answer. Was it five days? Possibly even longer. Was I better off over- or under-estimating? At least I knew it wasn't something horrendous like several months. Eventually, I decided on a conservative estimate of seven days.

'Thank you sir, that's all the information we need.'

I was left thinking: really … are you sure that is all the info you require? What about the size of my penis? Or the time taken to ejaculate? Surely you need these critical details for your database as well? I scurried from the clinic mortified with embarrassment. Did that all really happen? I sat in the car and burst into laughter, as I replayed the entire scene in my head.

One week later, I was yet to hear any word of my results. Eager to find out I decided to ring my GP to force the issue. Unfortunately, he was unavailable, but I asked the receptionist whether she could check in his absence. She hesitantly agreed. Meanwhile I waited expectantly on the end of the line. When she returned to the phone she made a noise like she was rustling through a mountain of paperwork. She mumbled to herself, giving me the impression that she was struggling to interpret the results, which put me on edge. Then, without warning, she remarked. 'Here it is … the result was … normal.'

I was elated to hear the word 'normal'— a word that is more often used to describe the customary or mundane. But in this context it sounded to me more like 'fabulous' or 'thriving'. I let the word wash over me and felt a surge of relief. 'Sorry sir, my apologies, actually it says here "effectively normal".'

'What? "Effectively normal", what does that mean?' I queried anxiously.

'I don't know sir, you'll have to confirm that with the doctor, goodbye.'

'But …'

Then I was left with the dial tone, unable to learn more of my result. The receptionist was obviously eager not to get caught up in trying to explain medical terminology. I couldn't blame her either. I would've done exactly the same in her position—which left me alone to ponder what 'effectively normal' meant. How does that differ from 'normal'? Clearly there was some qualification or distinction being made here. Were my sperm effectively swimming well, but backwards? When I finally got onto my GP he explained that he was no expert at interpreting these kinds of results and suggested that we arrange to see a fertility clinic. One minute I was giving a sperm sample, the next I was being sent to a fertility clinic so they could better decipher the results. *This couldn't be a good sign.* Rather, this was beginning to sound pretty dire and appeared to be swiftly escalating in a direction I was seriously hoping to avoid. It seemed that we were not alone in our pursuit for progeny as the relatively new fertility clinic Isis (named after the ancient Egyptian goddess of fertility) was already heavily booked in advance. We were keen to go to this particular clinic because it was locally owned and operated, more holistic in its approach and it treated couples in an individual and caring fashion—so we were willing to wait. We managed to secure an appointment in several months time, the same week we were due to return from our overseas trip no less. So regrettably I was left with ample time to deliberate, fret and stew over what may be wrong with my baby gravy. Great! That's just the kind of distraction I needed on our long-awaited holiday.

Chapter 10
Birthday party pressures

A week before our overseas departure Ali and I were invited to Tara's second birthday party. I recalled having enjoyed Tara's first birthday party which had been a first for me too. There had been lots of Ava and Niklas's friends from university in attendance and we all got to know one another while eating fairy bread and chocolate crackles. So we were thrilled to be asked and were looking forward to catching up with their many friends again.

We rocked up a little later than expected and the majority of guests were already mingling and had congregated in the backyard but the festivities hadn't gotten into full swing yet. As I surveyed the visitors I was surprised that I didn't recognise anyone from Tara's first birthday party. I did notice though that there were significantly more infants at this gathering, all of whom were around the same age as Tara, running around like crazed miniature adults, with their respective parents in tow. I did a quick head-count then turned to Ali with a look of horror and whispered, 'Guess what? I think we are the only non-parents here.'

'No!' she said, whipping her head towards mine.

'Yep, have a look around.'

'Surely not, there were heaps of *other* people at Tara's first birthday', she said scanning the guests rapidly.

'Yep, but not this time.'

'That's OK, we can still mingle with the parents.'

'Yeah, you're right.'

As we worked our way through the crowd, we started to introduce ourselves to various parents and tried to strike up conversations. But repeated attempts at this proved futile. We just couldn't get past the usual introductory pleasantries because the parent would be preoccupied with keeping a constant watchful eye on their child. I previously hadn't ever talked to someone who was so blatantly not listening and I found it pretty insulting and demeaning. At one point I was introducing myself to a lady when she quickly excused herself and grabbed her child who was engaging in some mischievous behaviour just out of her reach. To my surprise she didn't return to continue with our chat, leaving me stranded and feeling immensely awkward. Even trying to engage with Ava and Niklas was unsuccessful, as both of them were too busy running around trying to coordinate the birthday activities.

I did overhear the occasional conversation between tight-knit groups of mothers who were talking knowledgably about various aspects of motherhood. Not exactly the type of chat that either Ali or I could provide any meaningful contribution towards. Eventually, after countless failed attempts, we both gave up trying to get to know the other guests, as their focus was clearly elsewhere and why wouldn't it be? I would be mortified if I were a parent and got so distracted during a conversation with someone I had just met at a party that I failed to notice my child running around with a knife in hand.

So with no-one to talk to but each other and nothing really to do, we retreated into the shadowy periphery and became the estranged, creepy childless observers, watching the little tackers play contrived games closely supervised by their doting parents. At this point I was sure the majority of guests were wondering: *What are* they *doing here? They don't have any children?*

'This is a shocker', I whispered in Ali's ear as I held her in front of me like a shield to deflect the humiliation.

'Tell me about it, I feel like the invisible, childless freak.'

'Do you reckon they can all sense that we're pricks?'

'Pricks?'

'Partners Really Invested in Conceiving Kids Soon!'

'Cripes, probably', said Ali. 'And we've only been here for 15 minutes. Can you believe that?'

'Really, that's not good', I said. 'How long do these parties normally go for anyway? Surely all the little tackers can't keep up this pace for long. They are bound to crash for their afternoon nap soon?'

'That depends—they're having a heap of sugar.'

'So we could be here for hours?'

'Possibly.'

'Shit.'

At the conclusion of some drawing games, Ava announced it was time for a sing-a-long. I have always enjoyed a good children's ditty or two so I eagerly emerged from my retreat in the hope that I could participate. Ava started the CD player and the opening chords of the tune were instantly recognised by the entire throng—except for Ali and me. The kids and adults sang along in unison and made the appropriate accompanying hand gestures. I tried my best to keep up, but my pathetic rendition only added to my embarrassment for the day. But I was not too disheartened as I was hopeful that there must be some songs coming up that I recognised. The next song was another new one I had never heard, and the one after that. This wasn't looking promising at all. Whatever happened to the classics like *Baa, Baa Black Sheep* that I knew and cherished. Don't tell me these songs have gone the same way as other classic memories from my childhood like the TV show *Noddy*—relegated to the scrapheap because some supposed authority considered them inappropriate in today's society fixated on political correctness. Feeling even more like a useless spectator I returned downcast to Ali who witnessed the entire debacle.

'Well … that didn't go as expected. I didn't know any of *those* songs', I mumbled in a defeated tone.

'Don't worry, obviously we're from a different planet.'

'Yeah, PRICKS from planet DINKS.'

We both chuckled quietly, revelling in our own private joke. Eventually the singing ended and it was time for the highlight in proceedings: the cake cutting and present opening. Niklas noticed the sorry sight of Ali and me sitting in silence alone together on the fringe of the party and came over to join us briefly.

'Matt, can you film this bit mate?' Niklas asked, handing me the camcorder.

'Sure!' I said, keen to be given something to make me feel useful. Not realising that in doing so I was leaving Ali in the lurch.

Suddenly, I was thrust into the thick of things, filming amidst all the organised chaos. Watching all the kids' eyes transfixed on the burning candles atop a colourfully adorned cake—yearning for a piece. This was what I loved so much about children; how they could get so caught up in the moment that nothing else matters except getting a slice of that deliciously moist and sweet-looking cake. *I love cake, I need cake, I must have cake.* It was hilarious to observe them squawk and quarrel over who got to blow out the candles. The notion that this was Tara's birthday, and not their own, was understandably lost on all these youngsters. Subsequently, the parents were forced to repeatedly restrain their child so they didn't intervene in what was meant to be Tara's moment.

The cake was eventually distributed to the kids and virtual silence descended on the group as I tried to document the giddy excitement and sheer glee these kids were experiencing at devouring the cake. It was fascinating to watch how differently each of the children (all the same age) tackled eating this prized fare. Some used their hands with great dexterity and picked delicately and selectively at either the icing or the cake, others used cutlery with surprising success—all savouring every glorious mouthful. Except for one boy who looked delirious with pleasure as he picked up his entire piece and rammed it into his gob in an effort to try and consume it in one giant mouthful. *I love cake, I need cake, I must have cake.* He continued to push the cake into his mouth at a rate of knots but couldn't swallow it quickly enough, causing a cascade of crumbs to shower down from his mouth and leaving a thick smear of blue icing across his face. This icing soon combined with his saliva to create a continuous stream of blue drool—the likes of which I had never seen before—which ran down his mouth, off his chin and onto his pristine party outfit.

In the ensuing chaos my involuntary shakes of laughter made it exceedingly hard to keep the camera still. I looked over at Ali and she too was laughing hysterically, as were many of the parents. I gestured towards the boy with the face full of blue icing but clearly Ali had already seen him. Then I realised that the child's mother had noticed us laughing at her son. For a moment the mother looked mortified at our behaviour and she started to try and clean him up but she soon realised there was little point, besides the kid was obviously having the time of his life. So she too joined in laughing at the state he was in. Kids are classic. What an understatement to say that children enrich your life. I wanted one.

Suddenly I could appreciate why parents go to so much trouble to make these first few parties such a grandiose affair: because of the utter joy they bring. Children grow up so fast and the years fly by and there would quickly come a time when the simple birthday cake would no longer be held in such esteem, as other adolescent priorities take over. These early treasured memories last a lifetime and forever put a smile on the face of whoever was privileged enough to witness them.

Soon after the chaotic cake consumption we left the party and I couldn't help but think that kids' birthdays *are* always fun, provided you look at things from the child's perspective and don't expect to meet any new adults. How I longed that we would soon be celebrating the birthday of our own child.

Chapter 11
USA distraction

The day before our trip overseas Ali got her period. After so many months without impregnation I almost became fooled into thinking that the creation of a baby was a cumulative reward for effort. That the more attempts invested, the more likely the outcome would be. But human biology doesn't work that way. The start of each new month after our 'friend' had again dropped in uninvited was a new beginning—a fresh start—irrespective of how close we might have been before.

Despite being upset once again, part of me was marginally relieved because of all the months, this one—just as we embarked overseas—would have been pretty bad timing as it would have changed the dynamic of the trip. During our stopover in Hawaii, we had various recreational activities planned and I was not sure I would have been too comfortable letting Ali exert herself knowing she was pregnant. Then there was New York where Ali forgoing alcohol and certain foods would have undoubtedly raised suspicions from our friends, who wouldn't have been backward in coming forward and would have been sure to interrogate us with questions.

I tried to put a positive spin on our latest setback. We were going to be revelling in one of the most vibrant and breathtaking cities in the world for several weeks. Feasting on delectable foods and seeing spectacular shows and sites like Central Park, Madison Square Garden, Statue of Liberty and the Guggenheim museum. Maybe the change of scenery would be just what we needed to conceive. I saw this as one last-ditch shot to avoid the intervention of the fertility experts. We were going to go at it like a pair of zealous rabbits—'effectively normal'—*I'll show them*.

How I would relish being able to ring up the fertility clinic and cancel our appointment, saying in an overly smug tone: 'Sorry, but we have to cancel our appointment—we're "effectively' pregnant" —good day.'

Then, as is all the rage at the moment, we could call our child by some horrendous name that references to where he or she was conceived. I jokingly raised the idea of joining the 'Mile-High Club' but Ali was having none of it.

Hawaii was glorious, particularly Maui which was an unspoilt paradise. We could have easily stayed there for weeks on end, partaking in various outdoor activities. The surfing alone would have kept me endlessly entertained. But New York beckoned. On arrival it was a definite shock to the system, having just come from the peace and tranquillity of a tropical island paradise to the relentlessly noisy and hectic concrete jungle that is the Big Apple. Nevertheless, we were invigorated by the energy of the place and excited by the prospect of seeing our friends. We caught a cab to their apartment and were met at the door by one of our dear friends, who had kindly decided to work from home that morning so he could greet us. He showed us around their expansive apartment which had breathtaking views of the New York skyline and the Hudson River down to the Statue of Liberty in the distance.

'Where should we put our bags?' I asked, expecting to be shown into one of the rooms.

'Uh, just leave them here. You'll be sleeping on the sofa-bed here in the lounge room. I hope that's cool?'

'Sure, that's great.'

Normally I wouldn't have any issue with such sleeping arrangements, but Ali and I were on a mission this month to have as much nooky as possible. Sleeping in such exposed and communal surroundings was unlikely to be very conducive to achieving this goal. I was still hopeful, though, that come morning our friends would head off to work early, leaving us ample opportunity for some *private* time.

As it turned out, this window of opportunity never eventuated, as one of our friends would intentionally leave for work late so that they could spend some time with us. This was a wonderfully kind gesture, just not terribly helpful when you are trying to make a baby.

To make matters worse, the evenings were even more difficult a proposition. Invariably one of our friends would stay up in the lounge room until the wee hours of the morning, either watching ice hockey or playing computer games. Ali and I would typically adjourn to our sofa-bed relatively early, which was only metres away, wishing that our friends would somehow get the hint and head for bed as well—but this never happened. Sometimes I would whisper to Ali, trying to convince her to partake in a quick 'lazy dirty' despite our lack of privacy but Ali was always against the idea, foreseeing the likelihood of us getting sprung.

Often we would lie awake exhausted from a tiring day of sightseeing, fighting to stay awake, waiting for an opportunity to pounce on one another. Yet the yearning for sleep would always conquer the desire for coitus. Sleep, whilst not the priority, was an almighty persuader.

I would wake in the morning in a haze and after so many failed tries, I had the recollection of a drunken sailor, so I would check with Ali as to whether we had any luck that night. The answer was always a deflated 'no'.

I was beginning to wonder whether we were ever going to get some alone time. My unfortunate 'effectively normal' sperm wasn't really being given a fair go to prove its worth—until we saw an unexpected opening towards the end of our visit. We returned to the apartment after a romantic dinner, just the two of us, at a swanky French restaurant on the extravagant Upper East Side and were surprised to find the apartment in darkness as it was only around 10:30 pm. Surely everyone couldn't be in bed already? We gave each other a look of both disbelief and delight. Not wasting any time we quickly disrobed as quietly as possible and snuck into bed. Every movement, even the slightest shift in weight, was accentuated and broadcast by a tell-tale squeak from the sofa-bed. These conditions were going to be tough even for a couple with seasoned 'lazy dirty' experience. We were going to have to be extremely 'lazy dirty' if we were going to avoid waking everyone. But it was impossible not to make the mattress bounce and squeak in an obvious rhythm that announced our amorous actions. After all, sex without movement isn't sex. Is it? It is more like a deeply intimate cuddle. Initially, Ali and I found it hard to suppress our muffled laughter as we listened to the unmistakeable noises we were making, but eventually the trepidation of getting caught heightened the sexual intensity between us, the laughter ceased and we began to thoroughly enjoy being with one another. Eventually my swimmers got one final chance to seek and destroy, to reach the intended target. *Bon voyage. Do me proud, dudes.*

It had been a wonderful visit, even if it wasn't as sexually focused as we'd desired and we were sad to say farewell. The Big Apple: the city that never sleeps. Really? We slept more than we had sex unfortunately.

Chapter 12

One goes out, one comes in

On returning home to Australia we received terrible news. Ali's aunt Kate had lost her battle with cancer. The funeral was an understandably sombre affair and reminded us all how cruelly cancer takes life and how we take our good health for granted and feel bullet-proof, particularly in our youth. Kate's tragic circumstances served as a harsh reminder that we must not become too complacent about our wellbeing. I started to feel guilty given all the energy and focus Ali and I had been directing towards trying to get pregnant and how we had both begun to complain and moan about our circumstance—as if we were hard done by. As if we were owed something. The reality was we were owed nothing. Sure, most couples have little problem having children, but some do. Just like most people are of good health, but some aren't. Neither of us suffered from any serious medical condition, so we had a great deal to be thankful for. Apart from that we also had each other. A union that meant the world to me but could potentially be at risk if we did not spend quality time with one another. The importance of this last point was profoundly reinforced by Frank, Kate's widower, when he approached Ali and me after the funeral service, looked us squarely in the eye and said with heartfelt conviction holding back tears of his own: 'Enjoy it ... enjoy each other.'

I found these words of advice remarkably apt and poignant. One day you are here, and the next you are not. It is vital to cherish all those moments with the one you love because they will not last forever. But we tend to concentrate on all the negative inconsequential banalities of our day-to-day lives that distract us from our own happiness—without stopping to realise how unmistakeably fortunate some of us are to be able to share this journey with our soulmate. Not everyone gets this opportunity; some people spend their entire lives fruitlessly searching for their one true companion. I had Ali. *Better Together.* I was one of the lucky ones, baby or no baby. I knew I must always try and remember that.

Having all the generations present illustrated how important family is and the unique and special bond that is formed. I had been fortunate enough to have only ever been to a small number of funerals but what struck me so deeply was the significance of friends and family at these gatherings—without them present there are few to acknowledge the significance of one's life. During the service there was a slideshow of images showing Kate throughout her life. A moving montage that portrayed Kate, her husband and her two boys, all partaking in various family activities over the many years—from birthday and Christmas celebrations to family holidays and amusement parks. I was left thinking how different our life together would be without children. They truly are a key ingredient to making a family whole. Like a pie without pastry just isn't a pie, no matter how you look at it.

Would we somehow find ourselves relegated to a life of ordinariness without kids—ostracised into oblivion by our friends busy with their progeny-enriched lives filled with camping holidays, music lessons, sports carnivals, kite flying and trips to the zoo? Sure just the two of us could still partake in many of these activities and have a lifetime full of cherished memories together, but it would be *different.*

At the wake I gravitated towards my only nephew, having not seen him in months. Rebecca looked a little flustered and exhausted, so I willingly took over holding duties to give her a much deserved break. I wrapped my arms around him like an unbreakable vice. Was I being overly cautious? You could say that again. I was doing my utmost to ensure no repeat dropping performance—in the privacy of my own home was bad enough but in front of the entire extended family that was family inheritance suicide.

'That was a beautiful service', I remarked.

'Wasn't it.'

'Luke was a little champ, he didn't make a peep', I said, tickling his feet and making him giggle.

'He's been so good all day. I can't believe it.'

'Do you reckon that maybe he could sense the occasion and that's why he was so well behaved?'

'Possibly, but I doubt it,' said Rebecca, 'he's too young to have any real idea.'

We were joined by Olivia, the vivacious and articulate middle sister in the Field family.

'Hey Rebecca, I've got some food for you. All your faves, smoked salmon, camembert, olives and fetta', she said, shooting me a swift wry smile out of Rebecca's view.

'Thanks Olivia', Rebecca replied, looking a little uncomfortable.

'You *must* try the salmon, peeps, it's marinated with capers, olive oil and Spanish onion. It's divine!'

'Yum …' Rebecca replied unconvincingly.

As the three of us continued to chat it suddenly dawned on me why Olivia had given me such a cheeky smirk when she first gave the food to Rebecca. Olivia, being a journalist by training, was doing some investigative research of her own. Shortly before we'd left for our overseas trip, Olivia had mentioned to Ali and me her suspicion that Rebecca might be carrying number two. This was a revelation, as Luke was still a few months off turning one at the time. Her suspicions had been raised when she had had Rebecca, Mark and Luke over for a casual dinner. During the evening Olivia had noticed Rebecca avoiding alcohol and soft cheeses, behaviour that was out of character. Renowned for her forthright approach (no doubt a prerequisite in her industry) Olivia didn't hesitate in probing her with relevant questions at the time. Rebecca denied it but this failed to convince Olivia. Instead Olivia was now on a mission, her journalistic instincts told her there was a story here and she was determined to break it—front page headlines.

'Rebecca, you've hardly touched your food, are you OK?' Olivia asked, in a caring tone.

'No, I'm fine, just not that hungry, that's all.'

'Are you sure there's nothing *wrong*?' Olivia said, pursing her lips.

'I'm OK, just a bit tired. Luke hasn't been sleeping well of late.'

'I hope it's nothing *more* than that?' Olivia said.

'Don't worry I'm fine—really.'

'OK, if you insist.'

To my surprise Olivia seemed content to let it go. She was persistent but I felt she didn't want to force the issue, not at this particular moment. Many wouldn't consider a wake to be the most appropriate time or venue to announce a new arrival. But Olivia couldn't resist giving me a knowing smile. I could tell she was convinced Rebecca had a bun in the oven—as was I.

Later I excused myself and went and sat down in solitude at the perimeter of the venue. As I surveyed the congregation I noticed there were numerous children present, all of varying ages, from toddlers and infants—who were oblivious to the significance of the event—to testy teenagers and young adults who could better appreciate the solemn scene. Seeing all these children at various stages of development and thinking about the likelihood that Rebecca was harbouring another of her own, in the earliest stages of growth, I was reminded of another Jack Johnson song. The song titled *If I Could* tells a tale of a newborn entering the world around the same time a friend dies from illness. I began to softly sing some of the lyrics to myself, over and over: '… new life makes losing life easier to understand … *One goes out. One comes in.*'

These lyrics made so much sense, particularly on a day such as this. I found they really helped broaden my perspective and outlook—to better accept the painful loss and look at it in a broader context. *One goes out, one comes in.* It is the natural circle of life. I took comfort in the speculation that Rebecca was again pregnant —that the family tree was still healthy and being rejuvenated by the growth of a new branch to replace one that had so tragically fallen. I started to think that maybe a wake wouldn't be the worst place to announce a pregnancy. *One goes out, one comes in.*

Despite my best efforts, these ponderings over pregnancy soon turned to unease over the probability of whether Ali and I were going to have a chance to add one of our own to this natural cycle of life, and the impending visit to the fertility clinic. What if we couldn't contribute to the family tree of our ancestors? Where would that leave us if we were to bear no fruit of our loins? When our branches fell that would be the end of our graft onto the family tree. I forced myself to stop thinking so negatively and instead recounted the powerful words that had been uttered to me only hours earlier: 'Enjoy it … enjoy each other.'

Chapter 13
Contraception tips and tricks

The day of our appointment with the fertility specialist had finally arrived. Not that I was looking forward to it but it undeniably heralded a big step into the unknown. There was no turning back now. I was particularly nervous and anxious because I was expecting to get some clarification on my 'effectively normal' sperm result. I was quietly wishing that somehow there had been a laboratory mix-up and that my results were fine—no, better than fine—excellent.

On arrival I was immediately impressed with the interior design of the place. It wasn't nearly as sterile and clinical as I had imagined it would be. Instead, it was more like a fancy hotel lobby, with comfortable couches, soft colourful lighting and an assortment of ornate decor. I couldn't help but notice the reception desk was adorned with numerous 'thank you' cards and the like, which I assumed had come from rapturous parents proclaiming their new addition. As we waited, nonchalantly flicking through trashy celebrity-obsessed magazines, I wondered what would happen if friends or acquaintances of ours were to walk into the clinic at this very moment. Would an awkward conversation arise, where both parties tried to bluff the other with a contrived story explaining the reasons for being in such a place? Not dissimilar, I imagine, to bumping into someone you know in a porn shop. Or would common-sense prevail and honesty be the approach taken?

After a while we were called in by the fertility specialist. She introduced herself.

'Hi I'm Nicci Sides, you must be Alison and Matt.'

'Yes', we both replied in unison.

'You know … I've never met a bad Matt!'

'We're all pretty nice', I added, without thinking, then realised how stupid what I had said must've sounded.

Then, for some reason, the doc's last statement distracted me. *Does that mean she sees heaps of Matts in her line of work?* Was it feasible that my potential infertility was somehow inextricably linked to my *name* of all things—like Tiger by name, Tiger by nature. *Stop being absurd.* I quickly snapped out of my ridiculous speculation when Nicci said: 'Now Matt, your sperm results …' The words hung in the air for a moment.

'… your sperm count is around 113 million per millilitre …'

That's got to be good, you only need one to get pregnant right?

'… but only 5 per cent of those are what we class as "rapid swimmers" and that percentage is a fair bit down on where I would like it to be, because these are the ones that make it to the egg—the others are just spectators really.'

That sounds bad.

'… which accounts for why your overall result was "effectively normal".'

'OK', I replied, looking more than a little upset. In a matter of seconds the doc had disclosed such startling personal information that I was left speechless.

'Don't worry, there are things you can do to increase the number of "rapid swimmers".'

'Like what?'

'Firstly, eating lots of foods high in antioxidants like carrots, berries, cooked tomatoes and decaffeinated green tea.'

'Right.'

'I will also give you a list of dietary supplements to take, including zinc and a few others', she said, hurriedly scribbling notes on a blank piece of paper in classically illegible doctor scratchings.

'Sure.'

'And the least favourite: refrain from alcohol. Then, after nine weeks of doing all that, we'll get another sample and hope to see an improvement—happy with that?'

'Sure', I replied, still a little dazed and confused.

'And definitely no binge drinking, as this can wipe out sperm for up to two months.'

I found it all a bit much to take in at once. Nicci was clearly so knowledgeable but she spoke so swiftly that I struggled to keep up.

From what she said about my results I imagined the problem to be something like packing 80,000 people onto the Melbourne Cricket Ground pitch with there being a prize at one end like a winning multi-million dollar lottery ticket. This bounty is up for grabs to the first person to make it through the hordes and claim the ticket. All of the people should fiercely covet this prize but instead (it appeared in my situation) a vast majority are either too lazy or indifferent and are simply content to stand around and idly chat with other similarly minded individuals. All of these thousands of spectators make it near impossible for the keen and energetic people to make their way through the disinterested masses in sufficient time and as a result no-one claims the prized ticket and it jackpots to the next month. Strange analogy I know, but it worked for me.

I was pleased though that there were steps I could take to hopefully improve my count of those keen and motivated individuals. I was determined to follow the doctor's orders religiously and wasn't particularly fazed by any of her instructions. I certainly got the impression that advising men to abstain from alcohol was typically met with protest or even hostility. But I am in no way typical in this respect. In fact I have a horrifying secret to divulge that shakes my reputation as a true-blue, fair-dinkum Aussie bloke: I hate beer. I don't mind the occasional glass of wine or port, but beer—I can't stand the stuff—never have. There I finally said it! Believe me this is not an easy thing for any Australian male to admit because for many Aussie blokes beer is in fact a food group of its own. We were all taught about the healthy food pyramid at primary school and the importance of eating a balanced diet. For a vast majority of men this pyramid was soon replaced by a big square box: the slab of beer, accompanied by the occasional meat pie. Beer is so heavily consumed that for some it has become a currency more valuable than the almighty dollar, perfect for bets waged or favours repaid— ideal for some, but not me.

I remember when I was in my mid-teens, when under-age drinking was all the rage, I often felt pressured to get plastered with my mates. They all used to carry on about how delicious this amber ale was—nectar from the gods and all that. I recall my brother Steve, being of legal drinking age, was once eager to get a case of grog and get drunk with me and several of my friends one Saturday night when our parents were away. He saw this rare opportunity as a rite of passage. Everyone was notably excited about the prospect of consuming copious amounts of ale—except me. And when I was eventually asked what I thought of the plan, I replied sheepishly, 'I'm not that thirsty ...'

Steve found my response both astonishing and hilarious and subsequently set about berating me, in front of my friends, like only a big brother can. I was left scarred by the whole episode and forced myself to drink beer for many years to come, primarily because in Australia so many social events revolve around beer. Sure there are times when other forms of alcohol are completely acceptable. But men don't meet down at the pub for a glass of wine. It's as simple as that. Men typically bond over beer, while tending to the BBQ, talking about the footy. It's a cliché, but it's true, which is why my aversion to beer was ostracising to some extent.

As I matured, I grew tired of this façade and contrived a cunning excuse after reading an article about various food allergies. I started to refrain from drinking beer and saying to people that I had gone to a dietician and found out that I was allergic to some preservative used in beer. I was astounded by the reaction I received when informing people of my fabricated diagnosis. All my male friends considered this a fate worse than death—allergic to beer—what a cruel, cruel affliction. I got the distinct impression that some blokes would rather be diagnosed with a terminal illness than be told they couldn't drink beer. I'm not in the habit of lying or being deceitful but for me this sham was perfect. Besides, who was I hurting? My liver was certainly thankful. I maintain this pretence to this day. So suffice to say the need to forgo alcohol was going to be easy for me.

Nicci then moved onto talking about Ali and her results. My recollection of the details are more than a little nebulous, not because

I was disinterested, rather I was baffled by the complexity of the female reproductive system compared to the male. I was seriously out of my depth in terms of understanding. Nicci, with the aid of a large model vagina (that frankly I found intimidating as it looked like something out of a sci-fi movie), talked about a myriad of potential complications that could be preventing us from conceiving, such as uterine polyps, polycystic ovaries or endometriosis. She discussed the various procedures that Ali would have to undergo, most of which were not too invasive, that would be used to rule out some of these possible problems. All the while Ali nodded her head knowingly, whereas I seriously struggled to follow.

Then Nicci moved onto the plan of action for us, in a predominantly clinical and forthright manner.

'So, we're going to have those tests done as I discussed to check for any problems, but in the meantime we will get you started on some regular blood tests that will determine exactly when you're ovulating.'

'OK', Ali replied.

'Then when you begin "peaking" you must have sex twice a day, for several days either side of this fertile period to increase your chances.'

'OK', we both responded.

'Oh and preferably "doggy-style", because this is the most effective', she explained without missing a beat, as if she were a dentist merely asking a patient to brush their teeth in a certain way.

It was bizarre being told how you must engage in lovemaking by someone you only met moments earlier. But then again, from Nicci's perspective, love had nothing to do with it. This was straight-up sex advice—a crash course in Biology 101. She was looking at our problem like a mechanic examines a misfiring engine—looking to optimise the pistons and cylinder relationship.

Ali and I both nodded our heads, not exactly sure how to respond to her last comment. *Oh that's great we both enjoy that position—fantastic!*

'Also, you must ejaculate every two to three days. Some people tend to think that if you store it up, it's better quality—in fact the opposite is true.'

'OK', I replied, instantly red-faced like a previously pasty Pom after a day at Bondi Beach.

Gee, we were getting all the privileged info today. Nicci's last comment baffled me as it was contrary to what I had previously been told by other less qualified people who were adamant that holding off produced the 'Mother Lode'. I could identify with this ill-informed logic. Like space-shuttle launches, these are highly anticipated, infrequent occurrences, where the astronauts are primed to perform under intense pressure, having waited and trained for years for this once-in-a-lifetime voyage. This significant event culminates in a massive explosion that marks the start of a typically triumphant journey. I wonder whether these missions into space would be as successful if they happened every other day. Yet, apparently for sperm, regular missions are best.

At the conclusion of the appointment Nicci escorted us back to the reception area where she was set upon by an ecstatic couple eager to introduce their newborn.

'Look, James, it's your creator!' exclaimed the lady, holding her baby up to Nicci like he was about to be blessed by the Pope.

'Oh no, you both created him, I just helped along the way.'

'Stop being so modest, doctor.'

'Aren't you a cute little man … you look just like Michael Moore', said Nicci, probably trying to change the subject given her modesty.

Overhearing Nicci's last comment I did the biggest double-take. Never before had I heard the words 'cute' and 'Michael Moore' uttered in the same sentence. In fact, this was a blatant oxymoron in my opinion. If I were a parent and someone said my newborn looked like Michael Moore I would instigate a brawl and defend the honour of my son (or, god forbid, daughter) with all my might.

'Gosh … put a hat on him and he *is* Michael Moore!' Nicci added with conviction, without the slightest hesitation or malice.

Overhearing such a candid opinion I was desperate to sneak a peek at this supposed miniature clone of Michael Moore. I subtly walked past the couple pretending I had left something in the waiting area and quickly caught a glimpse of the baby and was stunned by how accurate Nicci's assessment had been. Then I turned around and was face to face with the father and he too looked like Michael Moore, only fatter and hairier—then it all made sense.

As we left the clinic I was of the view that the appointment had gone better than expected. Nicci was fantastic—affable and professional without a hint of austerity that so often permeated other doctors' bedside manner. Her approach was matter-of-fact but with a positive outlook that was cause for hope. This positivity was infectious making me confident that I could improve the state of my baby batter and that determining the 'fertile period' from regular blood tests wasn't nearly as invasive and clinical a process as I expected we would have to encounter. For the first time in a long while I was optimistic about our pregnancy prospects.

Chapter 14
Intercourse auto-pilot

We enthusiastically embarked on this assisted routine of unpredictability—where Ali would get her bloods done every few days at certain times in her menstrual cycle and, depending on the levels, we would be told to engage in either a minimal, moderate or massive amount of bonking for the next few days until the next blood sample. I know the cliché of the busy married couple who have to schedule in a time-slot to have sex, but this was taking it to a new extreme. The required concentration of fornication was pleasing but also overwhelming. Previously, when we were going at it alone without medical assistance, we were shagging frequently, virtually every two days without fail but, as Nicci highlighted, a lot of those attempts were wasted as they occurred outside the fertile period. Now we would be told precisely when to go at it like proverbial rabbits for a short and focused period.

Under this strict new regime I was particularly looking forward to having some 'morning glory' time. I had broached the topic previously with Ali, well before we even started trying for kids, and she was usually opposed to the idea during the working week, stating that there was too much to do in the mornings before work and that sleep was precious. Now we were under 'Doctor's orders' so I didn't even have to ask! Surely this was a major perk of the whole sordid affair. I was like a child with tonsillitis being *told* I must eat ice-cream.

During the first month of blood tests our fertile period coincided with the middle of the week. Unfortunately the first morning Ali needed the car for the day, so she was going to have to drop me off at the bus which departed at 7:48 am. We then calculated that in order to allow sufficient time to do all the morning rituals, like shower, feed cat, dry hair etc., we would have to wake up at 5:45 am and have sex. Let's get one thing clear: I am not a morning person. In fact I consider 5:45 am to be night-time, not the morning. The only time I ever see 5:45 am is when I have to travel and catch an early flight for work, which happens infrequently, thankfully, but when it does my body objects strenuously. However, in this instance there was no point trying to negotiate—Doctor's orders.

The next morning the alarm sounded and I was violently awoken from a deep, dream-filled sleep. My immediate thought was that the alarm must be wrong as it was so dark and cold. I rolled over and to my disappointment it was indeed 5:45 am—time to rise, unlikely to shine. Soon Ali emerged from her slumber and looked similarly disorientated and perplexed by the rude awakening. I could tell that neither of us were in the mood to 'get busy'. This was going to be harder than I envisioned and to think I was looking forward to *this*. It should be termed 'morning agony' any time before 10 am. This was a unique experience for me, never before had I been required to *perform* so soon after being fast asleep. I wondered whether my much maligned sperm were going to be as equally unprepared and unmotivated by their sudden pre-dawn call to action. Would they be caught napping and fail to make it to the launching pad before the rocket took off (so to speak)?

Passion certainly wasn't going to be the fuel for this sexual rendezvous, not at this ungodly hour. We were both lifeless but obviously motivated by the doctor's orders. Foreplay was limited to sufficient fondling to allow for 'all systems go'. We did the deed, following all the directives, and eventually made our way to work on time.

That evening we again engaged in intimate relations which were considerably more pleasurable than the earlier bleary-eyed encounter. The following morning our sleep was again interrupted by the hideous 'shag alarm'. Like on the previous morning we simply both went through the motions with minimal emotional attachment because both of us were still virtually asleep—operating on intercourse auto-pilot.

This same routine continued—it was Ground*shag* Day—until Ali's bloods revealed that she was past the fertile period—down tools. Then it was simply a matter of waiting, knowing we had done our best. If my recounting of this experience doesn't sound particularly romantic, well that is because unfortunately it wasn't. Invariably we were following orders, irrespective of either of our moods.

While we waited for the results I set about ensuring I consumed as much antioxidant-rich food as I could. This wasn't particularly arduous, apart from drinking the decaffeinated green tea. I had never been a huge fan of green tea but this decaffeinated variety was repulsive. It was virtually devoid of flavour as you drank it but it then left a potent and unpleasantly bitter after-taste that lingered tenaciously. My beloved French grandmother had a saying for such repugnant infusions: 'Wet and warm like cat piss!' Despite this, I ignored my tastebuds and guzzled at least three large mugs of this murky mixture every day. I was going to do all I could to improve my baby gravy and I had been told, in no uncertain terms, that consistency was the key. Sperm is produced daily but apparently what you do today doesn't equate to instant benefits tomorrow—it takes time. So there was little point in me only sporadically having the right foods.

The vitamins I was prescribed were also a bit of a challenge for someone not used to taking medication. Not that they were hard to swallow, just that there were so many of them and I would often forget how many of which I would have to take when. I was taking various quantities of zinc, fish oil, COQ10 and a multi-vitamin. I felt like a pill-popping geriatric but at least I wasn't having to take Viagra—well not yet anyway.

Chapter 15
Renewed optimism

The next several weeks wait wasn't as torturous as I figured it would be because my expectations were quite low given I seriously doubted whether the majority of my sperm, in their current state, were ready for the quest—far too many had no inclination to complete the arduous mission—and I knew it would take at least another cycle before any improvements in the ranks would be realised. I decided to keep these reservations to myself, rather than share them with Ali, as I didn't want to sound too pessimistic. I had noticed a positive change in her overall mood since meeting with Nicci and I didn't want to deflate this with any perceived negativity.

Nonetheless, when the end of the cycle drew near it was still hard not to feel just a skerrick of excitement and hope that somehow one of the vigorous, enthused and enterprising minority valiantly made it to the target. Unfortunately, the results told us otherwise. Once again we were not pregnant.

'Sorry Ali', I said, never really knowing what to say when we received the bad news. You would think I would have gotten better at it given successive occurrences but I was always floored.

'Don't be sorry.'

'Well I am, because it's my lazy sperm that are responsible.'

'We don't know that for sure.'

'Maybe not, but it's highly likely.'

'Look ... it was our first try and your sperm will improve, so I'm pretty hopeful—aren't you?'

'I s'pose,' I replied, 'I just don't like being the problem.'

'Who cares who's the problem, it takes two to make a baby.'

'You're right', I said. 'Do you still reckon we shouldn't tell our folks about this stuff?'

'No, I'd rather not at this stage.'

We had been discussing this topic on and off for many months. Firstly, we were both of the view that we would resist telling our respective families of the difficulties we were having because we believed this might bring unnecessary pressure from them if they repeatedly asked how we were getting on. We saw this as an additional stress that we could do without under the circumstances. Secondly, we were of the opinion that sharing this information would undoubtedly bring with it unwanted pity. We both dreaded the possibility of continual well-intentioned sympathy, which we suspected would be intensified given the recent arrival of Luke, the first nephew in either family. I would hate a family member to pity me as I held my nephew and have them think *Poor Matt, it must break his heart to hold that child, knowing he may never have his own.* Why I felt so deeply about this I am not entirely sure. We also considered that, if we told them, this might take the sheen off any future announcement, if and when we ever did conceive, and instead of our announcement being met with excitement, it could be met with a sense of relief.

A day or two after the result Ali rang Rebecca for her birthday.

'Hey Rebecca, it's Ali, I just wanted to wish you a fantastic birthday.'

'Thanks.'

'How's your day been, has Mark pampered you silly?'

'Not exactly. But we're going out to a fancy restaurant tonight and the grandpares are looking after Luke, which will be nice.'

'That sounds lovely', said Ali. 'How's the little man going?'

'He's great—growing up fast—I can't believe he's one next month.'

'I know.'

'Actually, I have some news on that front … I'm pregnant again!'

'Gee, that's fantastic. When are you due?'

'October.'

'You know we have all suspected for some time.'

'I figured. Olivia's been watching me like a hawk recently. She almost forced salmon down my throat at Kate's wake!'

'Well it's great news, we're really happy for you both', said Ali. 'We'll see you in a few weeks for Luke's birthday.'

'It'll be heaps of fun, see you then—bye.'

As Ali put the phone down she looked on the verge of tears. I hurried over to console her. I'm ashamed to say that my predominant emotion at that moment was one of jealousy more than joy.

'Bloody hell, another couple beat us to it! This is getting ludicrous', I said, in a mystified manner.

'Tell me about it …'

'Olivia always suspected that Rebecca would pump out kids once she was married', I added.

'I hate myself for not being happier about this—I feel like an awful sister.'

'Darling, your response is understandable', I said, squeezing her firmly. 'You're not a bad person for having these thoughts. Don't beat yourself up over it. Deep down we're both happy for them, you must realise that. It's just all the stuff we're going through at the moment brings other emotions to the surface first.'

'I suppose', said Ali. 'I just can't believe that Rebecca and Mark have been able to have another child in the time that we've been trying.'

'I know it sucks—plain and simple.'

There was no denying that this announcement was deflating as it served as a sad reminder of our inadequacies and fertilised our already sprouting seeds of doubt. We knew we needed a distraction, something to take our minds off what was quickly becoming an unrelenting endeavour. Unfortunately, we couldn't organise a holiday because we needed to be around for our fertility treatments. So we considered which home renovations we could concentrate on. We had both often talked about plans for a dream kitchen renovation but always joked that it wouldn't happen until the children were older because we couldn't afford it. Well the children were nowhere to be seen at this point, so there was a window of opportunity. So we both warmed to the idea of saving for a kitchen renovation and even if we were miraculously knocked up next month, we still had nine months in which to get the job done. Undoubtedly, part of the appeal of this project was that it enhanced the hub of the house and made it considerably more homely. On completion, our 'nest' would be ready for offspring.

This diversion worked as we quickly immersed ourselves in every aspect of planning for the renovation. We fussed over every minute detail: door handles, cupboard types, light switches, sink dimensions, colours etc. This distraction consumed us and our conversations became one-dimensional. Yet in reality we both saw this for what it was: a superficial façade. We knew we would both blissfully cast our kitchen plans aside in a heartbeat in exchange for a baby.

Chapter 16

Nephew turns one

Despite remaining upbeat we found we couldn't escape the constant reminders of our inability to conceive at will. We were invited to Luke's first birthday party in Sydney, which was yet another lousy reminder of how the months were flying by without success. Luckily for us, this event didn't coincide with our fertile 'sexathon' period, as it may have been difficult to fit in the necessary quantity of copulation. Needless to say, the well-rehearsed 'lazy dirty' would have again been a requisite to avoid detection.

This was our first visit to Rebecca and Mark's new home, which they had purchased several months earlier. They had been actively looking to buy for several years in an intensely competitive property market but struggled to find a place that ticked all the boxes: right location, right condition, right price, close to public transport etc. No doubt the knowledge of the impending arrival of 'number two' expedited their decision to finally settle on a suitable place. The house was more than suitable. It had ample space for a growing family, with a huge family/rumpus room that alone was more expansive than the small two-bedroom unit from which they had come. Sure it needed some work but it was in a remarkable location for the sprawling city of Sydney; the last house at the end of an impossibly steep cul-de-sac, backing onto a nature reserve where eucalypts and jacaranda trees provided ample shade for tree-ferns to thrive around slabs of smooth sandstone bedrock. The place teemed with wildlife, if you were patient enough to look closely, and you were more likely to be woken by kookaburras cackling than a low-flying jumbo. In years to come Luke would undoubtedly revel in mischievously exploring these surrounds.

I was in awe of the place as soon as we arrived. 'Rebecca, your place is amazing.'

'Thanks, we're really happy with it', she said. 'It's been a long wait though.'

'How's Luke liking it?'

'He loves it—now he's walking. Before, we were constantly saying, "No!" because there wasn't any space and he always got into things. But it's *so* much better now.'

The party was lively and, to my relief, there were more adults than children present and I in no way felt like an outcast observer. Rebecca and Mark both looked deliriously happy and relaxed to be celebrating the first birthday of their child in their glorious new home, contentedly knowing there was another addition to the family on the way.

The following morning Ali and I were up relatively early and went to the rumpus room to play with Luke. The room was overcrowded with all types of children's toys, some recent acquisitions, others well used and abused. Despite the vast array of toys to play with, he was fascinated with the least expensive and least complex. His primary focus was the inflated birthday balloons from the previous day. I wonder why this is often the case with young children—why they seem to get more enjoyment out of the cardboard box that the present came in, than the gift itself. Ali and I took great delight in entertaining Luke with the balloons. We would throw them around the room and he would chase them, excitedly letting out infectious, explosive shrieks of enjoyment. We repeated this game over and over and his exuberance never waned.

I was truly impressed by the speed with which he could cover ground as he had only been walking for a few months—he could really motor along—but I half expected him to trip over his feet (causing water-works and putting an abrupt end to our playtime) but it never happened.

I later modified the balloon game to one where I would carry him around under my arm and slowly lower him over a balloon on the ground and get him to pick it up. This wasn't easy for him as the balloon was nearly as big as he was but he soon got the aim of the game and persisted. Luke was like a claw on those arcade skill-tester games. He enjoyed this variation and I did too. He would giggle uncontrollably at times and I soon found myself doing the same—real belly-aching laughter that soothes the soul—is there anything more uplifting, pure and beautiful than a child's laughter? I'm sure nothing could be more satisfying than hearing your child having such a good time.

Ali and I found it blissful spending quality time alone with him. I can honestly say it was the first time I had *ever* had a chance to play with a child for an extended time. Typically, I had only ever spent time with kids for short periods, in the afternoon or evening, when playtime was invariably interrupted by a tantrum, feeding, nappy change, bath or a designated nap—sometimes all of these. This morning was so special, Luke was extremely enthusiastic about playing and nothing was going to disrupt that. He was rested, fed and feces free. He had boundless energy to burn, people to play with, and a room full of toys—life doesn't get much better than that for a one-year-old.

After half an hour of playing with the balloons, we coaxed him onto a more subdued game of building blocks because Ali and I were beginning to tire. I started trying to construct the tallest tower possible. Initially Luke would patiently observe my creation until it got to a height where he would come along and destroy it—laughing hysterically as the pieces came tumbling down, flying every which way. I would repeat the process but gradually he became intent on obliterating my attempted monolith to its foundations before it reached any great height. The game quickly turned into a race between Luke and myself; both of us knew it and neither wanted to be defeated—after all, boys are inherently competitive. I was amazed at how much he understood and learnt by simply watching this repetitive activity. He couldn't speak yet but that didn't hold him back. He was learning before my very eyes.

I had often heard parents refer to young children as sponges that absorb all that is around them but never before had I witnessed it first-hand. I was a little taken aback in realising the degree of responsibility that this brings—how so much of the personality and disposition of a child is moulded during those formative years and how pivotal the parents' role is. Previously, I would have been overwhelmed by such responsibility, but no longer. I was now well and truly up for the challenge.

After a couple of hours of non-stop entertaining the three of us were all showing signs of fatigue. Ali carried Luke down to his room for a nap and I returned downstairs where Rebecca was sprawled on a couch by the window contentedly reading a book in the late morning sun.

'Luke's too cute', I said, interrupting Rebecca from her novel. 'Can we take him home?'

'Sure', she said, raising her head. 'You haven't seen him super pouty and cranky though—he can be a handful.'

I gave a look of scepticism that Rebecca reacted to instantly, sitting bolt upright. 'You see this', she said, lifting her book up and waving it at me like she was surrendering with a flag. 'This is only the *second* time I've read since Luke was born', Rebecca added, with a look of sincerity that made me believe without question.

'He does have tonnes of energy', I said in support. 'But cranky … really?'

'Yep, sometimes—then it's *hard* work because he won't sleep.'

'Well, we seem to have tuckered him out this morning.'

'I know, that's great—thanks', said Rebecca, as she returned to her reclined position and began to reacquaint herself with the prose. I took this body language as a cue to leave her in some much needed peace. But as I vacated the room I couldn't resist making one final remark, 'So where do I place an order for one just like Luke?' At first Rebecca didn't react and looked transfixed by the page, so I assumed she hadn't heard me.

'I've got contacts, I'll see what I can do', she said finally, playing along, not lifting her gaze, still engrossed in the novel.

If only it were that easy.

Chapter 17
Help from nature?

During the last month of autumn, as the last few leaves finally fell from those deciduous trees that adorned our neighbourhood, Ali's fertile period arrived on cue. Once again we were told to have copious concentrated amounts of copulation, so we did as we were told. You certainly couldn't question our dedication and commitment to the cause. I was eating berries by the bucket-load, drinking gallons of green tea and taking a plethora of pills. But Ali wanted to do more. Sure Western medicine was helping us, but Ali sought to explore other options, as suggested by the fertility clinic, that were potentially more holistic in their approach.

Ali booked us both in to see a naturopath. I'm not a complete sceptic when it comes to alternative remedies but it is true to say that I was reserved in my enthusiasm. Maybe because I feared being given some intolerable exotic potion or lotion to redress my sperm inequalities or worse still acupuncture on my nether region. The visit turned out to be relatively uneventful. I had hoped the naturopath, whom I knew to be a woman, was going to look like a female version of Mr Miyagi from the *Karate Kid* movies—fluent in ancient proverbs, never speaking in full sentences, always answering a question with a question. But to my disappointment she was rather typically Anglo-Saxon in appearance and disposition, the only intriguing aspects about her being that she had eyes that made her look rather serpent-like. This, in my opinion, added at least a little to her credibility—ridiculous I know, but hey, we all have our own personal unfounded stereotypes that we like to see vindicated every so often.

The naturopath talked in intimate detail to Ali about her menstrual cycle for a considerable length of time, at which moment I questioned whether I should be hearing all this tremendously personal information that I regarded as secret women's business. Again, for the umpteenth time in the past few months, I was left wondering where the romance had gone. This made me think of a colleague whom I used to work with. She had been married for over 20 years and had three children. She was so intent on keeping an element of 'mystery' in her marriage— in an effort to, as she would put it, *Keep the romance alive*—that she would turn a radio on in the bathroom whenever she went to the toilet, to prevent any 'unsavoury' noises from being heard by her husband. I always believed this was a massive over-reaction. *Who cares if your partner hears you urinating?* But now, sitting listening to the naturopath give a comprehensive explanation of vaginal discharge, I was beginning to think that maybe my colleague was on to something. Sure she had taken it to the extreme but the foundations of her logic may not have been far off the mark.

Later the naturopath performed acupuncture on Ali and I waited patiently as she gave commentary about having identified a potential blockage, which sounded positive. I presumed I was next, but that was not to be the case—she didn't explain why—but I assumed acupuncture does more to improve the complex 'vessel' than the rather simple 'depositor'. She finally did turn her attention to me, towards the last five minutes of our one-hour appointment, by which stage I really was questioning why I needed to come along at all. I concluded that this did accurately epitomise the relative importance of the male input into the pregnancy process and the naturopath had allocated her time accordingly. Men simply supply the baby batter during a brief one-off encounter and that is all —job done in five minutes—sometimes even less. It is then up to the women to provide the ideal conditions, over many, many months, for the bun in the oven.

When my turn eventually came I was told to look into the distance while she examined my eyes through a hand-held magnification device. Within seconds she reared back almost in fright.

'You *are* stressed!'

'No, I don't think so.'

'I can clearly see stress rings in your eyes. Are you in a stressful job?'

'No, not particularly.'

'Well, something is clearly causing you stress', she insisted. 'It's important to get on top of it; otherwise it can eat away at your reserves. I will give you some special medication to help.'

'Sure, OK', I replied with little enthusiasm.

More bloody medication, that's all I need.

The medication was in a powdered form and had to be drunk each morning before breakfast. It was indeed a foul concoction that tasted like rancid Tang. I wondered what it was made of—probably ground leopard's testicles or something similarly as prohibited and foreign. Nevertheless, I was not to be deterred because we had once more received disappointing results heralded by the arrival of our 'friend' that month which meant I had to again dutifully supply a sample to the clinic and I was intent on providing a batch of the highest quality—the crème de la crème—and maybe this latest elixir, on top of my already strict dietary regime, would yield dividends.

Providing my second sample to the clinic was incident-free compared to the first adventure. I knew what was expected and all the answers to the curly questions they were going to ask. I was cool, calm and collected—with an air of confidence like that of a student who had studied hard before a crucial exam. This was truly a test that I wanted to get top marks in.

Two weeks later we had another appointment with Nicci at the fertility clinic, primarily to discuss my results. I was extremely edgy. As we engaged in pleasantries I kept wishing she could just cut to the chase and put me out of my misery.

Nicci opened our file and discussed various details, none of which related to my results. The mounting sense of anticipation was almost too much to bear.

'Here we go … Matt's recent results', she said.

My ears were ringing with expectation. I tried in vain to look casual and relaxed, as if I was just idly waiting for someone to tell me the time or something as comparatively inconsequential, but I knew my face was a picture of pent-up angst. She started reading various figures out aloud, none of which made sense to me at the time, until she said:

'Excellent … remarkable! Your "rapid swimmers" are up from 5 to 61 per cent!'

I thought this was an astonishing improvement.

'Gee, great!' I replied, with a broadening smile.

'Your "rapid swimmer" numbers have gone from being classified as poor to excellent.'

I was beyond happy, beyond elated. But it got even better.

Nicci then went on to say that my low levels of "rapid swimmers" were most likely the cause of our infertility. And that now, given such a dramatic improvement, she recommended postponing any surgical procedures for at least three to four months. Instead we were told to keep at it because she suspected we would get pregnant without major intervention—apart from a little help with the timing, care of regular blood tests.

This was an outstanding result and it was fantastic to think that a natural pregnancy was still within the realm of possibility. It was also an immense relief to be able to delay any intrusive medical operations, as these had various associated risks. The only downside, from my perspective, was that the improvement in my baby batter couldn't be attributed to any one thing. Given it was likely a combination of factors meant that I couldn't afford to selectively forgo the more repulsive consumables. Unfortunately, it was all or nothing, with no reprieve. If this, however, was the price to pay for exemplary sperm I was willing to sacrifice my palate.

Chapter 18
Life in limbo

Given the remarkable improvement in my results we both considered this to be a fresh start. Sure we had been trying to conceive in vain for over one and a half years but now that we knew the reason why, a weight seemed to lift off our minds. In fact, we began to really see the humour in some of the situations that we confronted. Like when Ali received the call from the clinic with her blood results. Previously, a senior nurse delivered the required message, which was all well and good. But more recently a new recruit dispensed this critical information and in Ali's opinion he sounded like a young teenager, who didn't come across as particularly confident in his delivery. Ali would usually receive the call soon after 3 pm, so we joked that maybe this was an after school job for some kid. Not quite as mundane as a paper round considering a typical call would go something like this:

'Hi … it's Matt … from the clinic. I have your monthly tracking results … Nicci says you're surging and should have intercourse tonight, tomorrow morning and tomorrow night. And she says good luck!'

If I were a teenager and had to ring up countless women to tell them when to have sex, I would have been in hysterics. I'm amazed that the kid could maintain any air of professionalism. Surely he revelled in telling his mates what he did for some spending money. Ali too said she found it a bit bizarre, not to mention the guy's name was Matt—coincidence or what? I often asked Ali how she responded to the caller and she said she simply said 'thanks'. On more than one instance I dared her to flirt with the guy instead of simply thanking him for the results. Saying something inappropriate like: 'So Matt … are you interested in helping me out with all this sex I'm supposed to have …?'

But not surprisingly Ali refused—never one to prank people she didn't know. Anyhow several months later Matt was gone and a different person was giving the results. I wondered what happened to the kid, whether one day his humour got the better of him or worse still he accidentally rang a wrong number.

Not everything was so humorous however. Rarely did the 'fertile period' coincide with the weekend—it was uncanny, almost as if we were jinxed. This meant we continued having to factor in our amorous romps in the wee hours of the morning before work. This ongoing routine of being rudely awoken by an alarm, then having to immediately engage in sex, was at times laborious and far too ritualistic for my liking—I regret to say. Up until this point in my life I had always held the view that sex was like pizza: sometimes it's not the best and fails to live up to expectation, but it's *never* really bad! The crust may be too thin, or lacking lavish toppings, but it's still darn tasty and you can rarely stop at just one piece to satisfy your craving. But I'm surprised and ashamed to say that there were nearly times when this analogy no longer applied. I was almost over pizza. Particularly when it was a freezing winter's dawn and the heater was yet to have any effect—the room would often be below ten degrees—not the most conducive conditions for impassioned undertakings. But we knew there was a job to be done and we were under strict orders. And for some reason, when the allotted time for intercourse was scarce, there were several times when, despite my best effort, I couldn't expedite the process. I tried reverse psychology but that didn't work. Both of us wanted a 'quickie' but often my body had other ideas. It was almost as if it were deliberately disobeying directives to prove a point about what part of the male anatomy has control—the head or the penis. *Well you want quick, well I want long and drawn-out.* So with each extra minute of intimacy I was well aware this was putting us more and more behind in our morning schedule. This only added to further distract me from getting the job done within a reasonable timeframe. Normally, men have the problem of concluding proceedings too soon. I was suffering from the opposite affliction. This was a new form of performance anxiety I had never experienced. And there was no billboard advertising where I could get help—*Spending too long having sex? Call 1800 quickie!*

In my youth there were times when I actively sought distraction to prolong my performance. Now, during these morning trysts when speed was paramount, I found I was often easily distracted by trivial things. Our bed, for one, started to plague me during these extended sessions. It was a poor quality inner-spring mattress that inflicted severe discomfort. I could feel individual springs digging into my knees when in certain recommended positions. At times the pain was like being subject to some modern Chinese torture test. Not the kind of mindset you want to have when early ejaculation is your objective. Another diversion was the radio, the alarm by which we were rudely awakened each morning. It often remained on as we got down to business because neither of us dared venture out into the cold to turn it off. If I heard the hourly news report, I knew that it was 7:00 am and I was taking too long. It then became hard to stay focused, and certain songs or particular lyrics would distract me. In particular the Kings of Leon song 'Sex on Fire' was being played with eerie regularity around this time. Many people have speculated about the meaning behind these lyrics. If my experience was anything to go by I suspected it may have something to do with having a sexual marathon on a dodgy inner-spring mattress as your knees burn in pain!

Another challenging aspect of our somewhat random regimen was planning our social calendar. More than once a close mate, who had no inkling about our trying to get knocked up, invited me down the coast for a boys' surfing trip. I was always itching to go but knew there was a possibility that it could coincide with a 'surging session'. So I repeatedly had to be unusually non-committal and give flimsy work excuses why I couldn't be certain if I could make it until closer to the date. Needless to say Ali often got the call and it was 'game on' and I had to bow out of these trips. My friend began to take my rejections personally so eventually Ali and I decided it was best that we tell him why I hadn't been able to go. He was wonderfully supportive which made me wish I had told him of our predicament earlier as it would have saved a lot of angst and dishonesty.

Despite religiously sticking to the routine and prioritising Ali's peak periods above all other pursuits, sadly we had four months without success. To make matters worse, our monthly misfortune always appeared to coincide with a weekend visit from a friend or relative with young child in tow. Given the growing number of these it was getting near impossible to avoid. Not that we resented or disliked their company one iota. It was simply that it would often take us a few days to get over the initial disappointment of another failed attempt and being surrounded by gorgeous kids was like pouring salt on the wound. But at least we had the love and support of some of our friends who knew what we were going through.

C&J, in particular, were immensely sympathetic, always asking after us every month, and wishing they could do more to help. I would often joke with Charlie, 'Sure you can help … would you mind providing a sample?'

During those arduous months of failure we welcomed three happy and healthy boys into the world, the progeny of the New Year's announcements by Ava/Niklas, David/Erica and Pat/Jade. Their arrivals served as a sobering reminder of how long Ali and I had been unsuccessfully trying to get impregnated. So too did our third wedding anniversary, unfortunately, as this heralded another unwanted milestone: the passing of another year since we first decided to start trying for a family. Instead of being purely a celebration of our love and commitment to one another our anniversary was becoming tainted by this pervasive pregnancy undercurrent. In hindsight, maybe it wasn't the best idea to have decided to embark on this journey on a day that already held enormous significance. Nonetheless, we maintained the tradition by celebrating our anniversary at the café where our reception was held.

'You know this place will always hold the fondest memories for me', I said, looking around at the striking assortment of colours that radiated from the stained-glass windows that adorned the café's outer walls.

'Me too', Ali replied, stirring her coffee hypnotically.

'How are you feeling about the last few months?'

'It's upsetting, and to be honest I'm starting to think that maybe I'm the problem.'

'Really ... what makes you say that babe?'

'Well ...' Ali said, staring down at her coffee, looking uneasy. 'Your sperm's no longer the issue and we've been trying for a while now without any luck', she added, methodically scraping the encrusted froth from the lip of the coffee mug. 'Maybe it is time we started thinking about the various procedures that Nicci was talking about?' she said in a hesitant tone, lifting the coffee mug to her lips while maintaining eye contact from across the table.

'What, like having the laparoscopy?'

'Yeah.'

'But isn't it risky?'

'Not really, some of Jen's other friends have had them and they said it was no big deal. It's really just a general clean-up down *there*', Ali said, pointing discreetly down beneath the table.

'Nicci made it sound so much worse than that.'

'She has to ... so we're aware of all the risks.'

'It's really up to you I guess. But can we give it a few more months?'

'Fine', Ali replied, reaching across the table and holding my hand lovingly. 'I just hate feeling our life is in limbo. It's the not knowing that's the worst', she added, squeezing my hand with unexpected firmness. 'If we found out we definitely couldn't have kids it'd be devastating but at least we could move on with our lives.' The intensity in her eyes revealed how deeply this sordid affair was affecting her.

Ali was right; our life did feel like it was in limbo. I know children shouldn't dictate the choices you make in life and that they won't always accompany you in whatever direction you choose to take. But already Ali and I had made decisions that were based on the expectation that one day we would have a family together. Our choice of home was the most obvious and telling example of this. We had bought the house well before kids were the hot topic of conversation but it had instantly appealed to us because of its inherent family-friendly qualities. Located at the end of a quiet cul-de-sac, it had a large backyard perfect for playing and was situated in close proximity to good schools, playgrounds and parks. Both of us could easily envision a contented life ensconced in suburbia, raising happy and healthy children. But if we were unable to have children then I'm not entirely sure I would want to live in this house, this city, or even this country for that matter—Ali and I would be more inclined to move interstate or work overseas for a time. Part of me would feel selfish for not letting another family enjoy this special home and let it live up to its full potential by becoming enlivened by the vitality and adventures of a young family. We both knew Canberra was where we wanted to raise our children because of the clean, uncongested, easy-living lifestyle that it offered. We had crafted our lives in such a way that we had everything ready for a new arrival. Instead, however, we were left treading water, month after month. Consciously avoiding making any mammoth decisions about our future because we were so unsure in which direction we were headed—whether towards the beginning of the stereotypical nuclear family or eternal DINKSville.

Chapter 19
Suicide

I decided to bury myself in work as a means of distraction from the pregnancy preoccupation. After a particularly hectic day in the office, as I began the long ascent that constituted my bike ride home, I found myself mulling over the day I had had—the tension building within. This behaviour, of fretting about work after hours, was something that I had been working hard to redress. *Stress less* I kept telling myself. This was my new mantra. *Stress less*. One thing the naturopath was adamant about was my stress levels and that this could in some way be affecting my reproductive abilities.

I managed to suppress the work worries and continue with the ride. By the time I arrived home I was suitably exhausted and had successfully left the troubles of the day behind. Strenuous exercise is funny in that respect, the way the endorphins can quickly alter your mindset—set you on an even keel and blow out the cobwebs of a dreary day behind a desk.

As I started to stretch my ageing muscles on the lounge room floor there was a knock at the front door. I answered it warily, not expecting any visitors in the early evening. It was Pru, an old family friend who lived nearby. She promptly told me she had come to have a brief chat. I offered Pru a cuppa but she declined, insisting that she wouldn't be long. As we sat down on the couch to talk, my mobile phone rang in the kitchen.

'You should get that', Pru suggested.

'No it's fine.'

Several minutes later the front door opened and in came Ali. This surprised me as I didn't expect her back from the gym for some time. I could immediately tell that something wasn't right. She hung in the doorway with a look I had seen only once before, a look that had previously foreshadowed terrible news. My stomach dropped with dread.

'Stephen's ... killed ... himself', Ali whispered.

The words took a while to register, thinking I must have misheard her. 'What?' I replied.

'Stephen's ... killed ... himself ...' Ali spluttered, as fat tears cascaded down her flushed cheeks. 'Nicole just rang me, she tried to ring you too...'

I began to shake as I felt rage surge from a dark place within, pulsating through my every pore. It felt like I was being savaged by a foreign enemy. Fight or flight was my initial reaction. So I lashed out to combat the onslaught, striking the wall with my clenched fist. Then there was silence. Ali rushed to console me. Looking down at my knuckles, oozing blood, I peeled off hanging chunks of skin expecting, hoping, to feel the sting of pain that tells you that you're alive. Instead my body and mind were numb. I felt nothing. I couldn't process what I had just been told. Then one clear thought entered my head: *I won't be in to work tomorrow.* At that time I was in complete shock. My reality was in free-fall. So my brain had processed something practical, a certainty, a skerrick of clarity during this intense period of distress. *I won't be in to work tomorrow.* It would be some time before I would again think clearly.

'I should go ...' Pru said, breaking the silence. 'Do your mum and dad know?'

'Nicole's told your dad but she hasn't been able to get onto your mum in hospital', Ali replied.

Mum had been admitted to hospital several days earlier to receive intravenous antibiotics for a debilitating obstructive lung disease she had battled for many years called bronchiectasis, which leaves her incapable of walking any considerable distance without becoming breathless.

'We must go and see her now—she mustn't find out over the phone', I said.

Then it dawned on me, would I be expected to tell my mum that her firstborn was dead? I couldn't bring myself to be the bearer of such sad tidings which were a mother's worse nightmare. After some discussion, Pru benevolently agreed to accompany Ali and me to the hospital and be the one to break the disastrous news.

Leaving the house, Ali drove while I sat zombie-like, my ears ringing as if suffering from a mortar attack. A familiar tune filled the quiet confines of the car. But I was in no mood for music—not now. Yet the car stereo, notorious for being temperamental, remained on despite my repeated violent attempts to turn it off. The volume too was stuck, compounding my agitation. 'Fuck'n' thing! … Fuck! … Heap of shit!' I yelled with such ferocity that Ali glanced at me from across the wheel, her face fearful. Every note of the music prevented me from being alone with my thoughts as I wanted. But there was no respite during the entire journey.

I had never endured a more torturous trip.

At the hospital, we anxiously made our way up in the elevator to the ward where Mum was being looked after. The room she occupied was shared with four other patients so it was agreed, on discussion with the nurses on duty, to allow us access to a private room where we could have some privacy at this devastating moment in all our lives. As we were escorted into the small room my legs gave way and I fell into one of the couches and began shaking uncontrollably, my face in my hands, dreading the ensuing encounter.

The door opened abruptly and I was galvanised into an upright position, fighting back tears. I heard Mum before I saw her—her motherly intuition sensing trouble.

'What's happened?' she said, her voice shaking with intense nerves. 'What's happened? *What's happened* … !!' her wails becoming more frantic as no-one had the courage to answer her.

Then Pru uttered the same unimaginable words that Ali had announced earlier.

From the reflection in the archaic television in the corner of the room, I watched Mum's silhouette slouch, like she had been instantly drained of life—as if a part of her had been taken forever. I rushed to embrace her, as she slumped defeated into the couch.

I was speechless. I searched for something timely and poignant to say that would reassure my beloved mother in her time of need. But I had no such well-conceived response at my disposal. We sat in each other's arms, rocking back and forth. Never before had she looked so haggard.

'I will never, *ever*, do *that* to you. *Never*!!' I finally declared, breaking the silence.

I pledged this with such conviction and at the time I considered this to be my new mantra. I felt angry and confused. Angry at Steve for killing himself; confused by how things could *ever* become that bad, that committing suicide became the only option? Steve had everything to live for: his beautiful wife Nicole, a lovely home, an excellent job, countless friends and family that adored him. I became preoccupied with these thoughts of confusion and anger, revisiting them over and over without resolution, until Mum broke the silence.

'What about Nicole?' she asked, sounding dreadfully feeble. 'You must go and see her.'

As we drove to Nicole through the dark in eerie silence I sat in the passenger seat oblivious to the world that passed by and paralysed by sorrow, as if I, like Nicole, had just lost the love of my life. The infrequent light of a passing car did little to snap me from my comatose state where confusion and anger fought with the sorrow. When we arrived at Nicole's parents' house there were several cars already out front. Good news travels fast; terrible news travels faster still. Ali found the nearest available parking spot a distance from the house. Walking in darkness across the unfamiliar street I spotted Nicole's brother Henry entering the house some way ahead of us.

'Henry …' I called, emerging from the shadows.

Henry turned cautiously, his face ashen and devoid of emotion.

'You sound so much like *him*', he said, in an almost resentful tone, as he turned and continued to make his way into the house, not considering to escort us into his family home. Instead leaving us alone at the threshold to contemplate what emotional scene awaited us inside.

We made our way up the stairs into the family room where we were greeted by Nicole's father. Greetings were exchanged, condolences were offered and embraces felt. This was to become an all too familiar ritual over the forthcoming days, weeks and months. All the while I was detached from the world around me until I spotted Nicole who was sobbing loudly on the family room floor in the arms of her sister. I knelt down beside them and hugged them both.

'I'm so sorry', I said.

'You remind me … so … much … of … him', Nicole stammered, then broke down in violent tears. No words of solace could suppress tears of such anguish—somehow we all knew this. We wished that the warmth and touch of our embrace could at the very least provide some comfort. But she was inconsolable.

After some time I excused myself and asked Nicole's dad for directions to the bathroom. Once alone I stared at my reflection in the mirror, noticing my bloodshot, puffy eyes from which salt-encrusted lines ran down to my cracked salty lips. Rarely, if ever, had I seen grown men cry. I never knew it could leave such a lasting imprint. Men don't cry. I was never explicitly told this, nor had my parents raised me on this ideology, but my experience over the years had reinforced this macho stereotype and part of me was ashamed by the limp vision before me. I splashed cold water on my face, closing my eyes to wash away the evidence of my sorrow—wanting desperately to wash away this entire ghastly experience—praying that somehow this wasn't happening, praying that this was some unimaginable dream. But reality was my nightmare. My brother had killed himself. In those first few moments of true realisation I felt faint and nauseous whilst at the same time my head began racing frantically, searching for answers.

I returned to join Nicole and her family, but as I walked past Nicole's dad he pointed behind me and said, 'Ah … Matt … you've got a passenger mate.'

I was a little dumbfounded by his comment and gave him a look of bemusement until I turned my head and saw a lengthy trail of toilet paper protruding from my trousers. Then the entire room broke into abrupt laughter through tears of sadness. I rushed out, back to the bathroom, embarrassed beyond belief and tidied myself. When I returned seconds later I announced that word of my toilet incident must never leave this room.

Over the next few hours, as the word spread to friends and colleagues, various people started arriving to show their love and support for Nicole. Again greetings were exchanged, condolences offered and embraces felt. When the room was full of grieving friends and family Nicole sat up from her foetal position on the floor and announced 'Guess what happened before …'

'On no … Nicole!' her mother interjected, giving Nicole a disapproving glare.

At which point Nicole took great satisfaction in recounting my earlier humiliation to the burgeoning masses, where it was met with subdued laughter.

'Matt said it mustn't leave this room—that's all', Nicole insisted.

Checkmate—she certainly had me on that one. What an incredible woman—so selfless and composed—that even though she had just lost her husband she still endeavoured to introduce some laughter into a room full of mourners. This was certainly a renowned behaviour of Steve's that had obviously rubbed off on Nicole over the years—resorting to comedy at all times—the more inappropriate the occasion the better.

Chapter 20
The funeral

During the days that followed I sought to find answers to the many questions that still plagued me—all the whys and hows that surround a tragedy such as this. Upon speaking at length with Nicole, my mum and dad, the full story unravelled. They knew much more than I did, as it turned out. These conversations were some of the most intense and emotional of my life, particularly discovering that Steve had been suffering from depression on and off for several years. Nicole and my mum and dad knew this, but it was something which he had knowingly kept from me because like many men, we both saw depression as a sign of weakness—so he was too proud to let me know. I was shocked to learn of his mental health issues and couldn't fathom how I hadn't noticed any symptoms, given how often we got together and the strength of our relationship. But as Nicole, and my mum and dad explained, his periods of depression had never been particularly prolonged, hence his ability to be able to hide his illness from many friends and family—myself included. At worst he only ever missed a week or so from work which he could easily conceal under the guise of a bad flu. So I learned that he had been depressed before and had gotten better—but not this time.

On the day of his death, he was home alone battling with a sustained period of depression, was drinking alcohol and took his own life.

He left no note explaining why, unlike many depression sufferers who attempt suicide. A detail I later found out when trying to learn more about what Steve must've been going through. But in many ways, despite Steve not having left a note, we weren't left wondering—it was clear the insidious illness of depression had taken his life.

With these questions answered I was able to accept, to some degree, what had happened. I was, however, far from the state of full comprehension. In an effort to delay this I turned my attention and focus to the funeral. Nicole and I were adamant this service was to be a celebration of Steve's life. I was again astounded by Nicole's ability to remain focused and not to fall into a blubbering inconsolable heap—she was an inspiration and made me believe that if she could get through this, so could I. We busied ourselves with the many tasks that must be coordinated to make such an event possible—like planning a wedding in a week—only with the added emotional burden.

Friends and family pulled together to assist wherever possible. Modern technology really came to the fore. Within 48 hours of Steve's death, Nicole had created a Facebook page in his memory, exhibiting photos from his adventurous life. Friends from all over the world posted beautiful stories and moving tributes. Ordinarily, I wasn't a huge fan of social networking websites, but I became an immediate convert. It was extremely uplifting to see how much Steve meant to so many people. But I was struck with a gut-wrenching realisation: if only he had been more aware of this in his darkest hour. Depression must be a powerful persuader to make someone so remarkable and talented feel so worthless, to the point where killing themselves is seen as the only option left.

Technology also allowed us to obtain photos of Steve from all corners of the globe, which we were going to use in a video presentation at the funeral, accompanied by some of Steve's favourite music. Other elements of funeral coordination were considerably more excruciating, particularly being asked to choose the coffin in which your dead brother must rest. Nothing can prepare you for such calamitous events—they are surreal—unimaginable. You grit your teeth, fight back tears and do what has to be done to ensure a fitting send-off for your beloved.

The task of writing the eulogy weighed heavily upon me. The magnitude of this duty was overwhelming: to speak openly about depression being a deadly illness and suicide an all too common conclusion. I knew I had so many vital things to say but doubted I could find my voice to articulate them—I feared I would be overcome with emotion. But I began to write nonetheless.

At times my thoughts and feelings flowed onto the page. But occasionally I would be distracted by the enormity of the task. The words would cease and I would begin to labour and fuss over every written word to make certain its desired message was conveyed. I spent many hours in front of the laptop, my eyes straining, sore from the extreme focus and concentration. I slept unusually little during the week leading up to the funeral and was always preoccupied with the impending deadline. Yet how do you say all that needs to be said in such a short space of time. You have a captive audience but limited time. But I got there in the end and completed the eulogy to my satisfaction, yet I was adamant that I would not be delivering the most poignant prose I had ever written. And there was no way I would be able to keep my emotions in check. So I approached one of Steve's best mates, Phil, to speak on my behalf. To my immense relief he graciously accepted.

Phil also asked if he could possibly sing a song at the funeral—a gesture that Steve would have loved. There was little hesitation given Phil was such a fine singer with a commanding voice and a larger-than-life presence. I too wished I was capable of such a fitting tribute but I could not sing. Because I had lost confidence in my singing voice many years earlier during a childhood incident that still scarred me.

During my formative years at Marist Brothers primary, at the young age of 11, I was an accomplished singer, being a choir boy at the private Catholic boys school. I sang at many church services as well as in several school musicals. Singing was something I was naturally talented at and I enjoyed it immensely. I was never happier than when I was singing—until I was pushed outside my comfort zone. One day, minutes before an all-school choir practice, I was approached by the choir teacher and asked to sing the verses of a particular hymn—solo, in front of 300 of my peers. This I knew would be difficult, as we had only practised the hymn a few times and there was a particularly challenging high note at the crescendo of the final verse. A note which I wasn't sure I could hit with confidence, as it was very high. The teacher assured me that she had faith in my abilities, so reluctantly I accepted.

As the other students arrived my anxiety heightened. *You can do this*—I kept repeating to myself as I fidgeted nervously in my seat at the front of the filling hall. During the course of the practice as I sang with the group, my confidence grew. My voice had warmed up and I began to enjoy myself once more. Then, towards the end of the practice, my moment had arrived. The Principal invited me up on the stage and announced the arrangement of the hymn: the entire school would sing each chorus and I would sing each verse—solo. As I stood there and looked out across the sea of faces I began to have serious doubts. Immediately, my mouth became parched and my vocal chords felt stifled by the private school uniform with its constricting collar and tie. I was handed the microphone and the band commenced playing. I started well—singing in a relaxed yet confident style. But I knew the real challenge lay ahead. *You can do this.* As I began the final verse I could feel my nervousness grow. *Remember to aim above the note*— critical advice the choir teacher had always pressed upon us.

'… above your Shouldeeeeeeeeeeeeers!' I sang with trepidation.

To this day I am not sure where I had aimed, but what is certain is that it was nowhere near a note of any description. What can only be described as an intolerable discord hung in the air—worse than the hideous sounds that emanate from a distressed cat in an ugly moonlit scuffle. There was a moment of stunned silence as the entire school absorbed what had just happened—then laughter. Sporadic, isolated and muffled at first. But such laughter is contagious and within seconds the entire school was engaged in belly-aching, side-splitting laughter— teachers included. I stood there on the stage alone, for what seemed like eternity, with nowhere to hide. Eventually the Principal stormed over to me and grabbed the microphone.

'Silence!' he boomed over the mike. 'How dare you all laugh, you should be ashamed of yourselves!'

With this, the cacophony of laughter was promptly gagged. 'I demand that you all apologise to Matthew.'

Following the choir practice, school broke for morning recess. Again I had nowhere to hide; wherever I went—be it to the canteen, jungle gym or handball courts—I was accosted by a schoolmate offering an apology, some more sincere than others. Eventually I realised that avoidance was futile, so I just sat down at the lunch tables. Within minutes an impromptu line of children formed in front of me that stretched into the distance—each offering their apology as directed by the Principal. These apologies continued, one after the other, each a painful reminder of what had happened and only ceasing when the end of recess bell rang.

This was without doubt the saddest and most humiliating experience of my childhood. Ever since that fateful day I have never sung in public. Something which fills me with sorrow because I genuinely believe I had some God-given talent. To this day I still thoroughly enjoy singing, but I restrict my renditions to occasional outbursts in the shower or to the confines of the car on the way to work—environments where I can guarantee anonymity.

So, I had no intention of singing at my brother's funeral. Until, that is, Phil mentioned he was hoping to sing *Indifference* by Pearl Jam, an iconic grunge band that exploded onto the music scene in the 1990s. *Indifference* was one of Steve's and my all-time favourite songs. In fact, I can recall the precise moment when I first heard this rousing tune; it instantly gave me goosebumps and still does. To me it has always spoken of resilience in the face of adversity and the importance of realising that each one of us can make a difference to others, even in the midst of hardship. The appropriateness of this song for the funeral was not lost on me. So despite my grave reservations I asked Phil if we could sing the song as a duet.

'That would be amazing', Phil said without misgiving.

From the outset Phil showed complete confidence in me and my singing ability. We practised a few times and sounded remarkably good together.

'You have a great voice', Phil commented.

I felt compelled to tell Phil the sordid story of my childhood nightmare. Again his words of reassurance quelled the reservations I was having in taking on this responsibility.

In the final days leading up to the funeral I hardly slept. Instead I would wake every hour or so in a cold sweat with my brain whizzing, jumping from one topic to another: the unlikelihood of Steve's death, the eulogy, the decision to sing and other details of the funeral.

I could sense a growing anxiety in my demeanour. Undoubtedly those around me observed this too. Worried about my worsening condition there were many words of concern and comfort from Ali, Nicole and others close to me.

'Matt, take it easy.' 'Matt, look after yourself.'

'I'm OK', I would reply stoically.

At the time I firmly believed this. The focus of all my attention and drive was on the funeral and making it the most fitting send-off for my beloved brother. After which, I expected I would have ample time to rest, recover and privately grieve. Grieving over the death of a loved one was, until this juncture in my life, something that I had rarely had to deal with—apart from the anticipated loss of a family pet or of relatives from old age. But dealing with the sudden tragic loss of my brother from suicide was uncharted territory for me mentally and physically. During the final days leading up to the funeral I was running on pure adrenalin—to get the job done.

The day had arrived. And I felt nervous as if before a big exam, with butterflies in the stomach and apprehension about the day ahead. I knew my father was speaking at the funeral as well and he had a reputation for preparing material but deciding to ad-lib on the day. Which, in my opinion, had potential for disaster given the profoundly emotive topic. Surprisingly, I wasn't anxious about singing at the funeral; my biggest concerns were about ensuring the service went to plan. This was our only chance to say goodbye and the memories of this day would last a lifetime.

As Ali and I drove to the crematorium I started to feel really jittery and vulnerable, thinking that we were about be involved in a car accident which would prevent us from attending the funeral. Ali could sense my increasing uneasiness and tried to calm me. We arrived safely, a good 20 minutes before the service was to commence. Ali and I decided to walk around the beautiful gardens that surrounded the crematorium building. We followed a winding pathway lined with garden beds filled with a mass of blossoming colour. Evidence of spring was all around. I intently watched a pair of Superb Fairy Wrens, with their striking electric-blue markings, twitter and bounce through the undergrowth, playfully scavenging for food. The closer I looked the more of them I spotted. They were everywhere, going about their business in an intent yet playful way. This was the first time I had thought of anything other than matters to do with Steve's death. I pulled down my shirt sleeve and read the words I had written on the underside of my forearm: *slow down, build, less is more.* These words were to remind me of how I needed to sing. Little did I know these words of advice would have greater significance in coming weeks and months.

The sweet smell of spring was everywhere. I brushed past a lavender bush and picked a few flower spikes and rolled them gently between my hands; the pungent release of the familiar bouquet was inviting. I breathed in deeply, taking the scented oxygen deep into my lungs; I repeated this meditative action and found it immediately calming. *You can get through this.* We continued to walk slowly through the gardens which were filled with memorial plaques, occasionally stopping to read one here and there.

David Frank O'Conner

1945–2007

Beloved Father and Husband

As we continued to stroll, I calculated the different ages of various people who had passed away.

45, 67, 76, 89, 66 …

None of the ages on the 20 or so memorials we visited were close to Steve's age of 33. Upon grasping this I was hit with yet another painful realisation: Steve had so much more life ahead of him. His journey was only partway through—he had children and grandchildren to look forward to and another lifetime's worth of happy memories, all cut short by the appalling affliction that is depression. This reflection nearly brought me undone but I somehow kept it together. I had cried so much in the previous few days maybe I had no more tears left. As I stood amongst nature and witnessed all its beauty and wonder I was left thinking: life is short, but even shorter for some.

'It's time …' Ali said softly, planting a gentle peck on my cheek.

'OK, let's do this', I replied.

We headed up to the entrance of the crematorium where people had congregated. I was greeted by various friends and relatives. Again condolences were offered and embraces felt. We made our way through the crowd to the front of the expansive auditorium where Mum was sitting. I gave her a kiss on the cheek and handed her a sprig of lavender which I had souvenired from my therapeutic walk. She took a moment to smell its rich aroma, then placed it in the lapel of her jacket. I knew Mum adored lavender. I held her and Ali's hands and waited, putting on a brave face. As the crowd filled the room I wondered how many people would attend my funeral when my days on this earth were up. People vote with their feet at such events—but is it fair to judge the importance and impact of one's life by the number of bums on seats? As I looked around the room I could see throngs of people. The place was filled to capacity with people spilling out into the gardens. The music, *All I Want Is You*, by U2, which featured at Steve and Nicole's wedding only a few years early, began to play as my dad and the other pallbearers brought in the coffin. Tears were imminent, so I tickled the roof of my mouth with my tongue, a trick Jen promised would stop me from crying. It worked. My nerves settled and I was satisfied no more could be done at this point.

Chapter 21
Tackling depression together

The funeral went as well as could be expected. All those who spoke gave moving tributes to Steve, my father included. Phil did an exceptional job at delivering my eulogy for which I am forever indebted.

Tackling Depression Together—Steve Barwick's Eulogy.

My name is Matt Barwick and I idolised and loved my brother Steve. He was my hero.

If the events over the last few days have taught me anything, it is the importance of open and honest communication between friends and loved ones. So given this opportunity I feel I should speak the truth, and in light of this I have a confession: I have battled with a terrible affliction from the day I was born, 'Little Brother Syndrome'. Its symptoms can be publicly embarrassing for the individual concerned: an overwhelming desire to constantly copy big brother's entire being—his actions, speech, taste, opinion, demeanour and appearance.

Initially I battled in silence, thinking I was the only victim of this cruel ailment. However, during my formative years I began to see others, not directly related to my brother, showing signs of the terrifying symptoms. All of my friends, previously shielded from the affable, outspoken Steve, were changed forever after their first encounter. Because invariably Steve, being more than two years my senior, was always compelled to speak his mind and dispense brotherly advice on all topics.

I am adamant he saw this as his calling, his public duty, to ensure his brother (me) and all my friends were on the right course. The path of 'Steve Barwick Style'.

Maybe that's why I may never fully appreciate that he is gone forever, seeing that over his entire lifetime he subconsciously worked to craft his own entourage—a band of brothers. Steve obviously would be the reluctant figure-head—the ever generous and reluctant star—and I his most loyal follower. Adoringly alongside him every step of the way—come what may (the diet and fitness obsessed calf-less brother).

To say that I have been channelling Steve over the past few days would be an understatement. I am not a firm believer in such ethereal subjects. So much so that I had to doublecheck the word's meaning on Google. Steve, on the other hand, was a believer and so, as many here today could attest to, Steve and I often had heated comedic discussions on the relative good and bad of so-called literary 'masterpieces' that contained these other-worldly elements, such as 'The Lord of the Rings' or 'Harry Potter'.

The past week has been an ordeal, in the true sense of the word. I have been to the darkest place. The place Steve was. But what's worse I had to contend with my nearest and dearest asking me to voice an opinion on various aspects of the coordination of today. So I responded— what else can one do?

When in reality all I wanted to do was to be completely silent, with some music that Steve and I both loved—playing it as loud as possible. If only I had sign language in my arsenal— to help me through. Unfortunately, all I could call on was our most common attribute—my voice. Some people think Steve and I look similar, even twin like. I never really have. But our voices ... the similarity is scary, even I will admit that, which is partly why Phil is speaking so perfectly on my behalf today.

I had pre-empted another tragic scenario (and quite frankly, one a week will do me just fine thanks). A terrible yet comedic circumstance where a multitude of adoring Steve fans gathered to worship my hero, and were instead constantly distracted by the similarity of our voices. What a waste, when I have such an important message to convey.

At first, all concerned could see I struggled to formulate an answer when my opinion was sought. The evidence is for all to see. I would get angry at myself. Focus! Focus! I would plead with myself. I can do better than this. I must do better than this for my hero. Let me be sure to clarify here. At no time did I EVER refer to myself in the third person, one of my pet-hates!

Then gradually, as the days blurred into one another, I discovered my inner rhythm. And eventually found I could help. Really help all those in need. I found my secret weapon was to simply ask myself: 'What would Steve want?'

And, thankfully, because of his constant tutelage over my entire life, these answers, whilst cloudy and difficult to articulate at this inconceivably complex time, eventually came like a flash and felt so right. Almost—as stupid as it sounds—as if Steve were working through me. Subconsciously, I think Nicole and I were aware of this connection and I personally would have found it even harder these past few days without her strength, reassurance and support.

There were also moments since the incident when I felt as if Steve were testing all of us one last time, in his unique playful manner. And I imagined him sitting back observing all this, with a big glass of inky red, his cheeky grin and at times absolutely cracking up with laughter witnessing the chain of events that this awful tragedy has perpetuated. Proclaiming to himself quietly, tapping his fingers together slowly like his favourite Batman villain: 'Let's see if all concerned can pull this off … Let's see if my legion of minions can give me the send-off I want. A celebration—as grand as a wedding—coordinated in under a week!'

But at other times over the past week Steve would have been hurting. Truly regretting what heartache and sheer torment he is putting us all through. I and many others here today have never laughed so hard, spoken so much, thought so constantly and slept so little in the past week. No sit-ups for a while at least. Yet here we all are, dressed up to the nines to celebrate Steve. Bad luck Bro, the joke's on you. You are getting the send-off you deserve!

Had I and the others not suffered from 'Little Brother Syndrome' then maybe we could have arranged the unthinkable and tried to derail this celebration into something that you, Steve, personally would have detested: put you in a gaudy, ornate coffin, all of us reluctantly participating in a plethora of epic Godly hymns, with some liturgical dancing. The icing on the proverbial cake being the release of 33 white doves to a Celine Dion classic of my choosing. Sounds amazing hey? One final attempt by me, at brotherly one-upmanship— a game which we played often.

But all concerned couldn't do that. Me in particular, I lacked the intestinal fortitude. Because as many of you know big brothers always get their revenge. Unfortunately for us, Steve was never that good at physics, unfamiliar with Newton's third law of motion. Subsequently his revenge would be something to behold. Because like everything he ever focused on and was passionate about, he would give it his all, plan every minute detail, fuss over every perceived angle, refer to GoogleScholar for the latest academic thinking on the topic and, most importantly, write a macro to automate the process where possible. That was Steve. I envisage him giving his new endeavour an ominous and catchy title like 'Shock & Awe'. After all he did love the Bombers!

Then all concerned, myself included, who were involved in putting this travesty together, would be cursed for years, maybe even decades to come. 'Shock & Awe' would enact nothing malicious of course. Always playful, at times inappropriate, but always with impeccable comedic timing: in true Steve Barwick style.

I have one final almighty confession to make. I always wanted to be a Bombers fan. Truly. What an obvious public admission of Little Brother Syndrome. How pathetic. So, conscious of this, I chose to support the Melbourne Demons and my loyalty has never wavered. I recall agonising over this decision because under Steve's guidance one of the most important teachings at the college of Steve was to PICK A TEAM !!!! And never waiver, even when things got tough.

The details of when exactly this was are fuzzy but what I do recall vividly is that my decision came when watching a Bombers versus Dees game and Melbourne won! In my childish simplistic mind I thought any team capable of beating the team my big brother adored must be a real long-term premiership contender. The rest is history. In support of our respective teams we have endured triumphs and turmoil—indicative of life. Steve would always say philosophically: 'When the Bombers have a good year I have a good year.' I suspect this had more to do with the copious amounts of beer he would win with the various bets and subsequent double or nothing success. No year was more profitable than in 2000—it is amazing his liver survived—when his beloved Baby Bombers became men and took all before them, included demolishing my Dees in the GF, who quite frankly were just happy to be there in my humble opinion—like I always was with Steve. The Dees had the attributes to win the 2000 GF but lacked the belief. I firmly believe this. It was a topic Steve and I revisited many times together —the head is in control—it is always mind over matter. Irrespective of how you much you hit the gym— this I am certain.

Secretly, I was happy because, deep down, nothing pleased me more than to see my brother happy. I can truly say that I have always found it near impossible to say no to him. Steve subconsciously knew this too—an unspoken certainty. At times Steve took advantage of this—but again never in a malicious manner—always playful.

The Force was strong in Steve. Like a true Jedi Master. He Knew.

Yoda Voice: 'Make brother do what Master wants … hmmm.'

Yoda Voice: 'Go to pub you will. Pick Master up you must.'

Steve used to have staying power, so these calls often came for me in the wee hours of a freezing Canberra morn.

Astonishingly, I would virtually always respond without hesitation. Sleepily. 'Sure … Bro… see you soon?' Often I had been ensconced with Ali in bed, so had to leave this sanctuary and leave Ali blissfully asleep and unaware.

But it wasn't all bad, because I sometimes raced to Steve. With Led Zeppelin or TOOL blaring—primarily to keep me awake but sometimes for the sheer thrill of it! Man those old REXies could whistle ... Sorry Mum. Dad—deep down you understand. So too does Gran.

In hindsight, I may have always suspected Steve would eventually be struck down by this terrible affliction— that his happiness, that dominated his life, whilst in abundant supply at times, was precious and volatile and could be sucked from him at a moment's notice. Sadly the specific details regarding Steve's suffering from depression were never fully articulated to me until now.

Steve and I had a tradition that was unspoken—like much of the foundations of our strong and loving relationship—which was to always get together when our teams played. This was easy at first, but became near impossible to uphold as we matured and all of the unnecessary baggage of modern life weighed on us both. Regardless, there would only be a handful of games that we ever missed each other's presence. Maybe that explains my utter contempt for the UK and for London in particular.

Thankfully though, this year in early August we both followed our unspoken tradition of watching the game together. We met at the Yowani golf club, a venue I had never been to before but one at which Steve spent many hours with many of you playing golf. Steve, the bastard, has the home ground advantage— I thought to myself.

Our preference was always to watch the game at either of our houses. But on this day an alternative venue was necessary because the game was not televised on free-to-air because neither of our teams was doing all that well (the Dons 12th on the ladder and the Dees languishing in last place). To set the scene Steve and I walked into a completely empty club. But there was a massive plasma with prime epicentre seating. Great.

You could hear a pin drop. To some, this may not have been the ideal venue to watch footy but to Steve and me it was perfect. No distractions. But again this understanding was rarely articulated, always understood.

I would like to take this opportunity to put a call out to all here today, particularly the boys from the ANU Footy club. If someone, somehow, has a copy of this game I would be eternally grateful. Not because it was a particularly high quality game, in fact it was pretty hard to watch. But it was close—which is all that mattered. Quietly Steve and I were having a ball. Stakes were as high as the 2000 GF. Every game was, because of what the winner would get. Beer? No chance. Bragging rights! The greatest brotherly currency and something that couldn't be spent or consumed and held all its value until the next epic encounter.

At half-time the game was still in the balance. And we discussed in great detail and delight how the second half might play out. Steve was lording it over me with his beloved team's effort— like McPhee who, if I recall correctly, was playing particularly well. I, on the other hand, was desperately trying to seek solace from the smallest sign of improvement from my boys. Trying to telepathically ignite the infamous come-from-behind, never-say-die attitude that once so proudly typified the heart of the Red & Blue. But alas in 2008, my boys were struggling with the mental battle all year—lacking the self-confidence to back themselves.

Then the strangest thing happened, in hindsight. When the football talking subsided I felt an uncomfortable silence—something which normally never happened. This would have been the perfect opportunity for open and honest communication between brothers, about any and all topics including depression. Had we been sisters the chances of such an exchange would have been highly probable. But many men, and young Australian males in particular, find it near impossible to discuss such topics. We often discussed other important topics in detail but rarely those relating to one's health. And mental wellbeing was somewhat of a taboo topic given the stigma and our Barwick family history of tackling depression.

So I am left with this encounter as one of my personal 'What if' Steve scenarios that I have been playing since last week over and over in my head. Many of us will have these. But rest assured Steve was surrounded by family and friends that loved and cared for him, many of whom are here to pay their respects today. Furthermore, I'm adamant no one in particular is to blame for these terrible circumstances given what I now know about depression. Instead all of us and yet none of us are to blame. Better communication by all of us would certainly have helped but communication is only part of the puzzle. Hopefully if we all support organisations like beyondblue we can better understand this illness—I myself will forever be a supporter of beyondblue.

So I see this eulogy to Steve as a unique opportunity to present a call to arms to all the Steve worshippers, to his closest entourage of loyal followers, minions and junior-burgers.

'Fell deeds await, Now for wrath … now for ruin and the red dawn … forth eorlingas!!'

Let us unite as one and commit to the cause. Not just by monetary donation, but by breaking free of modern society's leaning towards silence rather than frank and fearless communication between family and friends. And when confronted with uncomfortable silence don't let it linger. Tackle it head on. No regrets, no potential future 'What if' anguish. The latter, I know, is an arduous request but you have a secret weapon. Just conjure up the spirit of quintessential 'Steve Barwick Style'. And be always playful, and at times inappropriate. Because, as I always stress to my colleagues at work, mistakes are inevitable, no dramas—we are not working in a hospital—no-one is dying here! However, what I have never been able to tolerate, for as long as I can remember, is not learning from one's mistakes but instead wherever possible ensuring they never happen again. That is all I am really asking of you all today.

By the way the Dons ended up winning. Just. Steve and I stayed until the very end and both of us were happy—because Steve was happy.

Steve, deep down you knew surfing was never my focus, your happiness was, and I know we both cherished the rare times we spent surfing together with friends and family. At least now your surfing prowess will surpass all because as I kept saying to you ad nauseam 'All you ever needed was time in the water'.

Now, you have all the time in the world.

So I'll see you in the Line Up—I expect you to drop in for a party wave …

Love you—Aloha.

Just one last thing: I'm done talking. Apologies for being so blunt. To many of you this will not need explaining. For the rest, please grant me this request. Please come and give me your condolences if you wish—but don't be alarmed if I have difficulty responding because I'm done talking for a while. Please regale me with your fondest Steve memories— which I know Steve would have loved— because today is all about my hero, Jedi Master, champion footballer, whiz accountant and snowboarder extraordinaire. And I want you all to bask in the glory of his greatest achievement—but only if you want to of course.

The duet, *Indifference*, also went well—as far as I can recall. Although at the time I was in an emotional haze. Did I slaughter any notes like in my childhood nightmare? I don't think so. But to be honest I don't care if I did, because I am adamant I sang with raw emotion, from the heart, for Steve and no-one else. I have always been a firm believer in some form of afterlife—believing that somehow that which is the essence of us, which makes us unique, continues on in some way beyond death. So I'm convinced Steve witnessed his funeral, and was moved by it and undoubtedly seething with remorse for what he had done.

My only regret on the day was that we ran out of time and the final song *Home* by the Foo Fighters was never played. This was partly due to the length of my eulogy, but I had so much that needed to be said and I knew the opportunity would never come around again.

I have read that Dave Grohl, the musician who wrote the song *Home*, considers it to be his finest work and that in writing songs he tries to not be too explicit with his lyrics, so that people can draw their own interpretation from them and the songs can then help them through a particular time in their own lives.

Whenever I hear this song, it stops me. Particularly the last verse:

People I've loved
I have no regrets
Some I remember
Some I forget
Some of them living
Some of them dead
All I want is to be home

Chapter 22
The wake

After the funeral Ali and I drove to the wake which was held at a nearby golf club that Steve frequented. We arrived later than the majority of guests, as I had spent a considerable time in the gardens walking and talking with Nicole after the funeral. Again we were met by various friends and family and greetings were exchanged, condolences offered and embraces felt.

As I stood making idle chit-chat with relatives I hadn't seen in years, it dawned on me that I hadn't yet experienced the wave of relief that I had expected would wash over me after the funeral. A wave that I hoped would ease my agitated state of mind. I tried telling myself to relax but this had no effect. Instead I was suddenly struck with the feeling that there was still more work that needed to be done—that the evening represented a unique opportunity for people to speak frankly about their own lives—to 'cut the crap' and speak from the heart because attending a funeral in such tragic circumstances lends itself towards serious soul-searching about one's own life.

I wanted people to really open up. As I had tried to convey in my eulogy, honesty and communication are essential in dealing with depression. But I knew that time was against me, because the opportunity for introspection doesn't last long. I think most individuals are genetically programmed to avoid topics surrounding one's longevity.

So I approached various friends and asked them, 'How are you?'

Their immediate response was always: 'Fine …'

I would quickly follow this up with, 'How are you *really*?' This would get a variety of responses. Some people would instantly break into tears and start to confess their deepest darkest secrets or their gravest fears. Often I didn't know what to say in response—but I listened and for many that is all they needed. I was astounded by the number of people who told me they, or a friend or family member, had suffered from depression—suffered in silence for the most part. It really dawned on me how pervasive this disease was and how Steve's life may have been spared had he let those around him into his personal nightmare.

Other times people would say, 'I am fine … really. How are you?' I genuinely believed they were OK. I also knew there was nothing I needed to help them with.

I worked the room for several hours, trying desperately to get people to open up to me. No topic was taboo or too personal. I had barely slept and hadn't eaten, yet I was invigorated by the real connection I felt I was having with people I cared about—that was until I hit a wall of exhaustion. Within minutes I sensed my energy levels drop and mental and physical fatigue kicked in. I found Ali and asked her if we could go.

'C&J have invited us around to their place to hang out', she said.

I figured relaxing with close friends could be just what I needed at the end of what was a very intense day. We promptly said goodbye and made a quick exit.

Unfortunately, being amongst friends in familiar surroundings didn't provide the distraction that I needed. I still found my thoughts were racing. I stood in the kitchen surrounded by C&J and Ali, their faces showing their worry over my uncharacteristic demeanour. I too could sense that something wasn't right with me. My emotions were all over the place, on the one hand I experienced immense relief and was elated that the funeral had gone so well, but this was juxtaposed with feelings of absolute despair and loss. My behaviour became increasingly unusual and manic, which understandably really upset everyone.

'We are *really* worried about you', Jen said, on the verge of crying.

'What do you want me to do?' I countered angrily, 'I'll do anything you say.'

'We think you should call someone', Charlie said.

'What, like a counsellor?'

'Yep', Charlie replied, as if he was asking me to call for pizza.

'Fine!' I said defiantly.

In reality, the last thing I wanted to do was talk to someone. I was done talking, as I had stressed in the eulogy. But I desperately wanted to allay everyone's concerns for me and maybe prove to myself also that I was OK.

Charlie went and retrieved the phone book and looked up *beyondblue*. He dialled the number then handed me the cordless phone. The phone rang for some time then reverted to a recorded message that explained the business hours of operation were 9 am to 5 pm and suggested a message be left for contact during normal business hours. So that's exactly what I did. I went into some detail explaining the circumstances surrounding my call. Ali, C&J listened on as I rattled off details of the preceding week—leaving all the possible contact numbers I could be reached on. At the time I felt lucid and was buoyed with confidence at being able to recite these numbers with such ease. *I can't be going mad when I able to think so clearly,* I thought. But this call did little to alleviate their worry.

'What now?' I said with renewed confidence.

Charlie dialled another number and again handed me the receiver.

'Who's it now?' I queried.

'Lifeline ...'

'Seriously ...?'

At that point it was clear to me that my wife and two closest friends had grave fears for my mental wellbeing. As I again listened patiently to the ringing tone I became despondent—the previous call had lasted several minutes and had been mentally draining—and I dreaded having to go through it all again.

'You speak. I'm done talking', I said, handing Charlie back the phone. 'You know the story, give her the details ... then I'll talk.'

Charlie did as requested, taking considerable time to give the counsellor on the end of the line ample context surrounding how we came to be in this position. As he spoke I listened intently and was astounded at how unbelievable these events would have seemed a week earlier, yet this story had been my reality.

'You're up', Charlie said, handing me back the phone minutes later.

The lady on the phone introduced herself as Julie. She spoke in a wonderfully calm and soothing tone. I imagined her to be in her mid-fifties and a homely, mothering type. We spoke for several minutes and she asked me numerous questions, the most pointed being how the suicide of my brother made me feel. I gave concise, contrived responses because I believed talking was only further agitating my mind. We spoke for some time until Julie could sense I was keen to wrap things up.

'You'll get through this', she said with quiet assurance.

'I know', I replied unconvinced, 'thanks for listening.'

'My pleasure, and remember Lifeline is always here should you need to talk.'

'Thanks, I really need to get some rest.'

With that I hung up the phone. I wanted this day behind me. I wanted it to end.

'Bedtime!' I announced to the group, stripping down to my boxer shorts, marching down the corridor, climbing into their spare bed and falling asleep immediately.

Chapter 23
Spiralling Out of control

The day after the funeral marked a new chapter in my life which I understood had changed forever. Ali had organised the perfect day with the intention of making me relax as much as possible. We were going to spend the day lunching at a café at the National Botanic Gardens, then the afternoon lazily reading under the shade of one of the many eucalypts. I awoke mid-morning after having taken some herbal sleeping tablets the night before.

Charlie had kindly left me his iPod to borrow for the day knowing we share pretty similar music tastes. This was a remarkably kind gesture. Music had provided me with great solace since Steve's death and I was grateful to be able to access music on the go. We left the house and Ali drove towards the Botanic Gardens. It was a glorious day; the sun was beaming with only a hint of breeze to carry the aroma of spring through the air. I decided I needed some suitably uplifting music, so I navigated through the menus and promptly selected *Everything in its Right Place*, a Radiohead classic. I experienced an unbelievable sense of relief as the poignant keyboard intro faded in. *I can get through this.*

Instinctively, I continued to choose songs that usually put me in a positive frame of mind. It was the first time I had ever used this new portable music technology and I became an instant convert—having an entire music library accessible, when I needed it most in my life, was marvellously opportune.

After lunch we wandered through the serene gardens and marvelled at the sights, smells and sounds of the Australian bush. When in such surroundings it is hard not to appreciate and cherish the beauty and uniqueness of the Australian wilderness. The gardens were full of commotion with school groups being guided, mother with strollers, professionals on their lunch breaks and retirees leisurely occupying their day. We made our way up to a grassy slope, shaded from the midday sun by several large eucalypts.

'This looks like a good spot', Ali proffered.

'Sure', I replied.

We both read our respective books in silence. This was usually our Sunday ritual, normally accompanied by a warm beverage. On this day I found myself reading the same sentence over and over. I couldn't concentrate. I couldn't relax and find my rhythm to reconnect with the story I had been reading (and thoroughly enjoying) prior to Steve's death. All I saw were jumbled, unintelligible words. Again my over-stimulated brain began to speed up, recounting events of the preceding week. These memories rushed into my subconscious in random and sporadic bursts.

So I resorted to listening to music, as I found this slowed my zooming mind. I lay on my back in the cool and cushioning grass and closed my eyes, letting the music wash over me. I mouthed the lyrics and tapped the beat firmly. This instinctive behaviour momentarily helped until I started to automatically infer a meaning and a message in the lyrics of the songs I chose, that was directly related to my experiences of the past week. At times the interpretation or connection I made didn't feel like speculation. Instead, it was almost as if these songs had been specifically written for me, for this particular time in my life. These were not logical thoughts, I was delusional. *What's happening to me— am I having a panic attack—am I losing my marbles*? I was not in control.

With this behaviour I experienced unparalleled levels of anxiety and bewilderment, as if I had little control over my thoughts. I started to again feel terribly vulnerable, like I had the day before on the way to the funeral.

'Can we go?' I asked in a neutral tone, not wishing to alarm Ali.

'But we just got settled, and it's such a nice spot', Ali said, stroking my leg affectionately. 'Relax. Try reading your book some more.'

'I just don't feel like being here', I countered, again trying not to sound too forceful.

'Are you OK doll?'

'Yeah babe', I lied.

'Are you sure?'

'Yep', I said, smiling weakly, panic rising in my chest.

'OK let's go.'

I turned off the iPod as we promptly made our way back to the car and headed home. Music wasn't helping and I again drifted into an accelerated contemplative state. Once home I decided watching a surfing DVD might provide me with the necessary level of cerebral distraction. The opening footage showed a carefree athletic surfer riding a mammoth board in an exotic island paradise. Watching the DVD had the desired effect—I found it to be the best distraction possible. How I longed to surf with such style, in a location like this—right now. But my surfing apprenticeship was in its infancy despite it having taken years to reach an average level of competency. Living 150 kilometres from the ocean hadn't helped. But I was hooked regardless and gained immense gratification from the pursuit. Part of the appeal of the sport is that it's near impossible to master. Seemingly simple, yet requiring the surfer always to adapt to the nuances of every new swell—a skill which requires a lifetime of dedication but the rewards, I figured, are immeasurable. I hoped to one day surf with style, even if by then I was proudly displaying my Senior's card.

Having only started surfing in my mid-twenties made it all the more challenging. However, my passion for waves started in my early teens when Steve and I bought a bodyboard during a Christmas holiday in Newcastle—sold to us by the most decorated and respected professional surfer in Australia's history, Mark Richards. I recall entering the shop which had a uniquely blended aroma of fibreglass, neoprene and surfing wax, a smell which at the time was completely foreign to me but that would later foreshadow exhilaration. I walked cautiously around the room filled with towering surfboards shaped by Mark himself, emblazoned with his distinctive Superman-inspired MR insignia, fearing one wrong move could bring them all crashing down. I desperately wanted one of those perfectly contoured boards so that I could learn to surf, which to me looked like the epitome of cool and unbridled fun. How many kids from landlocked Canberra can surf I wondered? But unfortunately my parents saw surfing as far too dangerous and difficult, so Steve and I had to settle for the bodyboard, which had the reputation of being the much maligned, poor cousin of surfing. I recall that when choosing the bodyboard my brother was puzzled when Mark asked him whether he was Goofy or Natural. Steve had no idea how to respond. But I did. I watched as he stood there in silence, dumbfounded in the presence of an idol. Eventually I came to his aid but not before I was sure he felt deeply embarrassed by a true surfing legend. This encounter was a rare moment of younger brother triumph and one-upmanship that became legendary between the two of us—a constant source of derision—that only weeks before his funeral was again called upon during a heated but jovial exchange about our respective surfing prowess. I couldn't fathom that Steve was now gone and that this fond childhood memory, like many others, was now only mine to recount with such clarity.

Unfortunately, upon conclusion of the footage my obsessed, frenzied mind returned immediately, this time with even greater ferocity than before. I found myself speaking like I had a severe case of verbal diarrhoea without any self-censoring. I couldn't control the speed with which I was trying to articulate my thoughts. I could tell this unusual behaviour was deeply worrying Ali. Not good at hiding her emotions, her face showed grave concern as she fought back tears.

Some time later Jen showed up unexpectedly at the house. I was unsure of the reason for her visit. She too had a look of unease when I conversed rapidly with her. She immediately went into the kitchen and had a private discussion with Ali in hushed tones. When the two returned to the lounge room Jen, the master of diplomacy, spoke.

'We want you to come with us', she said in her usual chirpy tone.

I looked to Ali for reassurance. But the deep worry on her face only heightened my concern.

'Where?' I said. Ali remained silent as if in shock, tears welling in her eyes.

'You'll see', Jen replied, showing no signs of distress.

'Can I bring my surfboard?'

'No, sorry', Jen insisted, her voice softening.

I followed Ali and Jen into the car and off we drove.

Chapter 24
The Psychiatric Unit (PSU)

I woke the following morning with my limbs feeling as if they were cast in stone. I lay there immobile for several minutes, dazed and confused. I tried to get out of bed but was overcome with dizziness. My mouth was parched and my body clammy with sweat. Eventually I slowly sat on the edge of the bed with my head nestled in my sticky palms, feeling nauseous. Looking down I noticed I was fully clothed and when I saw my blood- encrusted knuckles then recollection of the previous day's delirium began to return.

As the brain fog gradually lifted and movement returned to my limbs, I surveyed the drab and sparse room which barely fit a single bed in the middle, with a small bedside table alongside and a minute wardrobe against the wall. That was it. The only window was laminated, preventing any outside vista. But I could tell by the softness of the light through the opaque glass that it was either early morning or late afternoon. I suspected it to be morning but my stomach was trying to tell me otherwise—that I hadn't eaten in days.

I stood up gingerly and staggered around the room looking for clues as to my whereabouts. Nothing. No brochure. No information folder like in a hotel, explaining the general housekeeping directions and guidelines. *Where was I? How long had I been here?*

I lurched over to the door and tried the handle, expecting it to be locked. To my surprise it opened into an expansive corridor like those in shopping centres. But eerily this corridor was devoid of people.I cautiously made my way down it. Every few metres there were doors either side, off to other rooms which I assumed were like mine. The corridor then intersected another. Suddenly I heard the muffled noise of a TV in the distance and hurried towards the familiar sound. I located it at the end of the corridor in some kind of community lounge room. As I approached the TV I could instantly see on the screen a morning show with the time 7:15 am in the corner.

Gradually, people emerged from their rooms and made their way to some communal tables where breakfast had been served, but I stayed glued to the television waiting for some clue as to what day it was—too shy to ask someone.

'Mornin' Matt', said a cheery voice from behind me.

I turned around hesitantly as I was set upon by an athletic-looking woman in her early forties— bounding with energy.

'I'm Roslyn your nurse, I've got your meds', she said hurriedly, handing me two yellow wafers. 'Pop these under your tongue and let them dissolve.'

I promptly did as requested and was left with an unpleasant after-taste.

'Where am I?' I inquired timidly.

'The PSU.'

'The what?'

'The Psychiatric Unit.'

This took a few seconds to register.

'… How long have I been here?'

'Oh … just since last night', she said. 'Have some breakfast; it's over there on the tables. There should be a meal with your name on it.'

With that Roslyn rushed off as briskly as she had arrived—stopping momentarily to dispense medication to other patients.

By this stage I was famished, so I made my way over to the communal eating area, where half a dozen men of various ages were eating intently.

'Good morning', I said bashfully, like a child on his first day of school.

This greeting was met with virtual silence apart from the barely audible grunt from one individual between mouthfuls. Picking up on this less than friendly vibe I found my steaming plate of fried fare. It had all the hallmark signs of unappetising mass production: rubbery bacon, soggy scrambled eggs and charred hash browns, but I devoured it nonetheless, partly due to overwhelming hunger but also because I had a burning desire to get the hell out of there. I was relieved to realise I had only been held overnight. Other patients looked well accustomed to this daily routine, which led me to believe they had been here for a considerable time.

Those initial few hours were the most difficult given my still agitated mental state. No nurse approached me to explain why I had been admitted, how long I would be staying or where the various amenities were. Instead, I had to glean details about the routines of the PSU simply by observing those around me. After several hours I had surveyed the confines of the establishment: apart from the separate men's and women's sleeping quarters, there were two courtyards, several activity rooms and a nurses' station. There was also the 'high dependency' wing where, I assumed, people at serious risk to themselves were cared for and monitored. I considered myself rather lucky, given I had a private room, whereas the majority appeared to have dormitory arrangements.

I soon discovered that the nurses' station was where most of the activity was centred. It was bedlam because it was from here that disgruntled patients jockeyed for position to pester their nurse for information about their release, more medication or most often simply wanting cigarettes from their private stash that were given out under close supervision. The nurses behind the glass window were hounded continually. Upon observing this harassment I vowed that I would try my utmost not to add to their burden while at the PSU. So, despite having many questions that I badly wanted answered, I decided to sit, watch and wait—in full view of the nurses' station—until a suitable moment arrived to ask for assistance. In the meantime this submissive, inconspicuous position allowed me to engage in one of my favourite pastimes: people-watching.

As I sat, with my back against the wall, I observed a hive of activity being played out in this highly unusual environment. I naturally wondered what psychiatric disorder each patient was suffering: schizophrenia, obsessive-compulsive disorder, bipolar. Surprisingly, the majority of patients were around the same age as me and there were similar numbers of male and female. As I watched patiently, I was struck by how 'normal' the majority looked—sure there were some troubled and dejected faces but no more than you would see in a normal hospital ward. There was only the occasional patient who was clearly struggling, evident by enraged ramblings, relentless agitation or the agonising strain on their face.

Initially the idea of being surrounded by throngs of mentally unstable people did fill me with fear—like I imagine a person wrongly convicted of a crime would feel being locked up with other prison inmates. But then it dawned on me: *I was obviously mentally unwell—yet I was not to be feared*. My beloved brother had suffered from mental illness, yet he was one of the most affable people I knew. I realised that my fear was unjustified and that I should treat these people like anyone else. So that's exactly what I did.

I got up and approached a compact guy wearing baggy American gangster-style clothing. This surly-looking character had been pacing aggressively in front of the nurses' station, spraying obscenities at his nurse demanding she give him another cigarette.

'G'day, I'm Matt', I said tentatively, proffering my hand.

The guy stared at me, sizing me up, his eyes barely visible from beneath his sunken cap. There I stood, arm out, exposed and wondering whether he was about to pull a weapon on me. I persisted nonetheless—what choice did I have—there was nowhere to run, nowhere to hide.

'Do you wanna have a hit of ping-pong?' I asked timidly, turning and pointing to the table down the lengthy corridor.

'If ya want', he said with a snort, not breaking his intense stare.

'What's your name mate?'

'… Bashir.'

We began to play, hitting the ball to one another in a non-competitive way. After several minutes of playing in silence I plied Bashir with questions about the PSU. As it turned out he was well informed and surprisingly forthcoming with details and I sensed he enjoyed the role of informant. He also thoroughly enjoyed openly expressing his disdain for his nurse.

'That bitch!' he hissed. 'She sees me behind the glass but ignores me. Bitch! Shit, all I want is me fuckin' smokes!'

I sensed these tirades were a real emotional release for Bashir—speaking ill of his nurse whether warranted or not—because it allowed him to focus his anger and vent. From my perspective it seemed that his anger was misdirected but I knew better than to try and voice this opinion to someone I'd just met (not to mention the fact that he looked like he could inflict some serious damage on me if he so desired). Nor did I dare ask the reason for his presence in PSU nor how long he had been incarcerated. These, I soon came to realise, were the fundamental unspoken rules at the PSU.

'Oh and the food here is fuckin' ords', he added. 'I feed me dog better crap.'

'Great', I responded crestfallen.

'Speak of the devil—grub's up', said Bashir unexcitedly, as he gestured down the corridor to the communal eating area.

I followed Bashir down the passageway and we sat and ate lunch with a bunch of other male patients.

Bashir was on the money. The food was remarkably bad again— modern aeroplane food is far superior. And for someone who likes good food, I knew this was going to be tough for me. Nevertheless, people around me scoffed down their meals like a pack of hungry hounds. I, on the other hand, picked, poked and prodded, eating virtually nothing.

'Not hungry?' the guy next to me inquired, looking enviously at the uneaten mess on my plate.

'Not really', I replied.

'You will be eventually', he said. 'If you ain't having it, can I?'

'Sure', I said, sliding my tray to the guy whose baby-faced complexion suggested he was barely old enough to drive.

'What's your name?' he asked between mouthfuls.

'Matt', I said, trying not to stare at the obvious scabs that ran down the length of his wrists.

'G'day I'm Nathan', he replied. Then he continued to devour my meal and ceased to engage in conversation.

After lunch I spent the remainder of the afternoon alone in my room trying to piece together my situation. I got nowhere because I found myself periodically dozing, against my best efforts to stay awake. Obviously this overpowering lethargy was due to the medication I was taking.

Later in the evening Ali came to visit in my room. She arrived unannounced but I was overjoyed to see her. We sat on the bed together as she emptied a bag she had brought, filled with all sorts of items: clothes, toiletries, books, magazines and most importantly Charlie's iPod. Not forgetting a delicious, steaming fresh serve of home-cooked chorizo pasta, an all-time favourite that I consumed in minutes. But once I had finished eating, and the excitement of her arrival had abated, I sensed a strangeness between us. I was still largely in the dark about what had happened to me, and the reasons behind my admission to the PSU, and she appeared unsure about what she should or shouldn't say or do given my seemingly fragile state. The vibe between us was disconcerting and not dissimilar to First Date nerves, as if we barely knew one another—both struggling to keep the conversation afloat and dancing around the sensitive topic of my incarceration. She appeared genuinely afraid to engage with me for fear that doing so might set off another manic episode. Nothing was discussed regarding any possible diagnosis.

'I love you so much', I said, rubbing her thigh slowly, trying to get her to relax.

'Me more', she replied, avoiding eye contact.

'Thanks for bringing all the stuff', I said, catching a glimpse of her eyes which were even redder than the day before.

'No worries ... I'll do anything for you doll ... you know that.'

'Thanks babe', I said squeezing her thigh again.

'Is there anything else I can get you?'

'Just keep the beautiful food coming,' I said, 'the meals here are disgusting!'

'Can do', she said, finally looking at me face to face with a weak smile.

'Oh and some eggs and milk please.'

Then we said farewell and gave each other a loving kiss goodbye before I escorted her to the exit.

'See ya tomorrow', I said as I watched her walk into the darkness beyond the security doors.

Chapter 25
Day two at the PSU

The next day began like the first. I again woke disorientated and enervated, only this time I quickly reacquainted myself with my now familiar surroundings. I lay in bed, waiting for my limbs to regain their faculty. After which I suddenly was compelled to do some exercise.

Normally, I keep myself pretty fit regularly participating in surfing, kayaking, mountain biking, swimming and the gym. Since Stephen's death I hadn't had time to do any exercise whatsoever and I really missed the endorphins, the natural high that comes with exercise. My physical activity was now limited by my surroundings. I decided to use the exercise techniques I had used in my early weight-training days because they required little in the way of equipment. I started with push-ups, then balancing between the chair and the bed doing triceps-dips. Then, like Robert de Niro in the movie *Cape Fear*, I did some chin-ups using the door frame and finished with some sit-ups. I repeated this routine for numerous sets until the familiar ache returned to my muscles.

I wanted to finish my work-out with the 'bridge'—a technique where you lie parallel to the ground on your elbows and toes and hold the position, engaging your core muscles for as long as you can. But there wasn't sufficient space in my room to allow this. So I made my way to the communal TV area and got into position. Thankfully there wasn't anyone around as I'm no exhibitionist.

As I was holding position I could sense someone sidle up next to me. I held position, determined not to be distracted. A minute passed until my curiosity got the better of me. I turned my head to look who was beside me. It was Nathan and he was trying desperately to mimic my 'bridge' position—shaking uncontrollably.

'Hold in your stomach muscles—think of bringing your belly-button into your spine', I coached.

After a few more seconds of holding the position Nathan's tall, lanky frame gave in to the ache.

'I can't do it', he said, dropping to the floor in a disheartened thud.

'Yes you can, try again', I insisted. 'This time just try and last a few seconds longer.'

Nathan tried again and this time held the 'bridge' for considerably longer than his first crack.

'See!' I said triumphantly. 'How does that feel now?'

'Great', he said with a reluctant smile.

I finished my work-out with some perfunctory stretches. Again Nathan followed my every move, while I gave advice and encouragement.

'Gee, you're one flexible guy', I said, jealously observing his ability to contort himself far beyond my restricted range of motion—not unlike a giraffe doing yoga.

'Do you surf?' I questioned.

'No, why?'

'You should give it a try; I reckon you'd be an excellent surfer.'

'Really …'

'Definitely. I'll show you some stuff after brekkie if you want?'

'Cool.'

After breakfast I sought out Nathan. He was sitting in the central courtyard with the majority of the other patients, smoking. It seemed this was all the majority of patients did at the PSU—sat around and smoked—Bashir and Nathan included. I know smoking's addictive but, given what we now know about the health risks, I find it hard to comprehend that people continue to smoke— and I find the smell downright repulsive. I knew I couldn't tolerate such an acrid odour, despite how anti-social it may appear. So I asked Nathan if we could go inside, as I had a few surfing magazines I wanted to show him.

'Check this out', I said, expectantly handing him one of the mags that Ali had kindly packed for me.

I flicked through the pages, pointing out the simplicity and beauty of the waves, the athleticism of the surfers and the expressions of sheer excitement and adrenalin that were so apparent on all their faces.

I turned to a page that illustrated how swell was generated from wind across vast distances of ocean. How, as the groundswell approached the shore, the amplitude of the peaks and troughs heightened. I ran my finger along the illustration.

'See, up and down, up and down', I said, repeating myself over and over. 'Up and down, up and down.'

Nathan repeated the mantra with me in a slow and hypnotic tone.

'Waves are like life mate, they have both up and down periods', I said. 'At the moment you're in a down period, all of us here are. But hang in there, soon things will start to feel better and you'll have an up period.'

I continued to flick through the pages. By this stage I had well and truly got Nathan's attention as he looked on, almost in awe, at the pictures.

'Do these guys look like they're having fun?' I asked rhetorically.

'Totally', replied Nathan, his eyes glittering with envy as if fun was an unattainable dream for him.

'You can too, once you're outta here. Remember that. Surfing's my passion—some of my fondest memories are surfing with my bro and mates. And even if surfing isn't your "thing" find that "thing" that you're passionate about and make it happen. Don't think you've gotta be the best at it either, I'm a pretty crap surfer but *so what*, I get heaps of enjoyment from it and that's what counts.'

Nathan nodded his head in agreement. 'OK, can I borrow this?' he asked.

'Sure, but I need it back later.'

'No worries', he said, ambling off to his room, head down, still engrossed by the images.

By this stage I sensed I really needed some time alone. Here I was trying to help others, but I needed to help myself. The medication had definitely calmed me but my thoughts were still rather uncharacteristically manic. I retired to my room to listen to the iPod. I immediately chose the most mellow tunes available: Jack Johnson, of course, with his ukulele-strumming, laid-back melodies which have been referred to as the ultimate 'anti-road rage' music. His music is instantly calming; one can quickly be transported to Hawaii with the opening chords. Thanks to Jack, I was on the mend.

The next few days followed the same routine: exercise in the morning, often joined by Nathan (my own raw eggs and milk for breakfast in preference to the slop that was served up), followed by some games of ping-pong with Bashir, a compulsory counselling session, some more surf talk with Nathan. Generally, Ali or some friends would visit for lunch, bringing alternatives to the flavourless rubber food on offer. In the afternoon I would savour some quiet time alone listening to music of my choosing—songs that made me feel good—lots of Pearl Jam, Jack Johnson, Foo Fighters and Radiohead, just to name a few. Sometimes, I would try and read a book but I usually found this too mentally taxing.

I continued to drink copious litres of decaffeinated green tea, not wanting this unfortunate episode to have a detrimental effect on my swimmers. I even started to drink it cold, which to my surprise tasted remarkably good. I would place the tea-bag into a plastic drink bottle with a pop-cap lid and leave the bag in indefinitely. The water would eventually turn an unappetising yellowy-green colour which, when shaken, would froth up and look remarkably like beer. Bashir, however, took great pleasure in broadcasting to all and sundry that I had gone completely bonkers and was drinking my own piss.

As the days bled into one another I could sense an improvement in my mental state. My thoughts weren't as hurried and I was gradually getting back to my usual self. Music helped immensely in my recovery. As someone far more eloquent than I once said: 'Music *is the medicine for the mind*'. I began to realise this and subsequently would carry the iPod around with me all day and listen to it continually. To keep myself active during the day I would do umpteen laps of the corridors that surrounded the PSU—all the while listening to the iPod. When other patients would approach me unguarded and begin ranting incomprehensibly about something or another, I would just leave one earpiece in to ensure I could nod and give suitable words of support at the appropriate time. Doing this enabled me to engage with them without being rude, while still maintaining my sanity to some degree by not being drawn into their confused discussions.

On occasion I would offer the iPod to someone, so they could try and pick a favourite song to listen to. This was not always a success, as their taste in music often differed from mine and they were unable to find something suitable. I tried to give other people the opportunity to feel the same emotional release and solace that I was receiving from the music I cherished. The PSU did have some radio headphones that some of the patients used. But these were plagued with static and obviously lacked the functionality of being able to select from one's personal music library. Generally, one of the nurses told me, the headphones were given to patients to stop the voices in their heads. I pondered what improvements to patients' mental wellbeing could be realised if, like me, they all could access an iPod (or similar device) with music of their choosing.

One night before bed, as silence descended on the PSU, I heard ungodly wails, shrieks and howls that shook me to the core. Sounds of such terror I could only assume were coming from the high-dependency wing. Although I'm not particularly religious I felt compelled to say a quiet prayer for whoever was suffering such hardship. Thankfully, the drugs were quick to take their effect and sleep descended on me like a heavy winter's fog and I dreamt of being far from this place with the woman I adored, making passionate love for the sheer bliss of it, rather than for BMS (Baby Making Sex).

Chapter 26
Bipolar

The following morning I completed my work-out ritual, but this time without Nathan alongside. As I sat down to breakfast with the others to consume my post-work-out protein-hit of raw eggs and milk, Bashir grabbed a chair next to me. Initially I had been wary of Bashir given his prickly personality, especially after hearing his tirade against his nurse. But I later began to observe that this animosity was infrequent and sporadic and more likely related to his severe nicotine addiction than his underlying nature. Sure he was brash at times and fired off obscenities like no-one I'd ever met, but I found him to be a genial enough fellow for the most part and we were rapidly becoming friends.

'Ahh shit, you drinkin' that raw egg crap again', he announced in disgust as he poured himself some juice. 'I'm gonna spew dude, that's seriously rank.'

'Sorry mate', I said, sculling the remainder to appease him. 'Where's Nathan? The lazy bugger was going to work out with me this morning. Is he sleeping in?'

Bashir leant towards me and hunched his shoulders. 'No man … Nathan tried to hurt himself last night, so he got moved to the padded cells.'

'Seriously?' I said, shaking my head in disbelief.

'No shit, didn't you hear the noises last night', he whispered, trying not to be overheard by the other patients.

'Is he OK?'

'I dunno.'

This terrible news saddened me. Obviously being admitted to high dependency was a major setback in terms of his recovery and would undoubtedly prolong his stay. Nathan was a great kid; sure he had his demons—but don't we all? He had become so keen to exercise with me, to make himself fit and looked so committed to getting better—he had even talked about quitting smoking. I deeply hoped that my discussions with him hadn't somehow triggered this behaviour. Had I given him a false sense of hope? I had no idea what he suffered from or how long he had been here, or for how much longer he might be required to stay.

I never saw Nathan again.

Despite how upsetting this was I was determined to stay upbeat. I quickly realised that was how things were at the PSU. Everyone was unwell. People got better, people got worse. People came and went. The important thing was to focus on getting better. Some lucky individuals were only days, hours or sometimes minutes away from leaving. They had been given the all-clear by their psychiatrist. I had observed the gradual process of departure, where patients were drip-fed a taste of life outside the PSU. Patients were granted short excursions free from the confines of the PSU, provided they were accompanied by a friend or loved one. Initially these excursions were only an hour or so, but were extended—as the patient's condition improved—until eventually the patient was released. I suspected my release was some way off, considering I had been at the PSU for a fair while and was only now seeing a psychiatrist. Yet this was a cause for optimism, as I saw this as being one step closer to my release.

The appointment with the psychiatrist was at 10:30 am. I had a few hours to kill before then, so I found a private corner and sat in a chair that was basked in sunlight. I again sought solitude and music. As time drew near I felt nervous about what I might be told—was I suffering mental illness? Was I deranged? Or was it simply grief? I tried to prepare myself for the worst, but my lack of knowledge of the topic did little to help. Medical TV dramas often have stories of patients with brain tumours that cause mental episodes. Maybe I had a tumour? I was subconsciously avoiding the most likely diagnosis: bipolar disorder. My father had bipolar from his mid-twenties and having grown up observing this terrible affliction I was terrified of such a diagnosis.

I spotted Ali as she entered the PSU through the security doors—her dazzling smile lifted my mood instantly. I felt amazingly fortunate and honoured that someone so beautiful, intelligent and kind, adored and cared for me so much. It's amazing how one person can mean so much to you that it's almost unnerving—they can be your lover, your best friend, your confidant. You have so much love for that person that life without them would seem impossible. My heart sank as I reflected on Nicole who had lost exactly that and now faced a life of uncertainty—a new chapter, without finishing the last.

'Hey doll, how are you?' Ali said as she kissed me.

'Hey babe, good', I replied.

We made our way into the doctor's room, sat down and waited in silence. I still sensed some unease in Ali's body language. We both stood up when there was a noise at the door and in came a middle-aged man, built like an ageing ex-football player, except his square-framed glasses made him look much more intellectual than most footballers. I was struck by how much he looked like the actor Alec Baldwin.

'Hello, I'm Dr Moreton—Matthew I assume', he said in a pleasant reassuring tone.

'Hi', I replied, shaking his hand. 'This is my wife Alison.'

We all sat down. The doctor commenced with the usual pleasantries then went into some of the detail regarding the reasons for my admission into the PSU. All this information washed over me—I was waiting anxiously for the diagnosis. Then I heard the word: bipolar.

I froze. My eyes glazed over; I was in total shock. The doc continued to speak, but nothing was registering with me apart from that one word which resonated in my ears. Bipolar. For the remainder of the consultation I managed to maintain a certain level of coherence, just to ensure the doctor didn't think my condition had worsened, because I knew such behaviour might delay my departure even more.

'So, I'll see you tomorrow then', the doctor said as he made his way to the door.

'I won't be going anywhere!' I replied, trying to infuse a little humour into the situation.

Then Ali and I were left alone in the room.

'You OK doll?' she asked, rubbing my back with a concerned look.

'I s'pose …'

Ali looked relieved to finally know what was wrong with me. I knew it wasn't a death sentence but I had many years of prejudice towards this illness. When I was much younger I didn't know my father was unwell. I do recall more than once being brought to tears as a child and yelling: 'Why … why is he behaving like this?' As I grew older I observed behaviour in my father that made no sense to me: his inability to get out of bed for several days during a depressed phase—meaning we might miss out on certain activities as children—or the embarrassment and frustration felt during a manic episode where reason and logic vanished. At times I suspected something wasn't right with my dad but for their own reasons my parents kept this from me and my brother. Steve, being two years my senior, had a better recollection of our childhood together and I later suspected he may have known much sooner than me. It wasn't until I was in my mid-teens that the truth was revealed to me. I don't recall the precise moment that I was told but I do remember it made things a little easier, as it answered the question *why?*.

I do regret not being more sympathetic towards my dad during my teens. For some reason I didn't seek to better understand his plight through my own research—instead I remained relatively ignorant and prejudiced.

'I brought us some lunch', said Ali, breaking into my thoughts.

'What's on the menu?' I asked, trying to sound upbeat to disguise my concern.

'Sushi.'

'Yum, you know me too well.'

'Do you want to go eat in the courtyard?'

'No way, that place reeks of cigarettes, it's repulsive!'

'What about the other courtyard?'

'I've never seen anyone in there; the door's always locked for some reason.'

'I'll ask the nurse if we can get access.'

Roslyn explained that the reason patients were normally denied access was because the brick wall at the north-east corner of the courtyard tapered to an easily scalable height from which freedom beckoned—not a particularly well designed facility for the containment of patients. But Ali and I were in luck. It took some persuading but eventually Roslyn reluctantly unlocked the door to the courtyard only because I assured her I wasn't a flight-risk and besides I was being chaperoned. She locked the door behind us to prevent other patients trying for an escape.

This courtyard was much more to our liking. It received considerably more sun, a few garden beds with plants that showed signs of some TLC and an inviting timber outdoor setting, unlike the mediocre plastic chairs in the other courtyard. We sat down and ate in virtual silence, both stunned by what the doctor had revealed. I sensed Ali wanted to provide me with words of comfort but didn't really know what to say. Despite the likelihood of the diagnosis we were both so unprepared for it when it finally arrived. We both finished our lunch quickly.

'I've been meaning to tell you something', Ali said, grabbing both my hands and shaking them as if trying to invigorate me with her energy and enthusiasm.

'What?'

'Rebecca had the baby, a girl—Amy.'

'That's a lovely name. When did you find out?' I asked.

'A few days ago', she replied sheepishly.

'What, the day I was admitted?'

'… Yeeeaaaahhhh.'

'Sorry about that.'

'What are you apologising for?'

'For ruining it all with my craziness.'

'You're not crazy!'

'How can you be so sure? I'm in the nuthouse aren't I?'

'Don't say that. You're unwell at the moment but you *will* get better. I promise. I'm here for you always, *Better Together*, remember', she said rubbing my wedding band with her hand.

'I s'pose …' I said, pulling my hands free. 'Thanks for coming.'

'Do you want me to go already?'

'I just feel like being alone at the moment … that's all', I said, avoiding eye contact.

'Can I see you tomorrow?'

'That'd be nice', I said with a weak smile.

I motioned to a nurse passing by the courtyard to let us out. I walked Ali to the security exit and we kissed goodbye. As I watched Ali walk off into the distance I hoped that she had meant what she said. I suddenly considered myself to be seriously damaged goods, less of a person and I felt incredibly alone. Prior to today I knew I was unwell, but I believed it was more directly linked to the shock and grief I was experiencing over the tragic loss of my brother. I hadn't contemplated the possibility of a long-term psychiatric problem—this really frightened me. The possibility of losing Ali was terrifying; I prayed our relationship wasn't in jeopardy.

I wandered back to my room and closed the door. Sitting on the end of the bed I subconsciously fidgeted with my wedding band, slipping it up and down my finger. Ali had said it: *Better Together*. Never had I needed to hear this song more. I promptly selected it on the iPod, lay back and recalled pleasant memories of our wedding dance together.

I spent the rest of the afternoon alone contemplating my diagnosis. Being told you have a mental illness was unlike anything I had experienced. Until that point, I had been fortunate not to have had any major medical problems in my life (apart from a few broken bones resulting from boisterous behaviour in my youth). Bones break, they heal, life goes on without lasting repercussions. Mental illness was different. We typically take our mental wellbeing for granted. Your sanity is everything about you. It defines who you are as a person, how you interact with the world around you, even how you interact with yourself. Mind over matter. The prospect of requiring medication to stabilise my mind was terribly unnerving. I rarely, if ever, took a Panadol to relieve a headache because of my unease over what it might do to me. I also started to become concerned that the medication may in some way be detrimental to my fertility.

My pensive gloom was interrupted by a knock at the door. In walked Roslyn.

'Hey Matt, I have your evening meds', she said handing me the pills.

'Cheers', I said, reluctantly popping them in my mouth. 'Do you have a sec?'

'Sure', she said standing by the doorway.

'I've got an odd question', I said, feeling my mouth become parched with anxiety.

'No such thing around this place', she said, sensing my unease.

'Are these meds bad for … male fertility?'

Roslyn looked a little taken aback by my question, I suspected she had been asked all sorts of questions at the PSU, but probably not this one, judging by her delayed response.

'… Nope, I'm pretty sure they're not. Why? Are you and Alison trying to fall pregnant?'

'Yeah, for nearly two years.'

'Can I give you some advice?' she asked. 'Don't let people tell you to *relax*.'

'Why's that?'

'Because it's got nothing to do with it', she said sternly.

'How come?' I countered.

'Why then do raped women get pregnant?' she said with a fierce glare. 'They weren't relaxed during conception.'

I was left speechless by the candid logic of her argument. She sure had a point.

'Keep trying, you'd be surprised how many people have problems conceiving', she continued, her voice softening.

'How do you know all this?' I asked.

'Oh … I'm training to be a midwife. Can I tell you something else? The best thing a father can do for a child is to love its mother— remember that.'

'OK I will and, who knows, maybe you'll be our midwife one day.'

'Maybe', she said with a wink.

'Goodnight, thanks for the chat.'

Roslyn left and I readied myself for bed. I gathered my towel and toiletries and headed down the darkened corridor towards the bathrooms. A long, steaming hot shower had become a daily highlight. During this indulgence I used more water than a household with five teenage girls. I would fastidiously lather, then scrub, every pore, hoping to rid my body of the filth that had accumulated since my brother's death—trying in some respects to cleanse not only my body but my spirit. I scrubbed and scrubbed until my skin burned red-raw, desperate to forcibly shed my skin like a snake—I too wanted a fresh start. On occasion I had even begun to whistle and sing while indulging in the massaging and soothing cascade.

As I ambled along I heard faint moaning sounds in the distance. Thinking the worst my heart stuttered in alarm. I tiptoed until I reached the intersecting passageway and turned to see two unidentifiable figures in the distance, both draped with white sheets and pretending to be ghosts.

'Oohh … ooohhh … oooohhhhh', they moaned in eerie harmony as they approached.

I got a whiff of one of the characters who emitted a pungent funk of BO and cancer sticks that made my eyes water and nose tingle. I recognised this unpleasant tang; it belonged to a patient who considered showers a burden, preferring to disguise his powerful scent with infrequent applications of deodorant, to little effect.

'Is that you Bashir?' I asked confidently.

'Noooo, I'mmmm a ghooooost…' , the person replied as they continued down the corridor, fighting back laughter, his rotund figure bouncing the sheet as they passed.

I started to laugh hysterically—like I hadn't in months. The ghosts too began to crack themselves up, continuing to moan through spurts of giggles.

'You guys are crazy', I said, then immediately realising the inappropriateness of my comment.

'We're *all* crazy, ohhh, ooohhhhh!' yelled the distant figure from the other end of the darkened corridor.

Maybe he was right. Maybe everyone, even those outside the PSU, were a little nutty.

Chapter 27
PSU monotony

The next day started much like the one before. The monotony was making it hard for me to keep track of how long since I'd been admitted. After breakfast I sauntered down to the nurse's station to get my iPod charger when I was overtaken by Bashir who hurried past.

'Come check it out!' he puffed.

'What?'

'Some fucker's ram-raided the front entrance!'

I quickly followed him, turning the corner, then stopping abruptly at the entrance to observe the carnage. Several tradesmen were busying themselves putting up safety barriers and boarding up the doorway with plywood—plunging the entrance into uninviting darkness.

'Fuuuuck … someone was pissed', exclaimed Bashir.

'When did this happen?'

'Around 3 am—me sources tell me', said Bashir in his usual cocksure tone.

'Did they catch 'em?'

'Na, the bloke bolted—but left his ride—was an ex-patient apparently.'

'Really …'

In strode Roslyn, through the side entrance, to start her morning shift.

'Morning gentlemen, a little excitement in an otherwise dull day I see.'

'Look, if the bloke wants back in 'ere, he can take me spot', Bashir quipped.

'Sure … I'll see what the doc says', she said jokingly, ducking into the nurses' station.

Bashir and I spent the majority of the morning playing ping-pong together. Bashir had an average backhand but a lethal smash which frequently meant my downfall. His trash-talking, with which he could break my concentration, was even better than his game. He revelled in beating me and started to keep score of the countless games we played over numerous days. I, on the other hand, was just content to have some physical pursuit to pass the time and distract myself from dwelling on my predicament. I also gained satisfaction from seeing how much gratification it brought him, with the added benefit of keeping the lazy character out of the chain-smokers' courtyard—at least temporarily.

By mid-morning it was time for my appointment with Dr Moreton. Ali arrived just in time and we headed into the consultation room together.

'What happened at the front?' she asked inquisitively as we sat and waited for the doctor.

'Just some cranky ex-patient making his feelings known', I said, leaning over and giving her a welcoming peck on the cheek.

'Oh, is that all.'

'I told you the food here was bad, didn't I', I said.

The doctor entered and wasted no time in getting down to business. I sensed he was a little pressed for time, appearing more agitated than during our previous meeting. He proceeded to inform me that tomorrow they were going to give me a precautionary CAT-scan to look for any tumour or brain damage. He tried to reassure me that this was simply procedural and that there wasn't anything to worry about. But I had seen enough medical TV dramas to think otherwise. On a more positive front, the topic of 'excursions' was raised. Starting that day I was to be allowed one hour's accompanied leave from the PSU. And depending on how that went it would be extended to two hours the next day. This development was cause for optimism.

After the meeting with the doctor, Ali and I were left to contemplate what we could get up to in the limited timeframe.

'How about we head home for a quickie?' I joked.

But truth be told my libido had vanished since admission into the PSU. I assumed this was due to the drugs I was taking and hoped my desires would return promptly once released and off the medication.

'Nice try', Ali said. 'We wouldn't make it home and back in time. How about we get an early lunch at the café up the road?'

'I s'pose, but I prefer my suggestion.'

We were forced to take the lengthy route out of the PSU, via the 'normal' hospital because of the damage to the usual front entrance. This frustrated me as it took considerably more time to get to the car. By the time we got to the café a third of our allotted time had already elapsed. We hurriedly ordered, then took our seats, holding hands across the table. My preference was to grab our food and go for a leisurely stroll through the neighbourhood gardens, to enjoy the lovely spring day, but time didn't permit.

'How are you today doll?' Ali asked with a genuine look of concern on her face.

'Better, I think, but it's hard to know really. Do you reckon I'm getting better?'

'Sure, you definitely seem calmer and more relaxed.'

'It's probably just the drugs …'

'Yeah, but they're doing what they're supposed to—making you better.'

'Maybe … but you know how much I hate drugs.'

'I know, but it won't be forever.'

'I s'pose you're right. I miss you …'

'I miss you more—it is so lonely at home without you', Ali said with a frown.

'Hopefully, I can get out soon.'

'Fingers crossed.'

Our meals arrived and we were forced to devour them quickly given the impending curfew. Then we hurried back, arriving just in time. We said goodbye in the car and I made my way to the alternative entrance to the PSU.

As I opened the large bifold door to the corridor I could smell the all too familiar stench of the PSU: a combination of stale aeroplane-style food, cigarettes and human excrement—all trying to be disguised by acrid sanitary bleaches and anti-bacterial products. This pervasive pungent aroma had been less noticeable day to day in the PSU. Now I'd been reacquainted with the fragrant freshness of the outside world both the smell and my confinement seemed worse than ever.

I walked past the smokers' courtyard and spotted a surprisingly vibrant rosemary bush hidden in the corner, surviving against the best efforts to kill it. I ducked in and picked off a handful of sprigs and took them to my room. I placed a sprig in my palm, closed my fist, then pulled the sprig through my hand under tension. I repeated this action several times, releasing the fresh familiar aroma which reminded me of a hearty Sunday lamb roast. I placed sprigs all around my room and found this gave me some reprieve from the pervasive stench. But this did little to improve my general disposition.

My confinement was beginning to depress me. The novelty of my surroundings had definitely worn off. Even despite the appointments with doctors and counsellors the days were becoming excruciatingly long and I craved proper exercise. My makeshift morning work-out was gradually having less impact. The PSU did have access to a fitness room that had a treadmill and bike, but this room was locked and limited access could only be gained by speaking with one of the nurses who, quite frankly, had enough to deal with. There were meant to be some art and music classes scheduled on specific days (which I would have thoroughly enjoyed) but unfortunately both of the staff members who took these classes were away and neither had a replacement.

Then I was jolted from my stupor by an inspirational idea. Was this my opportunity to make a difference—to help people in need. *Was this my calling? What I had been waiting my whole life for?* Or was this just the beginning of another manic episode that I needed to promptly dispel before it prolonged my confinement? I wasn't used to doubting the validity and sanity of my own thoughts. I was also not really prepared to deal with this idea yet as I was still feeling gut-aching pain for my lost brother and a determination to recover from my illness. So I consciously abandoned the idea because at this point every minute, every hour and every day was a mental and emotional struggle, and I was incapable of considering the future, particularly one without Steve in it.

The following day the doctor was pleased with my progress and granted me a two-hour leave pass, much to my delight. This meant Ali and I were able to have a much more leisurely lunch than the day before. The weather was sublime and it again felt glorious to be outside in the fresh spring air with my beloved. These excursions had come to mean so much to me—a fleeting escape from the all too familiar surroundings. The simple pleasure of being able to go and do as you wish is ordinarily something that you take for granted. I can only imagine how claustrophobic prisoners who are incarcerated for many years must become. When granted freedom you sometimes feel befuddled by all the options available to you, after having become so used to a far less stimulating routine. It made me really appreciate all that life has to offer and to take pleasure from the little happenings in life. The fact that Steve was unable to do this when he was depressed really played on my mind and upset me. I was having real difficulty with the choice of suicide as an option.

That afternoon after lunch I was escorted through the hospital to have my CAT-scan. The operator was very business-like and clinical in his approach (after all he had undoubtedly conducted this procedure on thousands of patients). But this was a first for me and I was rather tense. I lay down on the examination table and was told to lie completely still. The table then moved into the centre of the dome, the contraption made a whirring sound and within a minute or so it was all over and I was led back to the PSU.

The next day I was immensely relieved when Dr Moreton confirmed that the CAT-scan had shown up no irregularities. He was also particularly impressed with the speed of my recovery. The nurses had noted that I had been behaving in a lucid and controlled way for days now.

Upon hearing this Ali felt buoyed to raise the issue of an extended 'excursion' release.

'We have a close friend's wedding in Wagga on the weekend. Is there any chance that Matt might be allowed two nights off to attend?' Ali asked expectantly.

'I can't see why not, provided he keeps things low-key and I must stipulate: no alcohol.'

'That won't be a problem for me, Doctor', I said.

'Oh and no driving also', he added.

'OK', we replied in unison, Ali giving me a knowing smile as if to say I told you so.

Chapter 28
PSU release

The next day Ali picked me up in the evening and I spent my first night at home. It was immensely healing to again be in familiar surroundings. There *is* no place like home and I can see why musicians, who travel far and wide for their passion, often write songs about the magnetism and sanctity of home. As we crawled into bed together I inhaled the essence of clean bed linen that was tremendously calming. This smell brought nothing but fond memories of times spent between the sheets with my lovely Ali. We soon became ensconced under these covers and fell asleep almost immediately in each other's arms.

The next morning we left early en route to the interstate wedding. I found it very difficult to stay awake as the drugs seemed to be making me drowsier than ever. However, I quickly woke up when we arrived at our accommodation and were met by several close friends.

I was a little apprehensive at seeing everyone as I wondered how they would react to me having been in the 'nuthouse'. I really hoped they wouldn't treat me differently. I needn't have worried. These were some of my nearest and dearest friends and it was clear from the outset that they loved me—warts and all. I sensed that everyone was relieved to see that I appeared to be well on the road to recovery. Once they had asked how I was, the conversation turned to more trivial topics. I found it deeply relaxing to be amongst my close friends, thoroughly enjoying watching them fool around together. I found it difficult at times not to participate in their high-spirited antics, but I was under doctor's orders and the drugs helped to subdue me.

The wedding was a complete contrast to the monotony and sterility of the PSU. It was held at the bride's family home amongst magnificent manicured gardens. The food was delicious and plentiful. The alcohol flowed freely (for some) and live music drifted through the property. It was a perfect wedding. Several times during the night my mind cast back to another memorable wedding—Steve and Nicole's. That too was a perfect wedding, in my opinion, as it showcased the deep and abiding love that Steve and Nicole shared and which was meant to last and conquer any adversity. I was again struck with awe for the terrible impact of depression on people's lives.

As the guests gradually slid into further inebriation it became increasingly difficult to tolerate, despite our best efforts. Not that Ali and I weren't having fun—quite the opposite. But the past fortnight was without doubt the most abysmal and emotional of my life and Ali and I were still suffering the after-effects, both physically and emotionally. Nonetheless, I was intent on having the best time possible. However, at the point when the consumption of alcohol overtook that of food and people's inhibitions were left by the wayside, the dance floor filled to capacity and conversations become less engaging and intelligible we decided to call it a night. We said goodbye and made a relatively early exit.

My agreed release had turned out to be somewhat of a mixed blessing. I'd greatly enjoyed the wedding but the release had given me a taste of normal life and I badly wanted to return to that life. The next day during the monotonous three-hour drive back home I had ample time to contemplate my fate and I was filled with a real sense of dread at the idea of having to return to the PSU. I sensed that my condition had vastly improved since being admitted a week earlier but the question remained whether the medical professionals would see it that way— and I dreaded that they would err on the side of caution.

But I too had some doubts regarding my health. Mental illness was uncharted territory for me and I wondered whether these past few days of relative sanity were only temporary and whether I would regress and eventually become a permanently hospitalised manic mumbling mess. I didn't know whether the medication could stabilise my behaviour long term. You hear bipolar and other mental illnesses referred to as a 'chemical imbalance' of the brain which the appropriate medication can correct. Was it as simple as that? Was the brain just like a cake whereby you just had to get all the right ingredients in the right proportions? How could this be when the brain is the most complex human organ?

So it was with much reluctance that I returned to the PSU and its pungent odour. Ali and I proceeded to the nurses' station to report our arrival.

'Hi Roslyn, we're back', I said in a sullen tone.

'Hi guys, how was the wedding?' Roslyn said brightly, clearly trying her best to lift me out of my funk.

'Too good ...' I replied.

'You mean you didn't miss us while you were gone?'

'Hardly', I said churlishly.

'Well, do you want the good news or the bad news?'

'The good', I said, raising my eyebrows in anticipation.

'The good news is you don't have to spend the night here ...'

'and the bad ...' I said timidly.

'You don't get to have breakfast here tomorrow.'

'Why is that bad news?' I asked quizzically.

'Because we all know how much you of *all* people crave the food here—Mr raw eggs and milk!—but you do have a doctor's appointment at 11:00 am tomorrow—please don't be late', she said with a wink.

It was with absolute delight that I left the PSU arm in arm with Ali. Clearly this must have been a good sign in terms of my recovery—three straight nights of freedom without incident. Surely I must be close to complete release. And I was right. My greatest wish was granted at the doctor's appointment the following day.

'Matthew we have assessed your condition and have been extremely pleased with your recovery so you'll be happy to know that today you can go home for good.'

'That's fantastic, thanks.'

'Please, if you start to feel unwell again don't hesitate to contact the PSU immediately for help, 24/7, that's what we're all here for. OK?'

'Sure, and thank you so much for your time Doctor.'

'My pleasure—all the best.'

After the appointment Ali waited at the front reception while I returned to my room to collect a few belongings. I tidied the room, made the bed, and returned all the furniture to the position it had originally occupied before I had temporarily rearranged things for my morning makeshift gym routine. I wanted to leave the room exactly as I had found it, with no lasting impression that I had ever been there before. Maybe I was subconsciously hoping that this act could somehow erase the experience of my time at the PSU. I did, however, decide to leave the sprigs of rosemary strategically placed throughout the room, as a not too subtle hint regarding the unpleasant smell of the place.

With this job out of the way I knew I had to say goodbye to a few people. I sought out Bashir who, as usual, wasn't hard to find, taking up residence in the smokers' courtyard.

'Shit Matty, where ya been mate?' asked Bashir, lighting up a cigarette. 'I haven't seen ya in fricken ages. We figured you'd done a runner.'

'Nah man, I was at a wedding … but this is it mate, I'm outta here for good.'

'Shit no … ya fuckin wit me. You're nuts … they shouldn't be lettin' ya out!'

'I know, I must've got lucky.'

'Nah, it's all that sucking up to the nurses, mate—you sly bugger', he said, as opinionated as ever, blowing faint smoke rings into the air.

'Look after yourself, OK. Thanks heaps for all the games of ping-pong', I said proffering my hand.

Bashir stood there, arms folded, looking genuinely disturbed, nursing his treasured cigarette as it continued to bellow its acrid fumes around us. *Maybe I should have just left without saying goodbye? Was I rubbing my departure in his face?* He took another heavy drag on his cancer stick, then reluctantly but firmly shook my hand.

'Who the fuck am I gonna smash at ping-pong now?' he said with a wry smile. 'Take it easy Matty.'

'You too mate', I replied. 'Oh … can you do me a favour? If you see Nathan, tell him I said I'll look out for him in the line-up.'

'What?' he said, shaking his head in confusion. 'Le' me guess, more of your hippie surf shit.'

'He'll understand', I said as we parted ways.

I had one last goodbye. I approached the nurses' station which was unusually quiet.

'Roslyn, do you have a minute?' I asked.

'Normally I wouldn't, but you're in luck,' she said looking around in amazement at the relative calm around her.

'I just wanted to say thanks for all the care and concern you have shown me. All the staff here are amazing—so dedicated to such a thankless job. You should all be paid a king's ransom for the work you do—unlike those millionaire banker-wankers who just crunch numbers and gamble with other people's money.'

'Well thank you', she replied, blushing a little, seemingly unaccustomed to such compliments. 'It's my pleasure. I'd like to say "See you later" but that's a bit of a faux pas around here—take care.'

'Thanks,' I said with the broadest smile in many weeks.

Chapter 29
Needing normality

The week following my release was a relaxed one and things began to feel like they were back to some degree of normality. I was home free. Ali and I both took time off work and we enjoyed spending time together. Not that there was much action between the sheets. My drug-affected libido was still off the boil, so we agreed to skip the next few months in terms of fertility treatment and concentrate on looking after ourselves. So we lounged around the house and out on the back deck having late leisurely breakfasts, listening to music, reading and generally just being feline in our behaviour—eating, sleeping and lounging. It was unusually gratifying to again be able to read a book, something I'd taken for granted before my illness. In fact, I was surprisingly philosophical about my PSU experience and didn't give my recent diagnosis much thought. Instead I simply took great enjoyment in doing those pursuits that gave me pleasure, like cooking—something that I hadn't done since Steve's death. But I was still struggling to accept he was dead. You expect to outlive your parents but you assume you and your siblings will grow old and grey together. I had lost my closest friend, the person who helped shape me and now I felt like an only child.

During this week I did break this recuperative routine to do some exercise which I also craved. I went for a swim at the local pool which was fabulously cleansing—as if washing away the grime that had polluted my pores during the PSU experience—although while swimming laps the monotony of the black line below the depths allowed my head to wander into the all too familiar territory of Steve's death. I went kayaking alone on the lake and within minutes found myself preoccupied with the same topic. At times I welcomed the memories, as I desperately wanted to hang on to any connection with Steve. I constantly picked at the scabs on my knuckles to stop them from healing because they were a reminder of *that* day—the day I punched the wall when I was told Steve had killed himself. The day that my life changed forever and I didn't want to ever forget that. But at other times I questioned whether I would ever be able to be alone with my thoughts without them repeatedly reverting back to the tragedy. I had no idea grieving was going to be this hard. Steve was forever out of sight but never out of mind.

I soon realised that the company of others helped distract me from my thoughts. Ali and I visited C&J for our favourite Tuesday night dinner ritual. Laughter and good food was abundant but at times I would catch myself in the middle of laughing and feel a pang of guilt, as if I didn't deserve to feel any happiness yet.

I realised I needed more distraction so I decided to go back to work the following week. Although I knew no-one at work would know about my time at the PSU, I was still rather apprehensive as I speculated whether it would somehow be apparent to all—like a tattoo on the forehead—*Recently discharged from the loony farm.*

Before my unexpected departure I had been very upfront about Steve's death and had told everyone in my division, via email, that he had depression and had committed suicide. The last thing I wanted to do was pretend he had died due to other circumstances. So I also wondered how they would react towards me in general, what people would say. Whether there would be any uncomfortable silences or awkward moments.

I rocked up at work at my usual time, getting in before the majority of my colleagues. Then in walked my boss, only a few years my senior, with a look of complete astonishment on his face.

'What are you doing here?' he said from across the office. Then he sprinted over to my cubicle and gave me a bone-crunching hug—an unexpected outpouring of sympathy that was very welcome.

'Great to have you back', he said with a sniffle.

'Thanks boss.'

It was interesting to observe how my colleagues reacted to my return—as there is no text-book to follow in such situations, as I was quickly finding out. Some would offer kind words of support for my loss, others didn't even acknowledge my absence, let alone why I was gone. Maybe the latter group had also suffered a similar tragedy and knew from experience that words do little to quell the pain, or perhaps it was simply apathy. Who knows? Either way I was relieved when those initial few days were over.

In the weeks that followed work did provide the necessary diversion, particularly when I was in the middle of a task, with my brain focused on the job at hand. At these times I sensed glimpses of my old self returning. Again I found solace in music. Thankfully the work I was doing allowed me to listen to music while working. Virtually not a day would go by without listening to Pearl Jam's *Indifference*, Foo Fighters' *Home* and Jack Johnson's *Better Together*. I did begin to struggle though when moving from one job to another—where even the slightest idle time was ample opportunity for my thoughts to wander back to Steve. Initially, I recognised the warning signs and was able to minimise such occurrences by ensuring my work day was completely filled. But this became harder to do. In the evenings, away from work, I was doing a lot of soul-searching. Asking myself those big questions posed so simply by Jack Johnson in his lyrics: *Why are we here, where do we go and how come it's so hard?* But I was at a loss for answers—not surprisingly considering these topics have plagued mankind for centuries.

As I sat in my drab cubicle I started to question the passion I had for my day-to-day work. Prior to my brother's death I had gained immense satisfaction from the belief that the work I was doing as a modern-day cartographer made a difference. I prided myself on being diligent and committed. I viewed my job as a career with a promising future where I was respected by my colleagues. Previously, I had only taken one day of sick leave in eight years but slowly the days began to drag. In the past, the days and weeks would have been a blur of productivity from which I gained an immense sense of gratification because I knew I was contributing positively to society. Gradually the seeds of doubt took hold. *Do I really want to be here? What's it all for?* I was losing my motivation and drive—my work mojo. I no longer felt energised by work. The hours, days and weeks dragged and the weekends felt like an excruciatingly short reprieve.

I spoke about this change in my attitude towards work with a counsellor and she reassured me that these thoughts were a common stage of the grief process. I wasn't convinced. I needed some time out away from work to gauge these new emotions.

As luck would have it Nicole rang me at work to invite me down the coast for a few days. This was an enticing proposition but in the past the impromptu nature of such an invitation would have led to me looking for work-related excuses as to why (given such short notice) I unfortunately couldn't make it. This time I instead found myself accepting Nicole's offer without any consideration for the work implications. This reaction surprised me as it was pretty out of character. But I think it was the chance of being able to go for a surf which was the sealer. I hadn't surfed in several months, which always unsettled me—like a junkie trying to go cold turkey, I would ache to revisit my favourite pursuit—not purely because I missed the adrenalin rush but because I equally craved its therapeutic effects. A session amongst the waves cleansed your spirit and washed away the psychological gunk of modern-day life.

The following day we headed down the coast in the late afternoon and as soon as we arrived I hightailed it down to the beach for some waves. Labouring across squeaky sand dunes that obscured the ocean, the familiar taste of sea mist and the promising rumble in the distance lured me onwards. Cresting the final dune I came upon a flawless three-foot wave, holding up against a light offshore breeze, the wave eventually succumbing and peeling gradually along the shallow sandbank. The roller was almost mechanical in its perfection and I was astonished to find I had it all to myself. I hurriedly waded into the ocean, diving under an approaching wall of white-water—its cool turbulence massaging my entire body into an energised state—feeling more at home amongst the sand, salt and sea than ever before. I paddled into my first wave, sensing the surge of ocean beneath me, and then instinctively slid to my feet. I rode straight across its green face, not bothering to turn but instead content to just feel the energy of this swell—to connect with its source, running my hand along its glassy curve. As the wave dissipated ahead I turned sharply up the face and launched myself several feet into the air, landing with a clumsy splash. I surfaced and gave out a loud whoop—as a way of acknowledging the moment—claiming the ride. I then gazed across the beach and witnessed a breathtakingly picturesque sunset unfold, where a myriad of golden rays pierced an assemblage of cotton-like clouds.

'Thank you', I whispered to myself.

To whom I was talking I'm not entirely sure. Perhaps it was Steve, or Nicole for the invitation, or some divine creator, or Gaia. But I was compelled to give thanks for this serene moment. This was without doubt the happiest I had been since Steve's death and is a memory I will always cherish. All the stress, anxiety, angst and anger of the past month were released and I was rejuvenated.

I continued to have several more rides that were equally as uplifting and therapeutic. Then without warning the winds turned, the tide shifted and the conditions were no longer ideal. Nevertheless, I felt privileged to have been able to experience those exceptional conditions that are typically quite rare and brief—one in a million.

That evening Nicole gave me a book *Dying to Be Free* which documented real families' private accounts of dealing with suicide— from individuals who have failed to take their own life to those relatives left behind. I read the short book within a few hours and was struck by the similarities of some of the stories to my own experience. I found one particular quote profoundly comforting: 'I no longer fear anything, because I have lost everything.' I was determined to feel the same way about Steve's death, for it to eventually become something that made me stronger, something that I could learn from and that could make me a better person.

The next day Nicole put her renowned culinary skills to good use and served up an epic breakfast of crepes topped with seasonal fruits and various decadent condiments. This lavish spread delighted our tastebuds and was a welcome distraction but soon Steve was again being discussed, a topic which neither of us was shying away from.

'You know we were trying to have kids, but were having trouble', offered Nicole.

'Really, for how long?' I said, trying to sound ignorant on such a subject.

'Nearly a year.'

I was compelled to confide in Nicole about the fertility problems Ali and I were having. As it turned out Steve and Nicole had been having similar issues, although Ali and I were a little further along the path of getting help.

'If only people were more open to talking about these issues', I said. 'It can really help to know you're not alone.'

'I know', Nicole replied with a look of resignation.

'Guys in particular, we never talk about this stuff and it's gotta change!'

This revelation further strengthened my resolve to try and break down the stereotypes regarding men and their reluctance and inability to discuss with their fellow mates matters involving their health—whether it be physical or mental.

With advances in mobile phone and Web technology and the popularity of social networking sites like Facebook and Twitter, there is no doubt that men communicate with others all around the globe more than ever before. But do we communicate better as a consequence, engaging in meaningful conversations that make a difference in people's lives? I suggest not. Instead these sites tend to encourage the broadcasting of trivial information about people's daily lives: like the new toothbrush they bought or how irritated they were by the floury apple they had for lunch. People perceive they have a multitude of 'friends' around the world. But I would argue it should be more about quality than quantity, as only a select few will really be there for you in a time of need.

However, true friends can only come to your aid if they believe there's a problem. But men, in their desire to be the alpha-male, typically hide behind an impenetrable wall of machismo. So any concerns from loved ones regarding a male's wellbeing are met with a contrived and stoic response like 'Yeah everything's fine'. As if volunteering anything to the contrary would be an admission of fragility, a sign of weakness, that won't be tolerated. Are Australian males particularly reticent on such matters or does this phenomenon extend to other cultures as well? I'm sure it must be a more widespread problem—but why? Have men been genetically programmed to be a closed-book on such topics—to always give the stiff upper lip in preference to open dialogue? Or has media-manipulated modern society gradually encouraged this conduct and endorsed it as the epitome of manliness today?

There is no doubt that Steve and I were bound by this stereotype as much as anyone. We certainly didn't have open and honest communication on matters of physical or mental health. I will eternally regret not raising such topics with my brother. Sharing such information could have lessened both our burdens and made Steve realise that he wasn't alone. We would have certainly had a laugh comparing sperm sample results—after all, brothers are eternally competitive.

Our trip away definitely served its purpose; however, it came to a conclusion all too soon. But I was keen to get back to my wife, as I always was whenever we were apart for more than a few days. I think the separation anxiety that some couples experience is a definite sign of true love. They say absence makes the heart grow fonder. Well in this instance something else *grew*, in a physical sense, while I was away. I felt my lust and desire for my beautiful wife return—a glorious sensation that I had dearly missed. Ali welcomed me home and I immediately kissed her passionately like I hadn't in months. Things were on the up—in more ways than one. That evening we made romantic, sensual love for the first time since Steve's death. This time it was only about the two of us connecting completely and not about diligent baby-making. It was unforgettable.

Chapter 30
Bipolar: what goes up, must come down

Despite obvious signs of improvement in my general wellbeing, work continued to be the bane of my existence. Previously, all of my concerns were centred on what I was getting out of work—whether I was still finding it challenging and rewarding. But gradually, over a period of several weeks, my relentless obsession over work shifted focus. I felt that I wasn't coping. It started with simple things—like poor memory retention. So to compensate I started to write things down obsessively. Then I found I was unable to comprehend written documents. So all the things I had written made little sense to me. Sounds comical, but it was far from it. Initially I attributed this to a natural reaction to grief and stress—the brain was still in recovery mode from trauma I guessed—but when it didn't abate, my panic level rose.

My condition worsened so much that rudimentary tasks became complex and taxing. And the more difficult activities, that I usually relished, were like impossible, insurmountable feats. I wondered whether the medication I was still taking was causing my dysfunction. But my psychiatrist's view was that this was more likely a reaction to grief. This sustained period of inability really affected my self-esteem. I went from having a 'can do' to a 'can't do' work attitude in a matter of weeks. Again I turned to music as a means of comfort, reassurance, inspiration and salvation. I desperately needed music to rescue me from an ever-increasing negativity that was plaguing me. But to my astonishment this salvation never came. No song helped. I was all alone.

This unease about my job then turned to worry. Nothing I did seemed good enough, everything was sub-standard in my opinion—despite reassurance from my superiors to the contrary. The worry soon turned to deep-seated fear. Fear that I would lose my job due to outright incompetence. These ponderings were not based on logic.

As the incessant distress and despair took hold it affected my sleep, even though the medication I was taking was supposed to have a sedating influence. I was plagued by my thoughts of ineptitude and the negative voice inside my head was unstoppable, preventing me from sleeping. In the past I'd always been a 'nine hours a night' guy and any deviation from this was bound to affect me seriously. Several days of sleep deprivation took their toll on me physically and mentally. I was walking around like a zombie.

Needless to say my condition worsened without sleep. My inability to concentrate became unmanageable and my self-esteem sank to rock-bottom. I was a mess—plain and simple.

I arranged a meeting with my boss where I told him that I wasn't coping. I didn't go into too much detail regarding my issues apart from mentioning that I felt unwell and that I believed I needed to take several weeks off the job and return after Christmas. He showed real concern for my health and was extraordinarily sympathetic and supportive and didn't hesitate in approving my leave.

Unfortunately, being away from work didn't alleviate my unease. If anything it made my irrational thinking worse. I still truly believed my days at work were numbered and that this would cause a catastrophic chain of events:

1. that losing my job would make me unemployable

2. we'd be in financial hardship and at risk of losing the house

3. faced with the possibility of being forced to move back in with her parents, Ali would leave me.

Losing Ali scared me the most. I couldn't imagine life without her. I refrained from telling her about these concerns for fear such thoughts would signify a seriously irrational and agitated mood that might find me back at the PSU.

This scenario preoccupied my thoughts without reprieve, despite my best attempts to dispel it with logic. Instead, it became more and more plausible, more and more debilitating. I longed for respite and believed I was worthless and alone with no means of escape. I was lost. Until the unthinkable happened, one night I found the answer to my woes, a sure-fire way to release me from this constant nightmare.

I was going to kill myself.

I was surprised at how calming the thought was—a means to an end—a logical progression to the last resort. It was accompanied by a genuine sense of relief. And the more I repeated it in my head the more it made absolute sense at the time. Surprisingly, at no point did Steve's suicide enter into my mind, nor the inevitable consequence of leaving Ali permanently. For the remainder of the night I was busy considering the practicalities of various methods of suicide. Never did it seem macabre or immoral. I spent hours trying to recount all the movies I had seen that vividly illustrated suicide—calmly considering each method on its merits. I revelled in this clear thinking that had evaded me for so long.

But by morning I was still undecided as to my preferred suicide option. I was adamant that I didn't want Ali to be the one to find me after the event; I couldn't bring myself to do that to someone I loved so much. What was also clear was a burning desire for this day to be my last. This put me at ease knowing that I would not have to endure another agonisingly long sleepless night of mental torture.

'How'd you sleep doll?' asked Ali as she awoke.

'Fine', I lied, trying desperately not to make eye contact. I knew if I looked at her I wouldn't be able to go through with my plan.

'How do you feel today?'

'Fine.' Another lie.

Ali's face showed signs of deep-seated worry. We got up and had breakfast together in silence.

'Are you having a shower?' I asked afterwards, looking vacantly out the window.

'No', she replied, staring at me with furrowed brow.

'Why not?'

'I'm worried about you hon. Are you sure you're OK?'

I knew her questioning might weaken my resolve. I grabbed the car keys in an agitated and desperate manner. I needed to flee to do what needed to be done. But I initially had no idea where to go. Then it dawned on me: I was going to stage a fatal car accident. I envisaged driving into the mountains, taking a corner at excessive speed, then aiming for a large tree on the roadside. The ensuing crash was sure to kill me—sorted. This method satisfied all my criteria: quick, private and discreet.

In my distracted state Ali was able to grab my hands and pry the car keys from my grasp. Then she tried to hug me to comfort me. But I was having none of it. I had to have the keys. With Ali clasped around me tightly, I wrestled with her, only moderately at first, not wishing to inflict any harm. But when it became clear she was desperate to hold on, I found myself using considerably more force to retrieve the keys—something that was terribly upsetting, because I had never before used physical force towards my wife, or any female for that matter.

Ali looked overcome with anxiety as she stood at a distance, realising physical restraint was useless. She was powerless to stop me now that I had the keys back in my possession.

'Where … are … you … going?' she gasped, fat tears of anguish streaming down her face.

'Nowhere … just to the shops', I puffed unconvincingly.

'Please, don't go doll!' she begged, sensing my unusual desperation and disengagement. 'Look at me doll. Tell me what's wrong … please … I beg you!'

It was futile. I couldn't avoid her gaze any longer. Looking into her eyes I had no choice but to surrender. 'I want … to kill myself', I said.

'No … doll!' she stammered, shaking with terror. 'I can't live without you, please no …' she whimpered, her voice quavering.

Seeing her like this broke my heart and quickly snapped me back to reality. How could I knowingly inflict such pain on someone I loved so completely? Saying the words and seeing her reaction made it all too real, particularly the devastating aftermath.

'I'm sorry', I said calmly. 'The last thing I want to do is hurt you.

I won't harm myself, if you promise to be beside me, no matter what! *Better Together.*'

'I promise!' Ali replied, sniffling and wiping away tears with her sleeve.

We held each other for ages, both shaking from the ordeal. I could feel Ali's heart pounding beneath her chest.

'Go and have a shower babe', I insisted.

'No, I want to stay here with you', she said, squeezing me tenderly.

'You can't watch me 24/7. You have to believe me. I promise I'll be here when you get out—this is a trust exercise, OK.'

'OK', she said timidly.

That was undoubtedly the most honest, intense and confronting conversation of my life. *I want to kill myself.* Hearing those five words spoken had been a monumental wake-up call. I was shaken by how close I had come to suicide. How quickly and easily my mindset had allowed such considerations to develop, despite months earlier having vehemently declared that I would *never* perform such an act. I now understood only too well how it was possible for my brother to have tragically taken his own life.

But having voiced those forbidden words lessened the despair I was previously battling in silence. Realising Ali would help me through thick and thin gave me hope to keep living. If only Steve had told those around him of his feelings.

That morning we booked an urgent appointment with the psychiatrist. I had to again confess to my suicidal tendencies, which wasn't easy. He confirmed that I had become clinically depressed—the all too common flip side of bipolar disorder. I was prescribed a mood stabiliser and antidepressant medication, on top of the drug I was already taking since being at the PSU. The downside to the medication, the doctor informed me, was that it took some time, often several weeks, before it brought about any improvement in the disposition of patients, and in some cases a particular antidepressant did little to help and it was a matter of finding the right one for the individual—which could take months. I was horrified at the prospect of being this way for months on end. The news just kept getting worse. I was also told there were numerous side-effects but I told the doctor I didn't want to know about them. *Ignorance is bliss.* He did offer some advice, however, insisting that I watch my carbohydrate intake. This I took as a weight gain warning which I was intent on heeding.

In taking the first antidepressant tablet I yearned that by some miracle it could have an almost instant corrective effect—as immediate as a Panadol that combats a headache—as if by chance my condition weren't as severe as the norm and the drugs were able to take control more rapidly and easily. But of course this was wishful thinking. I was only at the beginning of my depressive period and unfortunately had a much longer road to recovery.

Chapter 31
The indifference of depression

At times the depression was like being trapped inside a murky bubble, where the absence of light brought constant darkness and tainted all aspects of life—colours were dulled and senses suppressed—gradually suffocating the spirit. Food became nothing more than fuel and music was muffled beyond recognition. Other times it felt like a severe lack of motivation or ambition to do anything. But it was much more complex than that. A lassitude like nothing in the world could satisfy you or make you feel any other way. Deep down, however, I was determined to make it through and I kept quietly singing some lyrics from *Indifference* to myself for reassurance: I will *make my way through one more day in hell.* These lyrics spoke to me now more than ever.

In the days and weeks that followed I continued to be tormented by depression, relatively unassisted by the medication. One benefit of the medication was that it allowed me to sleep and, by and large, that was all I wanted to do. Even after 10 or 12 hours of sleep, I was still content just to stay in bed all day, which was most unlike me. Most days I was listless and could barely get motivated to crawl out of bed. But I knew I must fight the depression and push myself, if I was ever going to get better.

My day became one of little challenges, mostly surrounding battling the lure of being drawn back to bed. Other challenges involved forcing myself to do some exercise each day, which I had been advised was an effective way to combat depression. Normally, this would have been something I would relish, but in my depressed state I was enervated. My limbs were unbelievably lethargic and heavy, much worse than at any time at the PSU. Physically, I felt a shadow of my former self. Typically, Ali and I would go for short walks together hand-in-hand around the block, only for a period of half an hour or so, after which time I would feel too fatigued. I was so weak that was about as much exercise as I could handle. My normal pursuits of surfing, kayaking, swimming, mountain biking or going to the gym just didn't seem to interest me, nor did I feel up to any of them.

Music also no longer invigorated me. Nicole kindly bought me an iPod filled with hundreds of songs from Steve's music library, in the hope that I would again connect with music, thus helping in my recovery. Unfortunately, this was not the case and my indifference was so pronounced that I didn't even unpack the gift for months. I hated being a burden on others, particularly Nicole, as the last thing I wanted was for her to be worried about me. More than anything I needed to be taking care of her but couldn't in my state.

Mostly during this period I watched an inordinate and unhealthy amount of Test Match Cricket. If there is a longer sport in history, I am not aware of it. The games last for five days, sometimes without a result. I observed hour upon hour to be honest, day after day— easily consuming an entire day's play. Not that I found it particularly interesting or stimulating but its monotony and predictability distracted me from my thoughts just enough to get me through another day.

All the while Ali was keeping a close and watchful eye over me: reading a book or doing a crossword in my company. It was reassuring to know that she was always there by my side. Not that we spoke much, but we didn't need to—actions often speak louder than words. Ali was a phenomenal carer, so accommodating, patient and tender with me. Often I would only summon the discipline to drag myself from the bed because she would gently suggest that I do so. Otherwise, without her coaxing I would have undoubtedly remained under the sheets in my vegetative state. It was during this vulnerable time that my adoration for my wife reached a completely new level. Prior to this whole sordid experience I knew our love for one another was deep and abiding and that our relationship was exceptional—one in a million. But the unconditional love and devotion that Ali blanketed me with during this period was staggering. She had always been my life, now she had undeniably saved it. It was Ali's love for me that brought me back from the brink. She saved me from myself. I shudder to think what might have happened had she not been with me that morning. And words fail to do justice to the intense gratitude I will forever feel towards her for this unimaginable act of salvation. I was determined to stand by the promise I gave Ali, to never take my own life. However, I couldn't always guarantee she would be in my company if those feelings ever returned to wage battle against common sense and rational thought. So I made a solemn oath with myself to always uphold a simple truism if I ever faced such a crisis again: honesty is the best policy—to tell those around me of these feelings—because the truth can save me.

Gradually word of my condition spread to close friends and family and I became inundated with support from them all. I decided from the outset that I must be honest about the feelings of suicide I had been having. I came to acknowledge that it was speaking the truth that allowed them to really help me—and I'm proud of myself for having had the courage to admit to such taboo thoughts.

On more than one occasion the loquacious C&J came to visit. Typically, I was stuck in the foetal position on the couch and barely acknowledged their presence. Yet they were unflappable, not perturbed by my less than sociable behaviour. Instead they tried their best to engage with me. And when that proved fruitless, they would happily converse with Ali about various trivial day-to-day occurrences, both as bubbly as ever, as if nothing were different. They knew that they simply couldn't cheer me up, or get me to 'snap out of it' but they were determined to show that they were there for me and it meant the world to me—although I didn't realise it at the time. Quite frankly I just wanted to be left alone, to fester and wallow in my own worthlessness.

Often during this period I would spend hours just lying there internally chastising myself. I was relieved that the suicidal contemplation had gone but I had ample time to contemplate what the repercussions might have been had I succeeded in killing myself. On reflection, I was mostly filled with an overwhelming sense of humiliation at how utterly pathetic and wasteful it would have appeared to all and sundry—considering some may have seen it as an act of brotherly devotion, one final attempt at imitation. Yet I knew depression was the sole cause of my near-suicide. The greater population hears a lot about depression through fantastic organisations like *beyondblue* and there is certainly more awareness and recognition than in years gone by. But with depression becoming more openly discussed and commonplace I wonder whether society in general is in danger of taking it a little too lightly and not appreciating the potentially dire consequences if left untreated.

Nothing it seemed could release me from my stupor. Even the prospect of going for a surf wasn't tempting. I just wanted to stay put and do nothing. So much so that I cancelled the traditional week's vacation down the coast over New Year's with Ali and C&J because I didn't feel up to it. This trip had been planned months in advance and I would normally have been anxiously awaiting it like a kid awaits his birthday. Christmas too was fast approaching and never was I more like the Grinch. *Bah, humbug!* As the weeks bled into one another I sensed that Ali was getting carer's cabin-fever. She had read umpteen novels and completed countless monster crosswords. But not once did she complain. She continued to be the loving, caring wife by my side 24/7. She did, however, suggest that we consider making the trip up to Sydney for Christmas to spend it with her family. I was starting to feel marginally better but I would have been content to spend the holiday plastered to the couch (after all the Boxing Day test match was going to be on). But I knew this would be a nice break for her from the humdrum duties of looking after me, so I reluctantly agreed we should go.

Chapter 32
The depressive fog lifting

I wasn't looking forward to being depressed around Ali's parents and away from home. In some respects depression is like any other illness; when you have diarrhoea or are projectile vomiting, the last thing you feel like is being in unfamiliar surroundings and around other people. And while I should have felt comfortable around Ali's parents (having known them for over 10 years) they were still, after all, my in-laws and no matter how long you have known them, there is always a sense that you must keep up appearances and be on your best behaviour regardless of your physical or mental condition. So I endeavoured to put on a brave face and not mope around too much but this was excruciatingly difficult to do as I was continually drawn to the comfort and refuge of bed.

It was unusually gratifying to see Ali with her family. She had been through so much during the past months and you could see her relax instantly in their company—with the three siblings partaking in animated sisterly ramblings, virtually incomprehensible to the onlooker. The visit also gave Ali time to bond with her beautiful newborn niece, Amy. It was hard watching them together, as there was no doubt that Ali was exceedingly clucky but she put on a courageous front and did an amazing job at suppressing her maternal instincts and desires in front of her family who knew nothing of our problems with fertility.

At one point I tried my best to play with Luke. He had received several new toys for Christmas and we started playing with one where you drop plastic balls down a chute and a fan blows them back out high up into the air. Luke was mesmerised by this contraption and took great pleasure in watching the balls fly across the room. He did require some help in retrieving the balls and putting them back in the chute, which I obliged in doing. We played this game for some time and I found it to be great fun, fun which I hadn't experienced since becoming depressed. But after a while, despite my best efforts, I became seriously fatigued to the point where I had to just lie there—my limbs leaden. Luke meanwhile, full of boundless energy, looked on perplexed, wondering why his uncle had stopped playing with him. As I lay there exhausted I pondered how someone in my condition would manage with a young family. For the first time in many years I was thankful that Ali and I didn't have a young family of our own, because I didn't know how I would have coped.

The trip to Sydney turned out to be better than expected but I was still glad to return to the familiar haven of home. My condition was slowly improving but I had to really fight to get out of the depressing bubble I was in. Some days, cracks appeared that let into my life some much needed light and warmth, but often the following day I would awaken to darkness once more. *I* will *make my way through one more day in hell.*

I recognised that right then I had been washed out to sea by a powerful rip and was caught in a ferocious mental storm and the seas of self-loathing were pounding relentlessly. But I sensed that if I could just hold on and keep my head above water, take every day as it came, eventually the battering waves of emotional anguish and disgust would lessen and I could eventually make my way back to the safety of shore. Surfing had taught me that the currents can shift, tides turn, winds drop and conditions can become ideal again. I was holding onto this hope. That's not to say they would remain so permanently. I knew there would always be a level of uncertainty: wipe-outs, monstrous rouge-waves that catch you unaware and the risk of predators lurking beneath the depths. But as I was learning, the key elements of surfing were applicable to life in general: be careful what you ride, be committed, look forward where you want to go and, above all, try and have fun.

Progress was slow but eventually I found I was having more frequent moments where life didn't seem so dire. It seemed that I was fortunate in that the first type of antidepressant I had been prescribed was finally working. So when C&J invited Ali and me around for a sumptuous New Year's Eve feast we decided to accept. Jen graciously allowed me to decide on the menu. So I chose an Asian theme. Jen also kindly asked whether I would be comfortable in the company of other guests. Unfortunately my socialising skills were still well and truly lacking, so I politely asked if we could limit the festivities to just the four of us. They were both more than accommodating—cooking a sumptuous feast of crispy pork belly entrée, succulent duck fried rice and delicious Asian greens salad, finished off with a mixed-berry compote—a sperm-friendly dessert! It was a wonderfully pleasant evening despite not being allowed to drink alcohol. The night came to a climax as we cheerfully welcomed in the New Year. We all embraced and Charlie felt obliged to make a toast.

'To a better 2009!'

'To a better 2009!' we all cheered as one.

Yes frickin' please!

I was eternally grateful to C&J for their kind gesture of hosting us for New Year's Eve. I recognised they were willing to forgo a celebratory gathering with other friends who would have undoubtedly been more vivacious than the depressed, recovering mental patient. It was truly humbling to witness the extraordinary lengths my closest friends would go to in order to try and make me feel better. Their unwavering friendship at the most difficult of times was an immeasurable source of inspiration for me. It also made me feel special—worthy of their affections—helping with a growing sense of self-worth that had abandoned me since the wicked depression took hold.

Thankfully, this was the start of the depressive fog lifting. Slowly, my interest in my hobbies returned. I became more energised and generally began to care more about those things I previously held dear. My outlook on life was no longer hopeless. I could see a positive future, whereas before every day was a pointless struggle where life held no purpose or meaning whatsoever.

After several months my condition had improved enough that the doctor was happy for me to return to work, initially in a part-time capacity. This was difficult for me to accept because I was so used to working full-time. But the doctor was adamant that I must watch my stress levels and ease myself back into work otherwise I ran the risk of falling back into a deep depression. This was truly a dark and lonely place that I wanted to avoid returning to at all costs.

Being back in the familiar surrounds of work was reassuring from one perspective but I was apprehensive and concerned about whether my performance would still be lacking. The doctor had informed my boss of my situation and he was again supportive and ensured my workload was appropriately reduced. Over the coming weeks I found I had lost all confidence in my abilities and honestly believed I was incapable of certain tasks—despite being surrounded by numerous examples to the contrary. This was an unnerving experience but gradually my boss challenged me and I slowly regained my confidence over many months.

Simply making it to work on time was often the greatest battle. Virtually every morning my mind and body joined forces to try and quash any desire to attend work. I hankered to stay in bed and avoid the stress and uncertainty of another workday but again it was Ali's quiet coaxing that persuaded me to get up and get going. Sometimes I would be in the midst of getting changed and I would look back at the warm inviting bed, undress quickly and climb back in for some prolonged sanctuary, until Ali would come in the room and again convince me to get moving. I would then drop Ali off and continue onto my work. But the torment was not over. Often, still gripped by the desire to snatch some more sleep, I would recline in the driver's seat for a half-hour powernap. This childish and ridiculous behaviour was very frustrating and out of character and subsequently I questioned how much of this habit was related to the various medications I was on.

Socially speaking, my recovery was much swifter and more noticeable. When amongst friends I found myself smiling and laughing more frequently and being much more vocal and extroverted. Before I was unwell, I took the blissful release of a belly-aching laugh for granted. Laughter truly is the endorphin of the soul—an act of sheer delight. Much to everyone's distaste I even started to again indulge in my own crass comic relief, a sure sign that my mood was vastly improving.

One of the more difficult aspects of my recovery was battling with weight gain. I had told the doctor that I badly wanted to stay under 80 kg as I had never before been over this weight. As the weeks and months progressed I exercised incessantly, much more than I normally would. Initially, in the early stages of my recovery, exercising was excruciatingly taxing and completing my usual gym routine became near impossible. I would labour through with my muscles feeling like they were filled with wet cement—impossibly restrained and restricted in their movement. But despite my concerted efforts I breached the weight limit. Even though I had only put on a few kilos they instinctively located themselves in the least desirable location—around my waist rather than somewhere like my calves, where I would have been more than happy with a little more bulk given my resemblance to a light bulb. Gradually my work trousers started to feel much tighter around the waist which was pretty disconcerting. This unwelcome development did nothing for my self-esteem which I was desperately trying to resurrect. I felt stodgy. At first I attributed the weight gain to eating too many carbohydrates as the doctor had warned. I was certainly guilty of having a large appetite, particularly when it came to Italian pastas. So in an effort to drop the weight I reduced my food intake, focusing on fewer carbs. Over the weeks this appeared to have little impact. My weight had plateaued, but it refused to drop below the set mark. So in desperation I resorted to running.

In my early twenties I had been advised by a podiatrist to avoid jogging if at all possible so that my knees would last into old age, and since then I have followed this advice. But confronted with my expanding girth I persuaded myself to give some light jogging a go—there is no better exercise for weight loss that I know of. I considered it best that I start on a treadmill, as this causes less impact on the joints. But running to nowhere in a gym with no windows and no scenery to distract you from countless pounding kilometre after kilometre was extremely uninspiring.

Despite my dislike of the treadmill I persisted over several weeks and gradually began to enjoy it. Not that I was seeing much reward for my efforts; the weight refused to budge. When I discussed this with Ali and C&J they suggested that maybe I was gaining muscle and hence weighing more. But I was not convinced as the tightening trousers continued to tell the true story. Later I ran outside—leaving from the house I would venture through the neighbourhood and up into the hills that bordered the suburbs then along a fire-trail that had breathtaking views that overlooked the bush capital. As much as anything, I enjoyed the solitude. A lot of the other sports I normally undertake alone require a degree of concentration on technique which prevents the brain from wandering. Whereas with running I was able to quickly get into a rhythm and could then indulge in contemplation about life. Not surprisingly, Steve was always close to mind, as was my mental health and thoughts of pregnancy.

Early that year the kitchen renovation was completed. It was project-managed to a tee—being on time and on budget, with no significant dramas whatsoever. This buoyed my spirits notably. We were also both relieved, as I'm not sure how I would have coped if there were any major stressful events during construction. We had both sacrificed a lot over the previous year and were proud of the end result. The finished product exceeded our expectations. The hub of our home was complete—our nest was well and truly ready. All we needed now was to lay the bloody egg! To that end we decided it was time to continue with our fertility treatment.

Chapter 33
"Unexplained infertility"

I was disappointed that due to my illness we hadn't engaged in any amorous activity for weeks but I was keen to redress the imbalance. Thankfully my libido, like my mood in general, was on the up and I was glad to be back in the saddle. I had a renewed enthusiasm towards making love to my beautiful wife. We decided to try a couple more times for natural conception, with the help of the blood tests to determine optimum timing, but unfortunately this again proved fruitless. So Ali finally booked in for the laparoscopy which had been delayed due to all the unexpected turmoil during the latter part of the previous year. I think I was more worried about the surgery than Ali was. Nicci had warned us in no uncertain terms that Ali could die (those were her exact words). The chances, however, were awfully slim but if the bowel was accidently pierced during the surgery this could have devastating consequences. Part of me questioned whether it was worth the risk—no matter how unlikely. I knew it was an important process to determine whether there were any blockages in Ali's reproductive channels. But I did feel we were rolling the dice somewhat and I am not a betting man—rather I'm of the opinion that the House always wins. Sure we both ached for children but was it worth potentially losing the love of your life for?

At this point we concluded it best to finally tell our respective families about our lengthy pregnancy problems, particularly given Ali was about to have a minor operation. We considered it to be inappropriate not to inform the family given the risks involved. But the circumstances surrounding Steve's death and my bout of depression also underlined to us the importance of being frank with those we loved. Our earlier concerns regarding receiving an unwelcome outpouring of pity had paled into insignificance given the chaos of the previous months. Our families had shown tremendous sympathy towards the both of us during this time—understandably pity was unavoidable. This latest announcement would only increase their compassion.

They all took the news well. I was surprised, however, that when I told my father he appeared either to dismiss the announcement as if it were commonplace, or he envisioned it would be simply a matter of time before Ali would be knocked up. Maybe I was just reading too much into the conversation; after all, I informed him one evening after dinner when he had happily quaffed an entire bottle of vintage inky red by himself because, as usual, I was forced to abstain for the wellbeing of my baby gravy. Dad and I always had a strong relationship and we talked at length about many things, like AFL football and current affairs. But this particular conversation was brief, as men rarely elaborate on such personal topics, particularly father and son—*why is that?*

I did notice Ali seemed to have a general sense of relief after she told her family. She is extremely family-orientated and particularly close to both her sisters and I knew she had been struggling keeping them in the dark for so long and having to deal with all the emotional baggage without their support. Sure she had support from some of our dearest friends but it wasn't quite the same. Rebecca, given her medical background, was able to provide Ali with useful advice about the medical aspects of the procedure, as well as put some of the risks into perspective—which certainly lessened my fears.

So on the day of the laparoscopy we were both generally more relaxed about what Ali faced as we waited together in the reception room. Sure Ali was a little apprehensive about it all but in some ways we were both looking forward to at least knowing if there was something wrong and, if so, hopefully sorting it out then and there.

Thankfully the operation went smoothly and we had an appointment booked several days later with Nicci to discuss the results. She was direct and concise as we had come to expect. She informed us that the laparoscopy revealed a small polyp in one of Ali's fallopian tubes that may have been causing our fertility issues but the likelihood of this, given the size, was only minimal. She also commented that the lining of the uterus was fine.

'So, really, based on the results of your laparoscopy, you now both have what is termed "unexplained infertility"', Nicci explained.

'What exactly does that mean?' Ali probed.

'It means there appears to be no medical reason behind your infertility.'

Ali and I were both unsure whether to be upset or relieved. Relieved because nothing serious was found to be wrong or upset because there was no explanation for our infertility and therefore no active treatment available to fix the problem. This inability of modern medicine to pinpoint a cause for our current sterile status made me feel more ostracised and biologically inferior than ever before.

If there was no medical reason behind our infertility what could possibly be the problem? Was it an incompatibility issue? I once heard a story about a woman who was so allergic to her partner's sperm that it caused her vagina to swell profusely. There were no obvious signs of that being our problem? But what about at the microscopic level? Did my sperm and Ali's eggs simply not get along? Had our determination to keep them apart for so many years via contraception caused a rift of resentment between the two parties?

Nicci was quick to snap me back to reality when she moved onto discussing what options were available to us from this point forward.

'The polyp, which has now been removed, may have been causing your problems. So you may want to persist with a few more blood-test-assisted tries', Nicci stated.

'We're not sure', Ali replied, looking at me for affirmation.

'Well there are two other options: IUI and IVF. IUI is assisted insemination and involves the female taking hormones to help follicle stimulation, then at the time of surging a sperm sample is collected, cleaned and injected into the uterus.'

She demonstrated the procedure on the now familiar enlarged model of the female reproductive system. But I was busy mulling over the details of what she had just said. *My baby batter will be cleaned?* I didn't like the sound of that at all, besides I presumed we had ascertained that my sperm was now in tip-top shape. *Don't mess with my manhood!* I felt like yelling, beating my chest. How exactly were they intending on cleaning my sample, with some all-purpose anti-bacterial like Glen20? *No you damn well will not!* I suddenly felt like an endangered species in a zoo where I required unprecedented intervention to conceive.

'Is the procedure performed under anaesthetic?' Ali inquired.

'No, you're awake the entire time; it feels like a Pap smear. There's nothing to worry about.'

'How successful is it?' I asked, always keen on knowing the probabilities.

'Around 20 per cent of couples are pregnant after three goes. But with IUI we recommend only three attempts because of the hormones taken', Nicci explained.

'So it's three strikes and you're out?' I replied, seeking confirmation.

'That's right. But then there's always IVF.'

I only partially listened after that, as Nicci explained the details of IVF, because quite frankly I didn't think we would ever go down that path. We had discussed this option previously and neither of us were in favour of this approach as it introduced a whole other level of hormone injections and medical intervention that just didn't sit comfortably with either of us. This left IUI as the only viable option for us.

'So go away and have a think about how you would like to proceed and let me know in the next few days.'

That evening over dinner we got talking about the appointment.

'So babe, what do ya think we should do?' I asked, trying to sound as positive as possible.

'I'd like to start IUI. What about you?' Ali said, her voice nervously hinting at the response she wanted from me.

'Really, given what Nicci said about the polyp maybe being our problem, I'm keen to try a few more months as we have been.'

'I just wonder whether we're wasting our time—it clearly isn't working for us and I'm not getting any younger. I just want to try something different, that's all', she replied, pushing her finished plate away in a defiant gesture.

'I get that, but what's a coupla months in the grand scheme of things?' I said, reaching across the table for her hand.

'I suppose', she said.

'Besides, we only get three tries at IUI then we're out of options. So soon we should know categorically whether we can or can't have kids—which will be something at least—won't it?'

'There's always IVF …' she said timidly.

'I thought we agreed it wasn't for us?'

'I know, but …'

Chapter 34
IUI (Intra-Uterine Insemination):
three strikes—you're out!

So after some persuasion Ali reluctantly agreed to a couple more tries with help from the blood tests. I desperately wanted this because I knew it was our last chance at creating an object of our affection the way nature intended rather than via a detached medical procedure. Was it too much to ask for this special moment to be solely between the two of us, instead of having to involve an intervening third party? I was relatively optimistic that the laparoscopy had cleared the way for my vigorous new-and-improved sperm to make it to the intended destination. So we followed Nicci's orders as usual and engaged in an intense concentration of copulation. I was much more focused than on previous tries—maybe because I had been given an ultimatum—nothing was going to distract me in the bedroom. Devastatingly though our respective biological representatives failed to cooperate and we again found our 'friend' dropped by on another two unwelcome occasions.

That was that. On our own we had tried and failed countless times to get preggers, now, much to our disappointment, it was time to call for serious assistance. I was raised on the philosophy that if at first you don't succeed, try, try, try again. This attitude had served me well over the years and rarely had I encountered a problem that I couldn't overcome with some persistence and focus—until now.

IUI was our last chance. Up until now time had been on our side. With every subsequent month of disappointment there was always the lingering hope that the next would be successful, or the one after that, or indeed the one after that. With IUI we no longer had this luxury. Three goes was the limit—no more. The pressure was now well and truly on. But in some respects, with the start of IUI, our pregnancy prospects looked strangely out of my hands. Correction: I would have to use *my* hand to provide a sample—surely I would be unassisted— and most importantly ensure I hit the target and collected all the contents in the cup. The rest of the process—sadly—would go on without me being present.

I was nonetheless apprehensive about my contribution to the process, knowing that I had to provide my batch of baby batter at the fertility clinic itself. My numerous preceding collections had occurred in the comfort and confines of my own home, devoid of significant scrutiny apart from my wife patiently waiting for me to get the job done. I decided to voice my unease to Ali and her sister Olivia when we were discussing the details of the IUI procedure, several days prior to my appointment.

'So, Matt, obviously you have to provide a sample for the IUI?' Olivia asked in her usual playful manner.

'Yep', I replied unenthusiastically.

'So how does that work, do you have to go into the clinic?'

'Unfortunately.'

'That's gotta be tough.'

'I know, tell me about it. I'm *not* looking forward to it.'

'*Oh please* … it's nothing compared to what I have to go through!' Ali protested vehemently.

'Really … I have to perform, on cue, like a trained circus animal. All you have to do is lie there!' I replied.

'Yeah … while some stranger pokes and prods up my nether region— like that's *real* fun', Ali countered.

'Matt does have a point though Ali. He's under *pressure* to perform. What if he's just not in the mood?' Olivia insisted.

'He's given adult material to help him along you know', Ali said with a smirk. 'Cripes … really?' Olivia said, her eyes wide open in disbelief.

'Yep, it's been a while … I'm kinda looking forward to that part at least', I said with a grin.

'Well anyway, good luck peeps! I have my fingers and toes crossed for you.'

The dreaded day arrived and I experienced nerves like a novice performer about to give a rendition to an eagerly awaiting audience. This show, however, had to be a one-hit wonder, with no opportunity for an encore—at least not today. I waited with Ali in the clinic's reception and as usual flicked through page upon page of pointless paparazzi print. After a short time I was met by a female nurse wearing a full surgical scrubs uniform complete with shower-cap and theatre slippers.

'Matt?' she asked as she approached.

'Yes', I replied.

'Do you want to come?'

I was stunned by her request. I knew why I was here; she knew why I was here. All I could think about was today's objective and then she asks me to *come* … I could feel my face flush with embarrassment. I know it's immature and inappropriate but understandable considering the circumstances. I nearly considered replying: 'That's why I'm here isn't it!' But my nerves got the better of me.

I must admit though I was shocked that this lady, who was a professional and encounters numerous men daily in the same predicament as me, couldn't think up a slightly less insinuating greeting— perhaps a simple 'Matt, please follow me' would suffice. Or maybe this was simply her way of injecting some humour into her day by watching men's reaction to her welcome.

I followed her down a corridor and into a small room. I took in the unfamiliar surroundings: the dimly lit room barely fit a single chair and had a sink and benchtop along its length, with a mirror spanning the same distance. There was a large plasma TV, that took up the entire wall, on the only available space, behind the door. The nurse then explained the process.

'I must first witness you fill out some sections of this form', she insisted.

I started to fill out the parts of the form she highlighted. I noticed that my hand was shaking which made my handwriting unusually difficult to decipher. This was far from ideal because the last thing you want is your quality baby batter mistakenly going to someone else due to a clerical error on account of your nervous penmanship. Once I completed the required sections of the paperwork she continued with her instructions.

'Please collect your sample in the container and make sure you fill out the details on the label.'

'No problems.'

'Then when you're done, complete the paperwork and pop the container with the paperwork into the deposit box.'

'OK.'

'Here's a selection of adult material', she said, pointing to a small pile of magazines discreetly concealed in a drawer.

'OK', I replied, sensing the blood again rushing to my face.

'There's also a DVD if you'd like, just press this button and it will start automatically.'

'Sure', I said, catching a glimpse of my ripened tomato-like complexion in the mirror.

'And finally be sure to lock the door … I'll leave you to it', she said, giving me a sympathetic smile in an attempt to ease my embarrassment.

'Thanks', I mumbled, not sure exactly what else to say.

As the door slammed shut I immediately locked it. Then tested it was locked. Unlocked it, opened it and repeated the process just to be absolutely certain—because I would have been mortified to be interrupted mid-collection. How could I have shown my face here ever again if such an embarrassing situation were to transpire? That would be it; our parenthood prospects would be over in an instant due to my stupid oversight. So I triple-checked the door like some poor OCD sufferer, then I checked my watch. It was 9:05 am. I knew the clinician was awaiting my sample on the other side of the wall but how long should I keep her waiting? I didn't want to dispatch my deposit in record time—what would that say about my sexual prowess: Mr One-minute Wonder. That was a reputation I could do without. I envisaged the staff in the clinic privately referring to me as 'Minute Man Matt' or something equally derogatory. Alternatively, I didn't want to take too long either, causing a backlog of patients in the waiting room and potentially being labelled 'Marathon Matt' by the staff. I started wishing I had done some research beforehand and Googled the average ejaculation time just to be sure—although conducting such a search on the Web at work would have undoubtedly got me fired. *I really must get the Internet at home.* I decided to stop over-analysing the situation and let my degree of stimulation determine the duration of my collection.

To that end I started to casually peruse the half-dozen magazines on offer. I was intrigued by their content and it was more than my curiosity that was aroused, particularly given the last time I browsed such publications I had been a sexually immature teenager. To my relief they were all in good condition, as I had envisaged the disgusting possibility that some may show foul signs of previous patients' perusal—such as pages being stuck together or telltale stains. Such a finding would not have been conducive to arousal. I was surprised to find that the clinic had thoughtfully catered to a variety of tastes: from the conventional *Penthouse* to the more risqué, 'taboo'-type publications and everything in between. I decided to resist viewing the audiovisual stimulation for fear that the volume, which I had no obvious means to adjust, may be up too loud and shrieks of 'Oh God, yes fuck me! fuck me harder …!' might bellow from the room, which I knew wasn't particularly soundproof given that I could hear muffled conversations through the wall. I was also concerned that if I turned the TV on I may have difficulty turning it off, which was a nerve-racking circumstance I would rather avoid.

After a few more minutes the magazines had their desired effect and I got down to business although I found my mind wandering from what I was doing to all the things that got me into this predicament. This distraction didn't help but I was able to maintain my attention enough so that eventually I completed the collection (thankfully not missing the mark). I tightened the lid of the container with unnecessary force. I recalled having once heard that light kills sperm, but I wasn't sure whether this only applied to natural light. Needless to say I was paranoid about my precious cargo being annihilated and wasn't taking any chances, so I momentarily put the container in the safety of the darkened drawer alongside the pornographic publications.

I then turned my attention to completing the paperwork. There was one question that I found particularly odd. It read: 'Was any of the sample spilt during collection?—Yes or No. If Yes, how much?' Fortunately, I was able to confidently answer 'No', yet I still found it puzzling. What possible reason could be behind this question? Was it there to enable patients to justify a sample lacking in quantity? Or was it a housekeeping aid so that the cleaners knew to look out for a spillage? Or was it trying to safeguard against any embarrassing 'hair gel' episodes as hilariously depicted in the classic Farrelly brothers comedy *There's Something About Mary*. Regardless of the reason, I have no idea how you're supposed to measure the quantity spilt.

With the questions complete, the ordeal was over. I placed the paperwork into the plastic bag and was about to drop it in the deposit box when I realised to my horror that the specimen container was still in the drawer. How dopey would I have looked had I forgotten to submit the sample? I quickly included the container in the plastic bag which I noticed had a large graphic on the front stating 'Biological Hazard'. This was a little insulting. My sperm weren't some lethal substance. I just prayed my swimmers couldn't read, otherwise they may become despondent and disillusioned by such a label. In sending them off I couldn't help but wish them a safe and speedy voyage—not dissimilar to when someone dispatches some vital mail to a loved one—and had to wonder about the destiny of my discharge—was procreation on the horizon?

I was relieved I had dutifully completed my part of the process without major drama. I observed myself in the mirror to see if anyone could tell what I'd been up to but there was no evident spillage, I was dressed properly (i.e. my fly was done up) and my face showed no obvious indication of exertion. It was time to return to reception. As I approached the desk the receptionist acknowledged my presence, nodded, smiled and said, 'Please take a seat'. This was a great relief as it spared me the awkwardness of having to state the bleeding obvious by saying 'I'm done' or 'I'm finished'.

Ali gave me a welcoming smile as I returned to sit next to her in the waiting area. She refrained from saying anything as we were in the company of other couples who, we assumed by the look of terror on the men's faces, were here to do what I had just done. As we waited while the clinician checked the viability of my sample I was surprised at how calm and relaxed I was given the importance of the impending result. Then again, my tranquil state was more than likely related to my post-ejaculation sedation. I did wonder, however, why partners weren't allowed into the deposit room to hasten things along. Maybe this was something I could drop in the suggestions box (if the clinic had one).

Several minutes later the nurse returned and said that the sample was fine and that we were free to go, but reminded Ali to be back in several hours for the insemination. While in the elevator Ali turned to me and said:

'Was it hard …?'

'It was before—now it's flaccid.'

'Oh Matt', Ali replied, rolling her eyes in a familiar look of disapproval. 'You asked!'

Chapter 35
IUI #1

We returned to the clinic at the agreed time and both took a seat in the waiting area that was again crowded with numerous other couples, all waiting silently. Some people were half-watching the Ellen DeGeneres show on a large flat-screen TV. Then in the commercial break an advertisement came on with an all too familiar catchy upbeat jingle for a baby clothing shop. Surely we had all seen this ad before and had undoubtedly loathed and resented it for its sickeningly cheerful overtones that insinuated pregnancy was as easy as (dare I say) 'falling over'. Instantly, you could feel the collective tension in the room rise. Nobody knew where to look or how to react. This ad was the elephant in the room that nobody wanted to acknowledge. Luckily for Ali the nurse came in to collect her mid-jingle. I was given the option of accompanying her but foolishly decided against it. Instead I sat through the remainder of the commercial and endured the awkward silence. I am not entirely sure why I didn't go in with Ali. I suppose I was in denial of the whole wretched affair. Part of me was still vainly holding onto the misguided belief that our fleeting sexual encounters could yield a child. And I feared that witnessing the assisted impregnation would destroy my hope for this unlikely miracle and heighten my feelings of inadequacy and failure.

Within 15 minutes Ali returned and looked no worse for wear. I half expected her to come out walking with a limp or at least showing some signs of soreness. Again we avoided conversation until we had left the clinic.

'How was it? Did I give it to ya good and proper?' I asked.

'Actually it wasn't that bad. Nicci was right—it was pretty much like having a Pap smear.'

'That's good.' Well I assumed that was good, although you do sometimes hear women refer to the terrifying Pap smear in a less positive manner.

We had to wait two weeks to see if the procedure had worked and the suspense was emotionally challenging. Neither of us initiated any sexual contact during this period because I believe we were both frightened that such behaviour could potentially upset the mix—despite being told by Nicci that this wasn't the case. We didn't want to cause any unnecessary disruptions, preferring to leave our respective reproductive representatives alone so they could both get well acquainted, without a million or so other unwanted guests crashing their intimate tryst.

Unfortunately, on the day that the result was due I was working down in Melbourne for the entire week (something I had agreed to many months before). It was bad timing, but unavoidable. This was a significant step for me, as it was the first time I had been away from Ali since being unwell and I was to be working on an unfamiliar project, in unfamiliar surroundings and with people whom I had never met—all of which was awfully daunting considering how much my confidence had taken a hit and the fact I was still recovering.

I arrived at the office in Melbourne and was met by various people who gave me a lengthy spiel about the job I would be doing, straight away diving into the technical aspects of the work. I found it rather difficult to concentrate when in the back of my mind I was constantly distracted by the looming call I was to receive from Ali. Her blood test was in the morning and she expected the result around early afternoon. Nevertheless, I carried my mobile around with me all day (not behaviour I'm known for). Then at 2:03 pm the phone rang. I didn't want to take the call in the small open-plan office, so I raced into the corridor and out into the fire escape.

'How did we go … ?' I asked expectantly in a hushed tone, my voice amplified by the vast concrete expanse of the stairwell. There was a long pause.

'No luck …'

I could sense heartfelt sadness in Ali's voice; she was either crying or on the verge of tears. I just wished I could have consoled her and not been 800 kilometres away.

'Oh babe, I'm sorry … I love you. I'll call you tonight after work. OK?'

'OK. I love you too.'

I stayed alone in the cold concrete fire escape for several minutes to let the enormity of the dreadful result sink in. I was crushed and utterly demoralised. I had been really hopeful that this latest intervention was going to work for us and now that it hadn't I felt an unprecedented level of despondency. Furthermore, I really pitied Ali. She had taken the entire week off work, now she was at home all alone, left to mull over this devastating news.

The remainder of the week was exceedingly tough. The typical Melbourne weather perfectly reflected my mood: grey with a chance of showers. I am not ashamed to say I shed a few private tears when alone of an evening. But I tried my best to contain my emotions when in front of my colleagues. In fact I felt I had no-one, apart from Ali, with whom I could confide to lessen the burden. Stephen's death had taught me the importance of open and honest communication and I know had I told my male friends that they would have been sympathetic but again the ever-stoic male stereotype prevented me from such emotional disclosure.

I rang Ali every evening we were apart as we had much to discuss.

'Hey babe, how are you getting on?'

'I'm doing better. It's always hard when you first get the bad news though', she said, sounding much more upbeat than before.

'I know, it's so deflating—gut-wrenching. I don't reckon people really appreciate how emotionally taxing it is.'

'Tell me about it.'

'I've been thinking …'

'Yeah …'

'You know how we said that IVF wasn't for us … well I'm not so sure anymore. I think I want to give it a try if the other two IUIs don't work. What do you think?'

'It's funny you should say that because I've been thinking exactly the same thing since we missed out with the IUI. I was beginning to worry that we only had two chances left, then that'd be it', I said.

'I know what you mean. I just think we should consider IVF as another option.'

'I agree.'

'That's a relief, because I thought you might be dead against the idea', she said, her voice clearly delighted with my endorsement.

'I'm still not a huge fan of the process, but if it means we have a kid, then I'm all for it.'

'I miss you doll …'

'I miss you more babe.'

Chapter 36
IUI 2 & 3 low expectations

It was remarkable how quickly we both changed our tune about considering IVF and it was a relief to know that IUI wasn't the last option available to us. Needless to say our expectations for the next two months of IUI were significantly lowered such that we both suspected we were destined to have to go through IVF. We were still committed to giving IUI another two tries but suddenly we began to pin all our hopes on the success of the last possible treatment available.

With the second shot at IUI came another trip to the clinic to provide a sample. I was much less nervous this time given I knew what to expect. The collection went similarly to the previous visit, with the exception of my decision to indulge in inspecting the DVD—after all, it was on offer for my viewing pleasure and my curiosity just got the better of me. To my relief there was no sound to alert staff in the surrounding rooms of my penchant for porno films. But I was disappointed with the quality of the production. I do not proclaim to be a skin-flick aficionado but I can spot a low-budget movie when I see one. The biggest give-away, in my opinion, is often in the quality of the performing talent. If the actors are well past their prime—flaunting flab instead of fit physiques—then I'm afraid it's highly likely the movie has been purchased from the bargain-bin. This did bother me because we were spending a significant amount of money on all of these procedures, you'd think it would be possible to purchase a pricier porno film. Needless to say I didn't spend too long watching the movie and reverted back to naked photos of the female form that have satisfied males for generations. The magazines again did their magic, the sample was collected, assessed by the physicians and the ordeal was over.

I found myself back at work 15 minutes later, immediately called into a meeting. This was a bizarre circumstance to be in—returning from an environment where carnal urges had to be satisfied then thrust into another where corporate cogitation was called upon. You couldn't get two more diametrically opposed states of mind—from masturbation to business planning in a matter of minutes. My mind was understandably elsewhere but none of my colleagues knew that I was distracted by the morning's activities. I tried my best to keep a low profile during the meeting but inevitably my opinion was eventually sought.

'Matt, you've been unusually quiet this morning. I'd be interested in your take on the draft business plan', asked my boss.

Normally I would be fully engrossed in such a discussion with all the necessary synapses firing but on this day I couldn't get my brain to work. I was lost for words, not a good position to be in when your superior explicitly asks for your input.

'Hmmm ...' I said stalling for time but trying to make it sound like I was about to respond with some particularly pertinent observations.

'Well then ...'

'I agree with the majority of what has already been said this morning', I replied in a vain attempt to deflect attention from me.

Thankfully the meeting ended soon after, which gave me time to gradually acclimatise back into the office atmosphere. Recalling my earlier display of ineptitude I was reminded that when you donate blood you receive a sticker to wear that states 'Be nice to me. I gave blood today'. This informs your workmates that your capacity to participate may be slightly impaired due to this altruistic act. I wondered whether the fertility clinic should consider a similar approach—although they would have to choose the words carefully so as not to offend. Maybe 'I just came in a cup, so cut me some slack' would do the trick?

Once the second IUI was completed we were again left to wait and ponder what the future held for us. Since Steve's death and the subsequent fall-out we hadn't really discussed, in any great detail, how our ongoing sterile status was affecting each other.

'I think we need a back-up plan', Ali announced, hopping in the car one afternoon as I picked her up from work.

'What do ya mean?' I said as I pulled away from the curb.

'I mean other options, in case the IUI and IVF doesn't work for us.'

'But babe, after that there are no options …' I replied, glancing across at her, surprised by the naivety of her comment.

'Not to get pregnant— I know. But what about other life options? I don't like having all our hopes hang off IVF—if that doesn't work what next? We just flounder around childless?'

'What are you saying? Do you want to get a puppy?' I said, somewhat confused and distracted by the crazy traffic jockeying aggressively to be home in record time.

'No, I'm not sure a puppy is the answer. I think we may need a change of scenery if we luck out with all the fertility stuff.'

'To where exactly?'

'Sydney … it makes sense: both my sisters are there, we have friends there and we would get to see more of our niece and nephew—which would be nice.' At this point I was beginning to wish we weren't having this important conversation during peak-hour pandemonium. As we pulled up to another red light I took the opportunity to give Ali my undivided attention.

'But Ali, don't forget we could go through IVF for months, years even', I said, rubbing her thigh.

'No, I don't want that!' she snapped. 'This whole process is too emotionally taxing. I couldn't stand it for that long. I'm sorry.'

'Don't apologise, it's much harder on you than it is on me. I agree, we should decide on a cut-off, otherwise we could just continue with IVF indefinitely, which would be hideous.'

'I say we give it one go at egg collection. Hopefully we get heaps of eggs, which gives us at least two or three goes at implantation.' I nodded in agreement as the procession of vehicles gradually got going again. 'I really don't want to go through the collection more than once. It's supposed to be pretty bad.'

'Fair enough, I understand', I said, my eyes fixed on the road, tapping the steering wheel, agitated by the horrendous traffic but equally by our pregnancy misfortune.

'Then if we still aren't pregnant, we consider moving to Sydney for a few years … yeah?'

'Sure, but let's hope it doesn't come to that.'

'I know, but at least we have a plan.'

Ali made a valid point and I was relieved that she was openly considering the possibility that we may never have children and looking positively into alternatives for our future together. I was also pleased that she wasn't expecting an abundance of pets to become the panacea for our pregnancy problem. Many months earlier, when discussions about a life devoid of kids first began, Ali expressed a view that getting several puppies would somehow be a suitable alternative—that miraculously introducing a menagerie of canine companions would satisfy our parental instincts. The harsh reality was that you can have umpteen pets but without progeny of your own you are just another pet-obsessed couple. Don't get me wrong—pets are marvellous companions—but your own flesh and blood they are not and never will be.

Several days later the possibility of eventually moving to Sydney looked one step closer when we again received the unwelcome result that the latest IUI had failed. Ali emailed me the terrible result at work, in preference to using the phone, as the modern open-plan office certainly isn't designed with privacy in mind and neither of us wanted to be overheard having such a personal conversation.

That evening a survey from the clinic arrived in the mail at home. *Talk about bad timing.* The last thing either of us wanted to do was think critically about the process we had just been through once more, without success. Nonetheless I tried to remain upbeat for Ali's sake. The survey asked whether we were satisfied with the clinic to which I immediately barked: 'No, we don't have a baby yet—so give us back our bloody money!'

The survey also asked whether there were any areas where improvements could be made. Here was where I considered I could definitely provide some valuable input based on my experience. My suggested improvements were that the clinic:

1. allow couples into the deposit room to 'assist' in sample collection (*I wish*)

2. invest in higher-quality pornographic films

3. ensure adult magazines are regularly refreshed with new content

4. ban staff from the use of the word 'come' in any context.

I articulated these to Ali but she refused to write them down—not surprisingly.

We weren't looking forward to another month of IUI as it was beginning to take its toll both on our minds and bodies. At least with the earlier blood test method Ali and I were engaging in an inordinate amount of amorous frolicking—which, despite having some trivial downsides, was predominantly pleasurable—and we were able to connect together on a physical and emotional level, unified towards the creation of something magical. But with IUI it felt terribly unnatural, as I had suspected it might, devoid of the human interaction that under normal circumstances is essential. At times it was almost as if we were working separately towards a collective goal. Ali would take her injections and I would pop my pills and consume my dietary requirements. I would ejaculate more in containers than in her presence and she would be naked in front of fertility specialists more than with me. And we both reluctantly refrained from sex for fear it may thwart the effectiveness of the procedures. This process was not how nature had intended *homo sapiens* to procreate.

Our attitude during the earlier IUI tries was expect the worst, but hope for the best. In contrast, we met our third and final try at IUI with a degree of scepticism and derision, as neither of us anticipated impregnation. Instead we held rather a defeatist view, as we expected another failed IUI attempt to be a fait accompli.

I was on auto-pilot, simply going through the motions, so much so that I barely felt any awkwardness when again providing my sample at the clinic. Now I was starting to wonder why we just hadn't gone straight to IVF instead of wasting our time and money on a treatment that was obviously futile for us. But we had both agreed, when we first embarked on this fertility-assisted journey, to exhaust all possible avenues before moving on to the next stage. After all, we could have gone straight onto IVF way back when we first visited the fertility clinic, but at that stage we were optimistic that our problems could be remedied with minimal intervention. It's funny how hindsight can sometimes make you question decisions you made in the past.

When Ali informed me of the outcome of the last IUI attempt I was not on tenterhooks as with the previous attempts, as my expectations were dreadfully low. So when I again received an unpleasant email stating 'No luck L' there was only an instant when the words were like a stab to the chest and I quickly moved on from that disappointment. I suppose the relative indifference in my reaction this time was because I immediately became focused on what lay ahead: the dreaded IVF.

Chapter 37

IVF (In-Voluntary Fertilisation)

It was rather disconcerting to finally be using IVF because not so long ago I held the stern view that it would never come to this. This was partly due to the fact that I harboured an incredibly prejudiced view of a typical IVF couple and for some reason I never saw us becoming one of *those* couples trying for a test-tube baby. But then neither did I envisage that I would lose my brother to suicide, an aunt to cancer, or that I would suffer from bipolar. In my naive and conceited mind, these were afflictions that happened to other less health-conscious, unfortunate people. But the reality of life is that no-one is immune from adverse circumstances and hardship.

There was little delay in moving from IUI onto IVF. Within a week we received a sizeable bundle of brochures explaining in great detail all aspects of IVF. We were advised to familiarise ourselves with this content prior to the consultation we would have with Nicci the following week. Ali wasted no time and conscientiously read all the information from cover to cover. In contrast, I was reluctant to trawl through the plethora of pages explaining the whole rigmarole. Not because I wasn't committed to the process—on the contrary—I just believed that in many respect ignorance was bliss when it came to understanding the finer elements of IVF. Besides, I knew my involvement would again be limited and there was little I could actually physically do to help Ali, apart from provide moral support. I suppose in some respects my actions demonstrated that I was again in denial.

Eventually Ali persuaded me to read the material, but I agreed to only on the proviso that she highlight the main areas I should concentrate on.

What I soon realised upon reading was that IVF was a whole other level of medical involvement, far in excess of the previous fertility approaches we had undertaken—this was *serious* scientific assistance. Before, I had complained that I found elements of IUI to be unnatural and unnerving, yet in comparison IUI was just the tip of the fertility iceberg—IVF got a whole lot worse. The booklet talked of: injections, nasal sprays, anaesthesia, ultrasounds, blood tests, pessaries. The list went on and on and none of the elements sounded pleasant. It mentioned how the drugs would dramatically alter Ali's hormone levels for a stage (potentially toward that of a menopausal woman) which could seriously affect her mood and general wellbeing. I really sympathised with Ali at the thought of her having to be subject to all this intrusion, not just once but maybe numerous times. I considered myself to be the fortunate individual in this situation, as my involvement simply entailed that I came on request. From this point forward I would make a conscious effort to ensure I ceased to complain about providing my component.

Another alarming aspect of IVF was the cost. Over the years I had heard varying figures bandied around that ranged between $5000 and $10,000 for each try. This was a significant chunk of change no matter how you looked at it. As it turned out, we were looking at a similar cost but at least it was at the lower end of the spectrum and there was the potential for some substantial government rebate. Nevertheless, I was worried about the financial pressure that IVF may exert on us, particularly if we decided upon multiple attempts. But I sensed it best to keep these concerns to myself—the last thing I wanted was to cause Ali to agonise over the financial considerations, seeing as she already had so much to contend with during the IVF process. To that end, I saw my most important role (apart from providing first-rate sperm) to be one where I buffer Ali from any potential stressor, to ensure she remained relaxed so that she could concentrate on the IVF.

Part of me couldn't help but feel ashamed for letting money considerations surface. After all, money shouldn't have anything to do with it—how can you put a price on a child's life? So, really when it came down to it, the money component was irrelevant to a degree. We had already spent thousands up until this point and were prepared to invest more because we saw the potential result as being the greatest gift. The difficulty with IVF, unlike IUI, was that it could conceivably go on indefinitely if you so chose. So at what point would enough become enough? I detest gambling, yet IVF had the potential to feel like we were pouring our funds, not to mention our souls and our bodies, into a machine that was never going to pay up. Always hoping that with the next one we would hit the jackpot. But Ali and I are both eternal pragmatists and realists and there would have to come a time when we ultimately had to cut our losses due to exhaustion on all levels. This was a discussion that Ali and I had already had. We had defined our limit to be based on the number of eggs harvested from the first collection but I questioned how resolute this decision was. Would we waiver if the collection yielded poor results and try again?

Only time would tell.

Deep down though I resented the fact that we had to pay for the privilege of having children, while the majority of society gets to experience the exhilaration of the ride for free. You can't imagine the overwhelming sense of irritation and indignation. Biology can be such a bitch. I liken the vibe to being unexpectedly confronted by a Door Bitch at Disneyland who takes an immediate dislike to you and your partner for no apparent reason and subsequently makes you wait at the gates for an indefinite period. Meanwhile, as you wait patiently for days, weeks, months, or even years, you are both tormented by watching and hearing the unconstrained merriment of those lucky patrons who are having the time of their lives in this amazing adventure playground. You become so desperate for this life-changing experience that you try to bribe the Door Bitch for entry as you have seen other equally as unfortunate couples around you do. But there is no flat fee. Some couples get through with minimal damage to the back-pocket, while others continually outlay coin without success. If she ever concedes, you know you have payed a premium to enter but in the interim she has been graciously letting others go straight through gratis—oh the discrimination!

I also loathed those couples who are so blasé about childbirth that they broadcast their pregnancy after having just peed on the stick.

They then go on to have no complications whatsoever and pop out a perfectly healthy bub in seemingly record time. *Wow, was that really nine months ... surely not!* They make it look so ridiculously easy that I'm ashamed to say it sickened me. It's almost as if they simply placed an order for some bespoke furniture then—voila—it's delivered on time, on budget and to specification. However, I suppose to be honest I actually just envied their good fortune and wished Ali and I could have experienced the same.

Above all else, though, what made me livid, more than anything, was hearing stories of unwanted or unexpected pregnancies. I was eternally baffled by the rate of teenage pregnancy conceived on an ill-fated alcohol and/or drug induced one-night stand. Although by far the most astounding of these stories was one where a lesbian in a night of frivolity became heavily inebriated and momentarily changed teams, so to speak (with her coach no less), and produced a baby nine months later. Unbelievable. It almost sounds like an urban myth, too farcical to be fact, but I can assure you it is true. I had zero tolerance for such stories.

During previous meetings with Nicci it had proved a challenge for me to absorb all the information, instruction and counsel she dispensed. Fortunately, on the day of the latest appointment, I felt better informed about IVF, having scanned the material. In no way was I knowledgeable on the topic but I anticipated I should be able to come away with some improved understanding. My optimism though was crushed soon after arrival when she launched into a well-rehearsed spiel explaining IVF, with an urgency and pace normally reserved for Wall Street stockbrokers. She rattled off words like endometrium, follicle, hyperstimulation, luteal and pessary. Meanwhile, I was scrambling to keep up, wishing I had read the material in more depth, or at the very least had a glossary at hand to aid my comprehension. Ali, in contrast, was continually nodding her head, indicating she understood what was being said.

Gradually, the tempo of the monologue subsided, much to my relief, and Nicci moved onto elements of IVF that I could grasp.

'It's important that you're aware that there are several advantages of IVF, compared to the other fertility treatments you've tried so far', she said, then paused to take her first breath in minutes.

'OK', we both replied expectantly, unfamiliar with hearing good news on the topic of our parental probability.

'With IVF you're 50 per cent more likely to conceive than a normal unassisted couple.'

'Really, that's good', Ali replied.

'Another benefit of IVF is that it allows us to optimise the timing. I like to use the analogy of the Melbourne Cup: with natural conception it's like having a bet two weeks out from race day, whereas with IVF it is like placing your bet 200 metres from the finish line', she explained.

'I see ...' I said, nodding my head in an exaggerated manner because for the first time in a while this wasn't a token response. I was surprised that I did actually understand, mainly because she had finally spoken in a language I could comprehend—a sporting reference.

'Basically, IVF is much less hit and miss', she continued. 'But by far the biggest advantage is that it enables us to gain a better understanding of what's going on and potentially where the problem may be. We then have a much greater chance of isolating and fixing the problem.'

'That's great', Ali said.

'I also strongly suggest that Alison continue having acupuncture at certain phases during IVF, as there have been some interesting studies that have shown acupuncture can improve success rates.'

'Sure', Ali said in an upbeat tone buoyed by the barrage of positive information.

After the consultation we were both left feeling a lot more comfortable about IVF in general. Nicci had demystified some of the more complex elements of IVF and I was relieved to notice that Ali appeared to be quite optimistic and unperturbed by what lay ahead. In the days and weeks that followed I was immensely impressed by her diligence in following Nicci's directives to administer the plethora of medical concoctions she was given. I can imagine how having to inject yourself in the stomach nightly could become irritating, but to her credit never once did she protest or moan. Her appointments with the acupuncturist were met with a similar unwavering dedication. And when she was advised by the acupuncturist to eat certain foods, she immediately modified her diet accordingly. She was clearly a committed model patient.

Fortunately, the drugs and hormones didn't seem to have too adverse an effect on Ali. Although her blood-test results indicated her levels dropped to menopausal lows, astonishingly there was never any noticeable change in her disposition. Some women become very emotionally unstable due to the drugs they must take whilst on IVF. With Ali, there was no evidence of such susceptibility—which was comforting. But with her coping exceedingly well on all fronts, my support services were not required, which left me feeling like a casual bystander—a spectator in a game that I was only allowed to be involved in for a brief, but climactic, moment. I knew my time would come (pardon the pun) but at that stage I just wished there was more I could have done to get actively involved.

Around the same time I had one of my regular appointments with the psychiatrist which had been scheduled every six to eight weeks to assess my condition since I had become mentally unwell. During the many preceding months my mental state had gradually improved, my positive attitude and outlook was slowly returning and the doctor was pleased with my progress. Over this period my antidepressant medication had been progressively reduced to incredibly low dosages but much to my dislike I was still required to take them. I was desperate to come off one particularly drug that was notorious for causing undesirable weight-gain. I had been exercising relentlessly and watching what I ate to try and battle the bulge but was seeing little reward for effort. My weight had plateaued slightly above the 80 kg mark, beyond the upper limit that I had set for myself, which was displeasing. So when the doctor gave me the medical reprieve I so deeply coveted I was jubilant. The doctor dampened my enthusiasm by highlighting that the drug was likely to remain in my system for another two to four weeks and not to expect any dramatic difference before then. Nevertheless, the change this had on me was close to remarkable. I immediately found I had energy that had eluded me for months and the kilos began to fall—not at an alarming rate but fast enough to encourage me. Suddenly, I felt almost as physically and mentally healthy as I had been before my brother's untimely death, which was an immense relief and a source of strength to consider I had come through such tortuous chaos and survived.

A week before Ali was due for egg collection I received word from Anthony that he and Isla were pregnant—again. Four to five months earlier they had told us they had started trying and since then, I'm ashamed to say, we were reluctant to visit them because we knew based on past experience that they were baby-making machines and would be expecting in no time. *How right we were.* Our behaviour sounds appalling, and in many respects I suppose it was, but Ali and I had decided to start trying for children way back on Anthony and Isla's wedding night when they had announced the same intention. So it was natural for us to compare our situation with theirs. Many years had since passed and many of those around us were now having their second child, yet we seemed no closer to conceiving. I am not overly competitive but it was like we were jogging on the spot and being lapped by everyone else—which inevitably led to harsh feelings of inadequacy, failure and jealousy whenever a new addition was announced. Obviously, my perspective was fundamentally flawed, as I somehow still viewed conception as an even playing field, when the reality—which I was having difficulty coming to terms with—was that Ali and I were like disabled athletes trying to compare ourselves to elite specimens. Comparison was the killer here, as it so often is.

Nonetheless, I congratulated Anthony on the exciting announcement. When I quizzed him on the details of the pregnancy he then dropped more astonishing news: they were having not one, but two—twins! *The lucky bastard—we can't even make one*, was my instant thought, followed by *Holy Shit! Three kids, under three—what a handful.* I didn't really know how to respond to this unexpected twist. Anthony indicated that he was keen to catch up but that would mean having to inform Ali. My preference was to delay telling her until we had gone through the first round of IVF as I wanted her to remain positive and upbeat and there was potential for this news to be met with some resentment and sadness, particularly the revelation of twins. This put me in an awkward position, in which I had no alternative other than to fabricate that Ali and I had an overly busy schedule over the next few weeks that prevented us from all getting together. Such devious behaviour did not sit well with me but over the journey I had learnt that at times it was unavoidable in certain circumstances. Besides, there are no rulebooks to follow in regard to such matters, so I was simply doing what I believed was best at the time—providing the necessary buffer for my darling wife so that she could concentrate on herself and making a baby.

Chapter 38
Give Up?

The day was already upon us before I really had time to get comfortable with the whole IVF process and concede without question that this was where we were. First I dropped Ali at the operating theatre where she underwent her egg collection surgery. This procedure took around an hour. In the meantime I supplied my sample at the fertility clinic without drama. I sauntered in like a seasoned professional. The receptionist had even begun to recognise me, calling me by name as soon as I entered the premises—an obvious sign of my frequent attendance. I nonchalantly took a seat in the waiting area amongst several of my brothers in arms. Unlike them, however, I was relaxed and familiar with the surroundings and what to expect. They, on the other hand, exhibited the telltale wide-eyed expression, like a kangaroo transfixed by approaching headlights, which was glaring evidence of unease and apprehension—a look that I surely mimicked on my pioneering visit.

Later I picked Ali up from surgery. She looked remarkably well and showed virtually no signs of wooziness or discomfort. We made our way to the fertility clinic where we had an appointment with one of the nurses, Doris, to discuss how the procedure had gone. Ali, who was typically an exceptional judge of character, had previously raved about how fantastic Doris was, so I was keen to meet her. Ali was right; Doris was adorable—the archetypal motherly nurse in her mid-fifties with a truly nurturing and tender attitude towards her patients. And, my word, did she know her stuff when it came to IVF. She was nearly as well-informed as Nicci.

'So, do you know you got eight eggs from this morning's collection, which is a good number. Not huge, but good—better than three or four', she said, in a reassuring and cheerful voice.

'That's good. I remember Nicci saying something like that to me soon after the surgery but I was still under the effects of the anaesthetic', Ali replied.

'So the embryologist will put the sperm together with the egg in culture and see how many fertilise within the next 24 hours. Then someone from the clinic will give you a call tomorrow morning to let you know how things have progressed. And, fingers crossed, transfer will occur towards the end of the week.'

'Maybe on your birthday Ali?' I blurted out without thinking.

'Really, it's your birthday this week? Wouldn't that be a lovely present', Doris said gleefully.

Doris then went on to explain some additional hormone medication that Ali had to take for several weeks called progesterone pessaries. She took out one of these pessaries and showed it to Ali in some detail (it was about the size of a jelly bean but conical and wrapped in foil like a chocolate bar). It was unlike any medication I had ever seen. Initially, I thought nothing much of this, simply adding it to an increasingly long list of medical technicalities I had learnt about during this infertility odyssey.

'You realise sweetheart you *must* take this vaginally', Doris said still with distinctive chirpiness in her voice.

Hearing this I nearly fell off my chair. Where was the necessary Secrets Women's Business Siren … *Whoop … Whoop … Whoop … All men to leave the vicinity immediately. I repeat, all men to leave the vicinity immediately!* Should I really be hearing this? Should I cover my ears? I looked around the room like a lonely and embarrassed child who finds himself in the wrong place at the wrong time.

'But if the pessaries aren't raising your progesterone levels enough, you'll have to start taking them rectally—OK sweetheart', she added slowly, all the while nodding to ensure Ali completely understood her instruction. 'I know most women's initial reaction to this is the same but many later find they actually prefer it!'

Oh sweet mother of God make these noises go away … enough is enough. Just when I figured things couldn't get any more uncomfortable, Doris had dropped another almighty bombshell. With that statement we reached an all-time-low in our romantic relationship. But it didn't end there. 'I must make it absolutely clear sweetheart that you know to take it either vaginally or rectally. Because we had one lady in here the other day who came in to complain about the taste. The poor thing had been eating them!' Doris added, shaking her head in disbelief.

And to add further insult to injury, I also found out that Ali had to pay extra for the privilege of the pessaries, and these little pellets masquerading as bon bons weren't cheap. Each one cost more than your favourite confectionery from Cadbury. So really, I wasn't surprised that the poor lady was trying to eat them; no doubt she was just trying to get some pleasure from them instead of downright discomfort. Forget nano-technology or the cure for cancer, the *real* money is clearly in pessary production. Next time you see an expensive sports car, check the numberplate, it'll probably say something like *Dr Pess*!

Most fortunate couples have the opportunity to conceive amidst candlelight, champagne and hastily removed lingerie, whereas for the past two and three-quarters years we had been having an entirely different experience altogether. Who was I kidding? I had been trying throughout this whole infertility venture to maintain some mystery like in an old-fashioned romance novel. But it was time to face facts, those days were long gone, it was time I truly woke up and stopped being so precious, squeamish and repulsed by such discussion and embraced the entire process—pessaries and all. Just as long as Ali wasn't going to ask me for assistance in administering them—but somehow I doubted that very much.

Soon after, we left the clinic and it was then that I realised that no mention was made of my sperm during the entire consultation—which was disappointing—some feedback on what *my* numbers were would have been nice. After all I had been working hard for many months to produce Ian Thorpe-esque 'Olympic-standard' long-distance swimmers and prayed my adherence to the strict dietary regime had paid off. So I assumed that 'no news' was 'good news' in regard to my baby gravy.

Nevertheless, I decided not to air my grievances which were pale and petty compared to what Ali was enduring, particularly in light of the pessary revelation.

On our way home we went through what had been discussed.

'Getting eight eggs is pretty good, hey? You'd think at least a few of them would fertilise', Ali said excitedly.

'Yep, you've done really well babe and you look so good. I'm surprised. I figured you'd be a lot more worse for wear.'

'It definitely wasn't as bad as I thought it would be. I have heard some women get around 15 to 20 eggs and can't walk for days. I'm not really in any pain at all. I'm pretty lucky.'

'It's strange to think that right now our bits are gettin' it on in a lab.'

'It's bizarre, isn't it?'

'Now we just have to hope all goes well.'

The following day it was useless trying to concentrate on work given the imminent announcement. Unfortunately I had a lot to catch up on having been away and was in and out of meetings all morning but would hastily duck back to my desk to check for any messages from Ali. When I hadn't heard anything by 10:30 am I was getting worried. Then I got the email which read:

Not great news, only four eggs left and none are looking too good.

I was devastated. Lost for words my response was brief and ineloquent:

F@ck. Sorry

My heart sank. A 50 per cent attrition rate wasn't good at all. And the remaining eggs didn't look promising. I was floored —shattered— as I had never contemplated the possibility of *none* fertilising. How could that happen? It didn't make sense. My sperm were good: spared any gruelling expedition, they shouldn't be fatigued. Ali had an abundance of eggs that were first-rate and ripe for the picking. They were both introduced in salubrious surroundings. This was supposed to be the perfect match on a blind date. There was supposed to be some primordial magnetism at play here. Perhaps even love at first sight?

Those all too familiar doubts I had before, about our pregnancy potential, reached an all-time high. I felt the prospect of fatherhood fall away in an instant. But I couldn't wallow in self-pity because I had to be in another meeting within minutes. The last place in the world I wanted to be. So I pushed this demoralising news to the back of my mind for the remaining hours of the working day, acting as if today were like any other in the office and that the next meeting held real relevance in my life, when the complete opposite was true.

That evening Ali returned home late from work after having taken the bus. We both said the usual pleasantries, interacting on autopilot, neither one of us keen to bring up the inevitable topic.

'How was your day?' I asked as I continued to prepare dinner.

'You know … the usual', she replied despondently.

'Same …' Then there was silence and the shortest time felt like the longest time.

'… They were pretty crappy results weren't they?' I said, trying to gauge her reaction.

'Yep …' she said, trying to not let her emotions get the better of her.

'Do they reckon any will fertilise?' I asked gently.

'They don't know yet, but they'll call again tomorrow', she whimpered, scrunching up her face to fight back the welling tears. I leant in and held her. 'I think … if we don't get any to fertilise … then we should accept … that it just isn't meant to be for us.' Ali sobbed.

'Really … so this could be it—the end of the road. Are you sure? You might regret it later.'

'I can handle not having kids … it's the not knowing that's killing me.'

'You know we'll be OK regardless', I said confidently for support but half looking for reassurance myself.

'That's just it—I'm getting sick and tired of the process. It just doesn't feel *right*. Maybe it's a sign that we should stop trying to force the issue', she said with conviction, shaking uncontrollably.

'Look', I pleaded, holding her face gently between my hands and staring into her tear-filled eyes. 'I know it's tough and especially tough on you. But remember there's still a chance that one will fertilise. It only takes one!'

'I suppose', Ali replied in an unconvincing tone.

'And if none fertilise I really think we should try for one more egg collection—and that's it—but it's easy for me to say, I'm not the one who has to go through it.'

'We'll see', Ali said, blinking away tears.

The next day things were looking up. Ali emailed me that two eggs had finally fertilised and transfer was tomorrow. I was ecstatic. This was a tremendous relief as it indicated that there was hope, a chance however slim. At last there was proof that our respective reproductive fluids weren't repulsed by one another after all. Even if neither of the eggs 'took' when transferred, at least we had seen some progress towards pregnancy and we could try again. If none of the eggs had survived or fertilised the whole IVF intervention would have been in vain.

In my elation I wanted to punch the air and shout with exuberance but my sterile work atmosphere inhibited such celebration. Instead I just muttered to myself with conviction: 'Yes! ... yes! ... yes! ...' We had become so accustomed to getting unwelcome feedback it was hard not to get excited.

I quickly replied to Ali, asking her whether they would transfer both at once. She responded saying that they would only transfer one and freeze the other which could possibly be used later if we wanted.

I found the concept of cryogenic freezing astonishing—how a living cell could be subjected to such harsh temperatures and not perish. You hear of snap-frozen vegetables that 'lock in the freshness' but I wondered what the process would do to our fertilised egg? Would it be better or worse for the experience? What if they don't thaw properly? You expect that fresh is best— it certainly was for vegetables in my experience—but clearly that wasn't always the case.

Chapter 39
Parenting future

So as fate would have it, on the morning before Ali's birthday, she was scheduled to be impregnated. I'm not sure why but I didn't accompany her to the clinic. This was odd behaviour as, up until this point, I had been beside her throughout the entire nightmare. Maybe my aloofness was an attempt to try and keep things low-key and not put too much unnecessary pressure on Ali at this crucial stage. Either way I don't think Ali was offended by my absence.

Later that day Ali emailed letting me know that everything had gone well but unfortunately the other remaining egg had died. She explained that, based on these results, Nicci was finally able to explain our infertility. Our issue was a condition known as sub-fertility and under these circumstances we had only a 3 per cent chance of conceiving naturally every month, whereas most couples have a 25 per cent chance. *Now they weren't good odds.*

That evening we were both as jubilant as we had been in months. Even the chore of cleaning dirty dishes became a playful activity.

'So now that you're "The Vessel" are there any things you have to do in particular, any foods you should avoid?' I inquired, flicking the damp tea-towel ineffectually towards Ali.

'Apparently I have to eat lots of figs, apricots, pistachio nuts and leafy dark green vegetables and drink dandelion tea.'

'Really, is *that* all?'

'Oh and Nicci also said I should eat heaps of chocolate and that I mustn't do any housework and I'm to be given a back massage at least twice a day.'

'Are you sure …?' I replied, with a degree of scepticism, whipping the towel towards her which gave out a sharp *crack!* millimetres from Ali's thigh.

'Oi, stop it!' she giggled. 'I'm positive. And no footy is allowed on in the house either … how weird is that. Apparently it's bad for the embryo's development—who would have thought!' she added with a cheeky grin.

'You almost had me going there', I replied, feigning to load up for another crack. 'But as usual you pushed it just that bit too far. I'm onto you and your scheming Vessel ways. So what does that mean if we have to do another round of IVF?'

'If we end up doing IVF again it'll be via the ICSI method, which is where they select an individual sperm and physically inject it into the egg', Ali explained.

'Gee, talk about needing serious medical assistance—let's hope it doesn't come to that.'

And hope we did, throughout the dreaded two-week interval, as we waited for a positive test result or, instead, the arrival of our unwelcome 'friend' which would herald failure. During this time Ali wasn't to participate in any activity that was too strenuous that would cause her body temperature and heart-rate to rise too dramatically. So following doctor's orders she refrained from going to the gym which she found frustrating. And after just a few days of relative inactivity she began complaining about how stodgy she felt.

I tried my best to not think about the approaching deadline but it was useless as Ali had to have almost daily blood tests to monitor her progesterone levels and ensure the pessaries (via the 'front door') were doing their thing. The poor girl was being treated like a pincushion but again, to her credit, never once did she complain. The first test was at the end of week one and remarkably pleasing; her levels were within range. Several days later, only a few days before the end of the all-important two-week waiting period, Ali had another test, the outcome of which was not so promising. Her levels had dropped significantly, which was a bad sign. We were both incredibly disheartened. Furthermore, Ali now had to take the pessaries via the 'back door'—which she was understandably embarrassed about. Initially, I thought I would joke about it with her, to try and make her feel more relaxed about the undertaking, but I rapidly sensed that she was in no mood for my banter. Then two days before the big day, on a lazy Sunday afternoon as we both lounged around, entangled comfortably together reading on the couch, Ali broke the relaxed silence with something that was even more cause for concern.

'I think I'll go to the gym this arvo', she declared, dejected.

'You shouldn't, you're not supposed to exert yourself, remember.'

'I think I'm getting my period', she said with a forlorn look on her face.

'Really … are you sure?'

'Pretty much.'

'Still, I reckon you should hold off just in case.'

'Fine, I suppose you're right.'

I prayed that somehow Ali was still pregnant despite numerous signs to the contrary. The next day picking her up from work she seemed in good spirits, so I gathered that maybe our 'friend' hadn't arrived. Unable to contain my excitement I was quick to inquire.

'Has our "friend" arrived?' I asked nervously.

'Yep unfortunately', Ali muttered with a rueful look.

'Why didn't you tell me?' I replied, unreservedly peeved.

'I told you yesterday, didn't I?'

'Yeah, but it wasn't certain. I would like to know too.'

'Sorry.'

We sat in silence for a while, the car idling. I was too distracted to drive home just yet. This turn of events really upset me because I resented the fact that I had been walking around all day hanging onto a glimmer of optimism. Meanwhile Ali knew we had lucked out again. What worried me most was that this behaviour typified a growing issue between us, in that we were becoming increasingly disconnected from one another as our sterile status drew on.

'So what percentage of first-time IVF attempts fail, do you know?' I asked, breaking the silence, not sure if it was the right thing to say but wanting Ali to engage.

'No, but what's it matter now anyway?'

'I'm just curious that's all. Do you reckon we'll have better luck next time?'

'Hopefully the ICSI will work. Otherwise there's nothing else they can do for us. But in some ways I'm glad that they have found our problem.'

'How do you mean?'

'Well, that we haven't gone through all this fertility hell for *nothing*, when we could have actually conceived naturally but were just too impatient to let Nature take its course.'

'Sure … so what's the plan with telling people that we missed out?' I asked.

'I think we don't say anything unless someone asks.'

'Fair enough.'

'And in future, if friends or family ask about our progress—like the number of eggs collected/fertilised and so on, then we just say to them that we would rather keep this info to ourselves.'

'So what—tell them to assume that no news is bad news?' I qualified.

'Exactly. It's just too emotionally taxing otherwise. Getting the result is bad enough, but then having to constantly repeat it to others is too painful. Do you know what I mean?'

'Totally. I agree', I said, leaning across the seat to plant a reconciliatory smooch.

It was naive of me to have second-guessed Ali's instincts about her not having a bun in the oven. What would I know? But in my defence I wasn't acting like a male chauvinist bastard—trying to tell a woman she hadn't menstruated—I was simply trying to be overly optimistic. But as it turned out I needn't have bothered because when the final test results came in Ali was right.

Our uninvited 'friend' was back in town yet again.

Chapter 40
Suicide vs. infertility

Ali didn't seem nearly as upset by the bitter news as I was, probably because she'd already come to terms with the likely outcome when her body started giving her all the unwanted signals. But both she and I were surprised when we were told we had to wait six weeks before we could start another full IVF cycle. They explained that this extended break was necessary to allow Ali's ovaries sufficient time to recover from the hormone treatment before another egg collection could be carried out. Had we been fortunate enough to have any spare fertilised eggs survive and be frozen one of those could have been used when Ali was next ovulating, but unfortunately this wasn't the case.

At first, the idea of having to wait for such a long period was discouraging, as it felt to me like we would lose momentum and further delays meant our precarious living in limbo would continue. But Ali viewed it differently. She saw the enforced vacation as an opportunity for the two of us to stop being so single-mindedly driven and obsessed by this pursuit and to start to reconnect with one another. Obviously she too had been sensing a growing distance between us that needed to be redressed immediately. Nurturing the stability and strength of our union was paramount—*Better Together*. As a couple we had endured so much over the past few years, and our relationship, while still fundamentally strong at its core, was in need of some attention and repair.

A few weeks into our forced fertility hiatus we celebrated our fourth wedding anniversary, a milestone that now brought with it mixed emotions as it served as a harsh reminder of yet another year of being the DINKS (Dual Income No KidS) who were PRICKS (Partners

Really Invested in Conceiving Kids Soon). At this point my concerns over our parenting probability were now amplified to an unparalleled extreme. I became resigned to the likelihood that it just wasn't going to happen. Ali too had reached the same agonising conclusion. Gradually, as the weeks passed, we both started to visualise life with just the two of us. We spent masses of quality time together and quickly reconnected on an emotional and physical level—making passionate love for the sheer pleasure of it which we hadn't done for ages. And slowly we became accustomed to this scenario: happiness and contentment without children. I even finally summoned the courage to tell Ali about Anthony and Isla's impending additions and she was delighted for them. This was pleasing as it showed that neither of us had become baby-obsessed emotional basket cases. In fact, we both jokingly made a conscious effort to point out to one another when we noticed a child or teenager having a repugnant public tantrum, as it served to reaffirm that there were indeed some benefits to living a child-free existence.

What I had also realised around this time was that this incessant and pervasive infertility cloud that had loomed over us for years now triggered emotions that were similar to the grief experienced upon the suicide of my brother and I regretted we'd never spoken about having kids. Ali and I were devastated by Steve's suicide and our infertility struggle and were going through the various stages of grief for both reasons: denial, anger, bargaining, depression and acceptance. But in some ways I found our persistent infertility problems to be more oppressive as there remained a degree of lingering hope that prevented us ever reaching closure. When someone dear to you dies, they are gone, never to return. In time, as you grieve, you slowly come to terms with the aching void you feel in their absence, until some day you heal and move forward with your life albeit with emotional scarring. I believe this is partly because deep down you recognise there is no alternative; you know nothing can bring back your loved one. In our case, infertility, in contrast, was a cruel monthly lottery where we both pined for success and with each recurrent defeat were saturated by grief: grief over the lost opportunity, the unborn child and the possibility that we may never be parents. This was an excruciating routine to endure month after month. But for many couples like Ali and me there was still the possibility, no matter how miniscule, that the next try would bring elation. So with a skerrick of optimism left we would show stoic resilience, dust ourselves off and try again, even though our wounds from the previous attempt were still painfully fresh. This loitering hope was insufferable torture, a roller-coaster of emotion. It fostered the dogged persistence to go another round, which inevitably brought another vicious cycle of grief from which we would never fully recover until the cycle was broken, either by becoming pregnant or finally accepting (the final phase of grief) our childless fate.

I also began to hold the pessimistic view that the odds were mounting against us. For years we had heard countless pregnancy stories from family, friends, colleagues and acquaintances, some of whom had been fortunate enough to get knocked up relatively easily. Others, like ourselves, had encountered difficulty, requiring tests, drugs, needles and/or surgery to conceive. Up until this point, however, *everyone* else we knew who had been trying for kids had eventually succeeded. While most people would find this encouraging, I did not. According to Dr Google.com, around 2 per cent of couples in Australia are unable to conceive. So, in my view, as more and more people we knew were getting preggers the numbers were becoming less and less favourable. Maybe *we* were one of the 2 per cent of couples in our random sample population.

I'll come clean and confess that I even began entertaining the prospect that we were jinxed—obviously no analytical or factual considerations at play here. But before you discount me as an outright fruit loop at this point—I did have my reasons. And it had to do with my father, whom I feared may have inadvertently cast a terrible curse on our parenting potential. To make matters worse this curse occurred on our wedding day, during the time at weddings that often offers up some of the more memorable moments: the speeches. I was nervous because Dad was due to speak on my family's behalf. He's a character—I'll admit it. Normally jovial and outgoing, he suffers from an over-inflated self-assuredness when it comes to public speaking. As I see it, his problems are twofold: firstly, his over-reliance on 'dad jokes' that typically fall on deaf ears and plunge the room into bamboozled silence. Secondly, he prepares little beforehand, rehearses even less and, most devastatingly, digresses onto topics that seem completely random. But it had been some time since I had witnessed him address a throng, so I desperately hoped he had improved, perhaps through some miraculous intervention.

As he started his speech it was clear that not much had changed, the speech had all the hallmarks of the old Dad—most notably several tangents that seemed to defy logic—to the point where (to my utter embarrassment) my reserved mother went to grab the microphone in an attempt to get him to wrap it up prematurely. This proved futile. Thankfully, though, there was no public family feud. Dad came home strongly to surprisingly riotous laughter from the crowd. I was pleasantly stunned. He had proven me wrong. But in hindsight had he cursed the newlyweds in the process? How, you may ask?

I will spare you the details of his speech and thankfully much of it is a blur, as I found most of it traumatic. Nevertheless, the crux of his verbose tale was thus: our surname has its origins in agricultural processes—more specifically the production of barley, hence Barwick—while Ali's ancestral lineage was equally clear—Field. So Dad surmised that he *expected* 'fertile' relations would ensue. This last line brought the house down— not surprisingly. That old chestnut of parents wanting, often demanding, grandchildren from their offspring is probably the oldest of all 'dad jokes' going around. Sure it got a laugh, but at what cost?

My concerns, however, over having been inextricably jinxed surrounded his flippant use of a certain word. Could having said the word 'expected'—which assumes so much— be the cause of our infertility? As is often the case the devil's in the detail. Had Dad tempted fate? If he had used a less presumptuous word—such as 'hoped'—would we be in a different predicament today—absurd, yes—but I wondered …

One thing was for certain: the Barwick/Field combination was yielding little for its labour. Correction. Our 'harvest' to date was zilch, zero, zip. And while I knew deep down that Dad's harmless quip couldn't really have any detrimental impact, it did add to the frustration—if only a tad. After so many treatments we still didn't have any real explanation for our infertility. Modern medicine left us none the wiser because so little is known about sub-fertility. So for a time my perspective changed, where I perceived anything as potentially the cause of our prolonged childless existence. Which is why, I suppose, I partly blamed my father for the situation.

Chapter 41
Man-to-man communication

After several weeks of ruminating, I decided to confide in Mum.
'It's not the end of the world', she said in a motherly tone.
'I know …'
'Kids *are* a hell of a lot of worry', she added.
'Gee … thanks ma', I said, slightly aggrieved.
'I don't mean it like that. You know I'm blessed to have had you both and you bring me such joy. But the reality is, there *is* worry.'

I wasn't at all surprised by this comment as my mum has always been a serial fretter about Stephen and me. Even to the point where she didn't like us travelling in the same car on trips to the coast, in case there was an accident—spread the risk was her thinking.

Although her comments were meant to comfort me, they did the opposite. Over the days that followed I kept thinking about what she had said and I just couldn't bring myself to agree with her point of view. Instead, I preferred to interpret her comment in a different way. I formed the notion that to have 'worry' can also mean there are elements in your life that you care deeply about. To have 'worry' often means your life is enriched with considerations other than your own. And to 'worry' about an individual means you have much more than a passing interest in that person's wellbeing. Therefore, in some respects, to live a life without 'worry' can be a pretty lonely existence. You often hear the statement: *In order to be a good parent you have to be selfless.* So wouldn't that mean that sometimes 'worry' must be part of that selflessness? If this is true, give me 'worry' over loneliness any day.

Wrestling with these concepts I started to feel that perhaps I had lulled myself into a false sense of acceptance out of necessity. Then I came across a quote from someone I respect, which read: 'It's interesting the whole fatherhood thing. Everyone says it changes everything but it's beyond that. It changes your chemical reactions, it changes your brainwaves.'

These words were yet another example of how parenthood can, for some, be the answer to the true meaning of life and hearing them left me tremendously depressed about our continuing sterile status. Just when I thought I had honestly accepted, and was comfortable with, not being a dad, it was obvious that I hadn't yet relinquished the dream. I had been hardwired from an early age to expect parenthood, almost as if it were a rite of passage, to continue the fundamental circle of life.

Why else does sex feel so fantastic? Think about it. Some may say that other pleasures surpass that of sex, such as chocolate, coffee or a hot-water bottle on a cold winter's night. But I would argue that they are misled and obviously aren't doing the sex thing right—if at all! It's obvious why getting your rocks off feels second to none: so that we yearn to repeat the practice to advance the species. When it boils down to it, this is our sole objective in life from a biological perspective— the rest is just fluff I'm afraid. Those who disagree may assert that we are in fact driven to evolve, explore, invent, conquer, own a 60-inch LCD television or endeavour to surpass 1000 Facebook friends. In my opinion they are all wrong—they've jumped the gun, by making the assumption that their own existence was guaranteed from the start. Unfortunately, when you struggle with fertility it becomes abundantly clear that the next generation isn't necessarily a done deal. So that's why procreation has to be the focus first and foremost.

Consider this, 200,000 years ago, when our earliest ancestors sat in their caves gazing into the hypnotic flickering embers, picking remnants of bison flesh from between their teeth, they rarely felt content to curl up and catch some Z's or turn their attention to some rock art drawing. They ached for something more: a primordial craving for some amorous action. This was an intense urge for a *reason*. Without which you and I wouldn't be here today—plain and simple. Whether they instinctively knew what to do in terms of the mechanics (what goes where) or instead relied on trial and error—who can say? Given sex sure feels a hell of a lot better than sticking your finger in your ear, they probably just went with what felt best—but it's inconsequential anyway. What's paramount is that they worked it out eventually.

You see we desire to extend our family line above all else and I was finding it near impossible to break this inherent presumption and see the childless alternatives as anything other than second-rate substitutes. Suddenly, I felt terribly alone. I recognised I could talk to Ali about this but there was also the potential risk that by raising such topics, her own doubts could resurface and I knew I must be her buffer against such negativity because this would only make matters worse for her in the midst of preparing for the next round of IVF. More than anything I yearned to confide in my dearly departed brother—he knew me better than anyone and would have been the perfect confidant. And unfortunately the select few of my male friends that were aware of our infertility turmoil, while sympathetic, weren't exactly the chatty type, up for a D'n'M, unless it revolved around football or beer.

I was at a loss, until I recalled several months earlier having seen Ali on an infertility Web forum reading stories from women experiencing the same emotional roller-coaster. At the time I remembered her saying she'd found these shared experiences a great support and gained a real sense of solidarity. In desperation, I secretly logged on and searched for any similar forums or posts from men. I tried various keyword searches but all proved fruitless. It appeared men just weren't comfortable talking about infertility. Desperate to find some reference to men on the various sites, I trawled through page upon page of posts from women. Immediately, I was amazed at how many women wrote, in great detail, about how their male partner was reacting to their hardship. But this wasn't what I wanted, as these posts were essentially from the women's perspective. What I needed was to read how they felt—what they were going through. To know I wasn't on my own.

I was flummoxed by my discovery that on the 'World Wide' Web no other blokes sought similar solace. Was I that effeminate? True, I disliked beer, but was I so dissimilar to the rest of the male population?

Surely not? I knew technology wasn't the barrier, given that men aren't averse to online chat sites (as I often frequented a Web renovator's forum for DIY advice and some blokes happily blabbed on about their latest project). These sites offered anonymity, so it wasn't as if guys were forced to open up face to face. I just couldn't make sense of it. So I concluded, yet again, that the problem must be men's incapacity to talk to fellow men about health or personal/relationship issues and confide in them when they have a problem: be it bipolar or infertility. I was guilty of this when I didn't talk about our fertility problems with my mates near and dear to me. It seems communication is an absolute no-no for some men as it undermines their alpha-male status and draws attention to their inadequacies. Our instinct is to not disclose. I'd like to encourage men to be more open—become more like our female counterparts—but such change will undoubtedly take time. But right then I was in need of immediate help, and ultimately I was left to ponder my fate alone.

Despite my feelings of isolation I managed to maintain an upbeat façade for Ali's sake. My role was to be a buffer and provide continual support—so that's exactly what I did. And I was by her side when we met with Nicci to discuss our failed first round of IVF.

Even before Nicci spoke I was put at ease, because I felt fortunate that we were in her care. She is a unique individual, particularly in her field of work. Exhibiting an interesting mix of country toughness, practicality and resilience intertwined with phenomenal medical smarts. On the one hand she exudes that uniquely Australian 'She'll be right mate' attitude that has little time for sentimentality or self-pity; on the other hand, she demonstrates compassion and warmth towards you in your fertility plight—which likely stems from Nicci having gone through IVF herself and come out the other end with three beautiful children. She revealed this detail when she sensed that this battle might be getting the better of us. She had gone through IVF when the technology was in its infancy and far more costly than today. Nicci recounted the trepidation when swiping her credit card to pay for another IVF treatment and not knowing whether it would come back declined, having been maxed out from previous unsuccessful attempts. And now Nicci was a partner in her own fertility clinic and gynecological practice. But despite this impressive achievement, somehow she maintained the perfect balance of country kindness and comfort with a positivity, confidence and urgency to resolve the problem. Rather than wasting time talking about the 'whys', she preferred to roll up her sleeves and get to work—the sooner the better—because she knew the clock is always ticking and our changes of conceiving are better in the coming months than they are one or two years down the track.

'So, you're not pregnant', she said in her usual forthright manner as she read through our records.

'Nope', we both replied in unison.

'Six sperm didn't penetrate the egg …', she added, still analysing the paperwork.

'So does that mean it's an egg or a sperm problem?' I asked, trying not to apportion blame but just wanting to better understand what was going on.

'It's hard to say. The egg has a shell around it, so the sperm may have difficulty penetrating it. Or the shell could be too tough. The next method we'll try is called ICSI where the sperm is inserted directly into the egg. With the previous treatment the sperm were just put in the vicinity.'

'How do you mean?' I asked.

'Well previously it was like putting your best football player in a clapped-out car to get to the Grand Final. In your case the car broke down and never got there', she explained.

'But hang on,' I challenged, 'wasn't *it* right next to the field to start with?'

'You're right, that's a lousy analogy. I suppose it's more like *it* was right outside the MCG on Grand Final day but all the entrances were locked and there's no way in. With ICSI the best player doesn't have to travel at all on the big day and gets magically dropped into the middle of the action—right on cue.'

'Ohhh', I groaned, my eyebrows raised, as the analogy finally made sense to me.

Initially, I didn't like the sound of the sperm-injecting business at all. How could Nicci be certain they had selected the 'best player' in the absence of natural selection, which ensures that genetically superior sperm are chosen? Under normal conception conditions only the strongest, healthiest, most tenacious swimmer triumphantly induces fertilisation. Physically injecting just one sperm meant there was no opportunity to weed out the inferior, sluggish bystanders. It seemed with the ICSI method the selected candidate didn't necessarily have to be able to swim!

So, could this treatment of impregnation influence the personality of the child? Would they be inherently lacklustre, incapable of sustained effort and forever expecting a free ride in life—just like the process that started it all? I couldn't let the conversation continue without getting some answers to these pressing questions.

'How do you guarantee only quality sperm are selected?' I asked.

'We make sure the sperm are strong specimens during cleaning.'

'What exactly does this *cleaning* involve?' I asked, not completely convinced.

'The sperm are put through a granule solution that prevents abnormal sperm getting through.'

'You mean like a sperm fitness test?' I clarified.

'Exactly', she said, nodding enthusiastically, clearly amused by my analogy.

Now I liked the sound of that! This information certainly allayed my concerns about the sperm selection process and the ICSI method in general. Nicci went on to explain that this procedure was the last avenue of intervention available to us—we had exhausted all other means. When we left the clinic I was somewhat numb to it all. I tried to remain as neutral as possible, refusing to be either upbeat or downcast. This was a difficult mindset to maintain given the magnitude of the outcome but as usual I resorted to humour to try and lighten the mood.

'So, Ali, Nicci said we really don't know which one of us is responsible for our infertility, right?' I asked.

'Yeah, that's right.'

'Do you wanna know what I reckon?' I said with a smirk.

'Not really', she replied, sensing an inappropriate comment on my lips.

'I bet the problem's your German genes constructing a Berlin-type wall around your eggs!'

'Really, I disagree,' Ali shot back, with an indignant stare, but the hint of her dimples suggested otherwise, 'I think it's your French genes, content to just laze around, quaff wine and gorge on creamy cheeses.'

'Of course, what'd you expect? They have better things to do than invade foreign territory— unlike some!'

'Touché.'

Chapter 42
Reflection on bipolar

Despite not feeling in the most upbeat frame of mind as we waited eagerly for the weeks to tick over, I was nowhere near returning to the dark depths of depression that had plagued me earlier in the year. This period became a time of sober reflection on how I came to be diagnosed with bipolar. I tried to deconstruct every event during that period from when Steve died to my eventual recovery from depression. I hoped that, with the benefit of hindsight, I might be able to explain or at least justify my actions—not to anyone but myself and not because I was ashamed of my behaviour—so that I could learn from them and maybe prevent a relapse of such mental anguish.

Looking back I suppose I should have seen it coming (and maybe others around me did). What goes up must come down. And in retrospect there was no denying I was up, way up there in rarified air for a time. No wonder I was eventually admitted to the psychiatric ward. When Steve died, I thought his death must have happened for a reason. So quickly but unsuccessfully I searched for it. Then, at the wake, I received much praise for the poignant message I conveyed in the eulogy. To my surprise people were overwhelmingly supportive of what I had done and for the first time ever I felt I had accomplished something extraordinary and articulated what is too often left unsaid. I believe it was being exposed to a skerrick of positivity at a time when all else was shrouded in abject despair that started to tip the scales of my mental health.

Sure, there was a justifiable explanation for my severely altered mental state—the unthinkable had happened—my life, and the lives of many around me, had suddenly changed forever. But in my unstable mind I took it one step further—beyond any normal reaction. I was adamant that Steve's untimely death had somehow granted me what I had been waiting for my whole life: my calling—a driven commitment to make a difference in the field of mental health—to speak out on the topic for the rest of my life. And when I was eventually admitted to the PSU, with virtually no feedback on what was happening to me, that's when my mind ran wild and became increasingly frenzied and illogical.

That first tumultuous morning in the PSU was particularly confronting. From my perspective I felt of relatively sound mind (considering what I been through), so was perplexed as to why I was in a psychiatric ward. So I surmised that my admission to the PSU was part of one big covert operation. An extraordinary measure designed to immerse me in the complex and challenging issues of mental health treatment. Ultimately putting me at the coalface—so that when I emerged I could provide meaningful insight into what improvements could be made from a patient's perspective. The scenario I mistakenly envisaged was one where I had been chosen by mental health bureaucrats to be deployed as their undercover operative to complete this secret mission. They assumed I was none the wiser—nor were any other of the PSU patients or staff. But I had cottoned on to their cunning and ambitious plan. Sure I asked myself: why me? Why had I been chosen? This answer came all too easily given my fragile mindset. I wrongfully and naively assumed that somehow senior mental health administrators had heard of my plight and the devoted pledge I gave towards mental health in Steve's eulogy—a welcome omen which they had been eagerly awaiting— that the messiah of the mental health fraternity had finally arrived. I assumed that Steve's death had shocked many people to their core and forced them to reassess their lives, igniting in them a passion to join me on a crusade to destigmatise depression and help sufferers. Clearly, my hyper-stimulated imagination was on overdrive.

I was overwhelmed by a heightened sense of purpose and meaning in my life that I had never experienced before. It was a wholly foreign state of mind but emphatically welcomed. Because to be honest it felt marvellous thinking I was *really* making a difference. I have since been told that some people suffering from mania feel God-like. This can be immensely dangerous and potentially life-threatening because some sufferers can attempt to do things that mere mortals are incapable of—like jumping from a building and attempting to fly. Thankfully, I never felt such unbridled euphoria, invincibility or ethereal qualities, but I certainly sensed I had suddenly had a calling thrust upon me.

Talk about illusions of grandeur and certainly not your celebrity-driven garden variety type we normally hear about! Yeah I had it pretty bad. But I kept it to myself because, as I understood it, if I were to have blown my cover and announced to all and sundry at the PSU that they needn't worry—that I was fine and that I knew my sage advice would be heeded—then the entire operation would have been foiled. So instead I just started to write down all that I witnessed and document the many issues that I was confronted with during those first few hours and days at the PSU.

My misconception about my predicament was being fuelled by the most unlikely of events. Like when Ali rang me for our bank details so that she could do some online banking in my absence. In my delusional state, I took this as further affirmation of my perceived newfound reality. I wrongly assumed that Ali's request was yet another crafty tactic to enable *beyondblue* to donate money to us, so that I could become an official sponsored spokesperson on their behalf. Seriously, I am not kidding! My mind was on optimistic overdrive—serendipity reigned supreme through my eyes to the point of absurdity. I was impaired by misguided judgment that transformed even the most mundane transaction, conversation or interaction with people, into perceived tangible benefits to mental health care down the track. In my delirium I was making all sorts of fanciful connections where previously under normal circumstances I would have assumed no such linkage. I suppose it was like thinking you're a genius or savant.

I also tried my best to help other patients. When flicking through the various surfing mags I saw the complete opposite of the people I was surrounded by in the PSU. Page after page was filled with athletic individuals, undertaking an act of pure pleasure, often with an infectious grin—something that was noticeably absent within the walls of the PSU. To me this was pictorial paradise. So I tore out pages and left them at various places around the corridors devoid of any stimulating images or artwork—in a futile attempt to try and invigorate others. I focused on helping them because I considered all was well with me. I couldn't have been more wrong. I can only imagine how my behaviour must have appeared to all that witnessed my bizarre transformation. When drinking excessively, back in my uni days, on the odd occasion I did say or do things that were nonsensical, that I regret, or that I just plain can't remember. And while my recollection of this chaotic time at the PSU is fairly sound, I'm sure there were periods clouded by a similar haze despite the complete absence of alcohol—which is disconcerting to say the least.

All the while I kept writing notes, documenting the shortcomings of the PSU and proposing alternatives. But my incessant eagerness to provide frank feedback was short-lived. Gradually I came back down to Earth (assisted no doubt by the sedative meds) to the humiliating, humbling and scary realisation that I *was* actually mentally unwell and not part of some grand scheme to make a difference. And as the weeks and months passed it became apparent that Steve's death, however tragic, was just one of the many daily suicides that forever devastate all those close to the victim. The period when I realised that the whole horrific experience was not so unique and that Steve's death was for nothing—and that I had lost my mind in the process— was the most difficult.

I am fairly certain that any psychiatrist examining my file would see it as a textbook case: family history of mental illness + devastating stressful occurrence = bipolar for life. It hardly seems fair how one minute your brain is in harmony, the next there is conflict and a permanent imbalance and nothing you do can ever get it back to what it was before. But is it really that simple? Could there have been other triggers? Was my slide into bipolar inevitable? Were there some factors that if avoided or included could have prevented what happened? For example, had I exercised, as usual, during the time after Steve's death, could the endorphins have countered those 'other' chemicals that caused the imbalance and my eventual admission into the PSU? Could having gone surfing momentarily cleansed my mind and spirit and given me some much needed resilience? Could it have provided a necessary distraction, albeit brief, where the need to focus wholly on the ebb and flow of this unfamiliar waterworld would have calmed me into a much needed meditative healing state of mind?

Could things have been different had I not written my brother's eulogy which called upon all my cerebral focus and resolve to divulge such private thoughts? Would a rested brain have impeded imbalance? Could things have been different had I not chosen to sing at the funeral? This gesture certainly compounded my mental and emotional cyclone. On the one hand, I experienced immense jubilation at being able to perform, particularly given the gravity of the occasion, the relevance of song and apt message it conveyed. This was truly a natural high and was intertwined with the deep emotional low of the occasion—an event of unrivalled sorrow. Clearly there was a lot going on in my head at the time—let alone trying to still process the appalling circumstances that initiated this entire unimaginable event. Was it trying to deal with these emotional extremes that tipped the scales?

The reason for these ruminations, I suppose, is that I wondered whether my diagnosis could have been prevented. Prevention is better than cure. Something my father, who was a doctor, always stressed to me from a young age (well before I had any idea what he was talking about). I often wonder at what point my imbalance occurred? Was there one identifiable moment or was it like a fuse had been lit in my head the split second Ali uttered those haunting words and nothing could have stopped the inevitable mental explosion? Or did the horrible announcement trigger some other reaction more akin to an elaborate domino chain whereby it *wasn't* an inevitability that mental disarray would result? Were there enough early warning signs that, if known and communicated, could have helped me and those around me change course—removed just enough dominoes further down the line to have put an end to the frenzied chain-reaction of collapse and prevented my eventual mental pandemonium.

There were ample eyewitnesses to my uncharacteristic change in demeanour. And, sure, people who saw the change in me asked 'Are you OK?' but that's a pretty generic sympathetic enquiry. In retrospect, maybe those loved ones around me should have asked what I suspect they were actually thinking 'Matt, are you losing your mind?' or 'Matt, do you feel manic?' or 'Matt, you may have to be sedated?' These are incredibly tough questions to ask—I can appreciate that—particularly given the ones closest to me were simultaneously struggling to comprehend Steve's sudden death. Also, I suppose for many, this was uncharted territory, witnessing mental breakdown, and many probably felt ill equipped and unsure of how best to intervene.

Which begs the question: why isn't there a national PR campaign and/or first aid type training to help educate people on how to look for these early warning signs, to enable early intervention and to possibly stave off the onset of a lifelong mental illness such as bipolar? A perfect example of this type of effective strategy are the simple yet compelling advertisements that are aired regularly which highlight the early signs and symptoms of stroke or heart attack. Being alert to these symptoms can save lives—why can't a similar approach be applied to mental illness prevention? Unfortunately, I suspect the answer is because not enough is known about the causes.

Nevertheless, would circumstances be different today had I been heavily sedated soon after Steve died, as a precaution, and slept for 20 hours plus under medical supervision? Not too extreme a measure considering my family's mental health background. Could this recuperative action of being isolated from all external stimuli have kept my balance in check? Of course, while you sleep you dream. You can't simply switch off the brain during sleep, no matter how hard you try. So it's possible that despite sleeping I could have still eventually reached my chaotic mental state.

Perhaps a preventative solution then is in the form of meditation? It may enable the individual to wholly rest the mind and recharge when confronted with such calamity and bolster their mental resilience — possibly buffering themselves from their genetic disposition towards mental illness. Who knows? One thing is for sure: it would take an extraordinarily centred and stable-minded individual to be able to shut out all stimuli and become truly ensconced in a meditative state, ignoring the incessant voices in one's head that are ever-present during such a time.

The lack of preventative measures aside, I believe more could be done by government and the medical community to educate sufferers and carers alike, because it is absolutely terrifying to not be completely in control of one's mind. Even more so during the depressive phase of bipolar. After my release from the PSU the psychiatrist didn't discuss with me the likelihood of a depressive episode after the manic phase. Ali may have been told of the risks, but I was left in the dark. Which I believe was a mistake—forewarned is forearmed. Had I been more conscious of the early warning signs—those negative voices in your head that become increasingly vocal and overwhelming—then perhaps I could have received help far sooner and not gone so close to the edge. But who can say whether that would have honestly made a difference. One thing is for certain, the manic phase was a cakewalk compared to the listless recovery from depression.

I liken it to how I imagine the sensation of BASE jumping to be, which begins with the adrenalin rush and thrill of the initial undertaking. The sun is shining, you can see for miles, you feel as free as a bird. All is beautiful in the world—there are boundless possibilities ahead of you. But the high is fleeting. Because, before you realise, you find yourself at the bottom of a deep, dark and dank canyon—where an eerie fog has descended making it impossible to see the direction in which to travel in order to escape this torment. Soon you feel trapped. All alone with no means of escape, despite continued efforts to climb out of the chasm you are in. You feel lost. The initial exhilaration is but a distant memory—you berate yourself for letting this happen. Your confidence is shot and you start to second-guess your every move—sensing danger and despair everywhere. As your situation becomes increasingly hopeless, you exhaust the last of your energy—often losing your grip, plunging you further into darkness. You are a shadow of your former self—you feel like a fool, not deserving of anyone's love or affection. You feel the end is near. But somehow you persist. For days, weeks and months you clamber, unsure if you are making progress because you encounter the same drab surroundings. Until one day you finally see the light and make it out.

That was how my battle with depression felt. Recovery was such a slog and so gradual that I wondered whether I had fully recovered. Nor was it a linear process—more like a game of Snakes and Ladders measured not in days but by thoughts—positive versus negative. Some days the negative murmurs outweighed the positive by 50:1 and I slipped further from my true self. And for the most part I had no idea if my disposition was improving.

In this respect clinical depression is unlike few other afflictions—a cut will bleed and a scab will form and eventually drop off, indicating the wound has healed. But with depression it was not as if the doctors could tell me that I was all better—that I had recovered. They would simply ask, 'How do you feel?' This is difficult to respond to and makes you second-guess your own mind, resulting in continual obsessive introspective interrogation, 'Am I OK? Am I of sound mind?' I found this propensity to doubt my inner self particularly taxing and unnerving. Compare this to a broken limb, where medical practitioners can test for strength, treat with physiotherapy and reassure the patient that they have recovered—sometimes to the point where the limb is stronger post injury— and that it is only the hesitation of the individual that holds the person back. The patient may still perceive there to be a problem and feel that they must still nurse the impairment. But I had no way of categorically knowing whether I was back to my old self—whether I would ever be *that* person again. How can you test your mental resilience? How do you know when you're no longer clinically depressed, particularly when you have lost your brother along the way? It's as if the sheen is taken off everything around you and his loss leaves a gaping void in your world that can never be replaced?

Chapter 43
Movember

My psychiatrist, however, did notice a change in me. Subsequently, he decided he no longer had to see me as regularly and that a session in a year's time, to see how I was getting on, would suffice.

'That's great. But what does that mean in terms of my diagnosis? Do I have bipolar? Or was this whole episode a reaction to the shock and trauma of my brother's sudden death?' I asked nervously.

'It's difficult to know at this stage. If you don't experience another depressive episode in the next 12 months then it's possible you don't have bipolar. But if you do suffer from another down phase, then unfortunately you probably do have the illness', explained the doctor in a coldly clinical tone as he went on to insist that I continue to take my mood-stabilising medication.

This was not what I wanted to hear. Unfortunately bipolar wasn't like pregnancy where a simple blood test can confirm or deny diagnosis. Nevertheless, part of me had always been sceptical of the doctor's diagnosis of long-term illness. Sure, I had spiralled into a terribly vulnerable and troubled state mentally after my brother had died but these were extraordinary circumstances that had triggered my fallout, steamrolling me psychologically off the rails. But I refused to concede that I was incapable of reclaiming my once robust psyche. The problem was there was no real way of knowing and unfortunately perception is often not the reality when it comes to mental illness. Which left me in a socially precarious and awkward position because sometimes I speak fast—always have—and yes I can get agitated and animated when discussing topics I'm passionate about. So, now, would such behaviour be perceived by friends and family, who knew of my illness, as a warning sign, eliciting whispers and sideways glances predicting the return of the prattling nutter?

Furthermore, the doctor gave no indication that I would be weaned off the medication any time soon and this troubled me because I was concerned this meant that my mind would always be precariously fragile and easily distressed without intervention. I wanted to be drug-free. I needed to be drug-free. I wondered how much my meds were altering my mindset. Were they suppressing surges of happiness, natural highs, because these could possibly escalate into a manic episode? Could the buzz and euphoria of riding an exhilarating wave put me over the edge? Were the drugs preventing me from feeling the full range of emotions— leaving me in a perpetually altered state of equanimity?

Althought I thought I had gradually come to accept my brother's death, I couldn't be sure because, since his suicide, I had been on some type of mind-altering drug or another. Could these drugs be preventing me from truly grieving—buffering me from myself? Up until this tragedy I always felt I had a healthy relationship with my inner self: that voice inside your head that you casually converse with, that helps guide you through life, defines your moral and ethical compass, shows you the right direction to take in good times and bad. Now I didn't know what to think. Was I going to be mentally compromised forever? My world had been turned upside down; I had lost my brother and gained the added burden of a mental illness in the process.

Little brothers are often hard-wired to blame their senior siblings solely for any hardship they endure, even if the siblings had barely any involvement. But, try as I might, I couldn't bring myself to blame Steve for the onset of my illness. Nor did I think any less of him for taking his own life. Since having been to the brink myself I experienced first-hand how easily life can slip away when clinical depression takes hold. It only takes one fleeting thought of volatile negativity amongst a lifetime of affirmative thinking to end it all. However, my biggest regret will eternally be that I never asked my brother about his health, mental or otherwise—virtually everything else—but not these supposedly taboo topics. I never dared venture into such uncharted brotherly territory. It's just not the done thing. Maybe because, more often than not, it's futile because men stoically uphold a façade of invincibility if questioned. This may partly explain why in Australia more men die from suicide than women. But had I the courage and foresight to break this social norm then maybe we could have engaged in a rare conversation between brothers that could have made all the difference and may have initiated the turning point for him. Instead my brother was just another statistic, another suicide to add to the list of desperate people that take their own life each year. Astonishingly, the highest cause of death for people in Australia aged between 16 to 37, almost twice as many as the annual road toll, is depression-related suicide yet it receives proportionally little exposure in terms of public education campaigns to promote greater understanding and address the issue.

Because of this lack of understanding I have little doubt that some people in society slander these individuals as cowardly, selfish and pathetic—which only compounds the problem. This ignorant viewpoint infuriates me as it belittles the relentless agony suffered by the victim. When someone dies from cancer or a heart attack the broader community shows an outpouring of compassion. Suicide should be met with the same instinctive supportive response, but I dare say it rarely is. Instead the general public seem to find it hard to look beyond the horrifically unexpected end result that overshadows the underlying cause which is often the insidious, vicious killer, depression. The reality is that depression is an illness as life threatening as cancer. Maybe even more so considering it can take a life in seconds: the pull of a trigger, the step off a precipice. Too often people suffer in silence when maybe all they needed was to speak up or have someone ask after them. But in order for them to do this, depression and suicide must become destigmatised so that sufferers feel they can come forward and communicate their woes to others without fear of being misjudged, ostracised or labelled as weak. I was determined not to be ashamed of what had happened to me. I suffered from an illness— nothing more—I kept telling myself. So in my recovery I tried to be honest and upfront with those around me about my battle with depression and bipolar. This was my way of trying to destigmatise this destructive illness that took my brother's life and nearly took my own.

To that end I was deeply committed to entering in the Movember challenge, which is an initiative supported by *beyondblue*, where men get sponsored to grow a moustache in November to help raise funds and awareness of men's depression. I already wore the *beyondblue* wrist band every day since my brother's funeral to bring attention to depression and the organisation, but I understood being involved in Movember would aid the cause even more.

The campaign was launched in Australia in 2003 and has since spread to five other countries. Since its inception it has raised over 60 million dollars worldwide to aid in research to better understand the illness. I made sure not to sugarcoat my reasons for participating. Instead I explained how, over the past year, depression had come to change my life forever. I sent an invitation to donate to everyone I knew—work colleagues included. It wasn't easy being so frank but Steve's untimely demise had taught me that reluctance to speak up is a huge part of the problem.

I was also motivated to participate by the memories of Steve having embarked on the Movember challenge in previous years. Maybe this involvement was his way of trying to tell people that he too was battling depression. I recall his moustache was a pathetic stab at old-school machismo but, despite his best efforts, he unexpectedly grew a large barren patch beneath his nose that was devoid of hair—a look which was quickly dubbed the 'two-slugs' and 'reverse Hitler'. I remember finding this altruistic behaviour admirable, particularly given how grotesque and comical it looked. But when I began the challenge I was very worried this hideous fragmented appendage would again make an appearance because Steve and I had the same genetic deficiency on our upper lip. But there was no room for vanity here. I completed the challenge but it wasn't a cakewalk. The month was like an eternity; living with such an unflattering, prickly and irritating thickening. It was worth it though and to my astonishment I was inundated with overly generous donations.

The stark likeness of my feeble growth was also a comforting reminder that Steve and I had many common traits and that in some respects part of what made him so special lived on in me. Inevitably, this realisation made me reflect on the genetic implication of having kids: how you pass on aspects of yourself to them. They become a mix, a blend, an amalgam, hopefully of all the desirable elements from both parties—but there are no guarantees. There was a chance that if Ali and I were to have a son that he too would one day model the same embarrassing slugs—not from birth surely? In some ways this was a pleasing possibility to think that a future child of ours could display a peculiarity that not only I possessed, but one that Steve and I also shared. I saw this as an opportunity for our child to in some odd way get an appreciation for who Steve was without ever having been able to meet him. I can understand how absurd this may sound, but sometimes you look for even the slightest positive when you lose someone so close to you.

I realised also that any future child of ours would be likely to inherit a predisposition towards bipolar. It was disconcerting to accept that this cloud of mental illness could overshadow generation after generation of the Barwick clan—subjecting individuals to a drenching from their own deluge of despair and plunging them into darkness when the forecast was supposed to be for sunny days ahead. Fortunately, depression and bipolar weren't death sentences, but I understood that they must be taken seriously, as they had the potential to kill.

I felt that I had lost a part of myself when Steve died. He was my only sibling—the only other child on the planet who shared many of those cherished childhood memories from within the inner sanctum of a family—so close in age that we may as well have been twins. Sure, some friends or relatives may have on occasion seen glimpses of this life, but Steve was always right there by my side, particularly between the ages of four and 12 when we were as thick as thieves. As mischievous as two puppies from the same litter and of an age where the elder wasn't too proud to hang with the younger sibling and the younger unashamedly idolised the other.

And, yes, our parents witnessed much of the shenanigans but their perspective often lacked frivolity—the key ingredient when reminiscing that makes memories appear far more vivid and exuberant. Certain memories are predictable and less unique like chaotic Christmas celebrations or elaborate Easter egg hunts. But others are decidedly more personal like the exhilaration of constructing BMX jumps out in the bush unsupervised, free from parental concern and questioning, or the shared torment of rainy camping holidays that seem to go on for eternity.

Sadly, many of these fond memories would now be mine alone and, when my parents eventually died, I would become the sole guardian of *all* our family memories. Before Steve's death I had imagined I'd always be able to share these memories with him, and with our children and grandchildren. But now, with our continued fertility woes, these treasured memories seemed at risk of never being passed on at all— which only added fuel to the fire of our fertility frustrations. Needless to say I remained anxious about our fast-approaching final shot at IVF, as the destiny of the Barwick lineage hung on it.

Chapter 44
IVF #2

The day had arrived. Highlighted in our calendar weeks in advance, yet we needn't have bothered with this reminder as the date was etched in our memory from the outset. We had both agreed on one last egg collection, so this was it—the last hurrah—one last roll of the dice for the couple who detested gambling. *How would this all play out?* The outcome from this day would determine so much about our future. However, unlike those choose-your-own-adventure books I read as a child, today we weren't given a choice to decide which option we preferred or which direction we found more appealing. The outcome was out of our hands—a challenging scenario for a couple of Virgo control freaks.

We both coolly followed the now familiar routine. Ali's eggs were collected while I went to the clinic to provide my sample.

It was 8:25 am and I had been waiting in the reception area for a while when I caught a glimpse of a man as he burst through the front door, rushed past reception, down the corridor and disappeared around the corner—which I thought was a little odd. Seconds later my name was called by a middle-aged male nurse I hadn't met before. I dutifully followed him down the corridor as he led me towards the all too familiar collection room.

'So Mr Barwick, have you been here before?' asked the nurse, trying to make polite small talk.

'Yes, several times', I replied.

We turned the corner, then the nurse came to an abrupt halt, so suddenly I almost bumped into the back of him.

'Oh … sorry Mr Barwick … um … it seems there has been a mix-up. Please follow me', he said, ushering me backwards but not before I spotted the same hurried bloke I had seen only moments before being led through the collection procedure in the one-and-only collection room. I returned to my seat in reception, not impressed by the clerical blunder.

'I must apologise, Mr Barwick. The room is currently occupied. Sorry for the wait. It shouldn't be too long', the nurse said apologetically.

At 8:40 am I didn't think much of the delay. By 8:55 am I had become a little annoyed. But after 9:00 am I was downright cranky, mostly because this guy had jumped in front of me then was taking his sweet time to get the job done. In my anger I reluctantly pictured this guy 'doing the business'. Then, to my utter disgust and distress, I couldn't get this repulsive image out of my head.

After 40 minutes—still no sign. *What the hell was he doing in there?* The images in my head worsened. During all my previous visits to provide a deposit I hadn't seen another male patient called into the collection room before me. This was remarkably fortunate as it allowed me the naive luxury of imagining these facilities were exclusively mine. But now that I had actually witnessed someone else ahead of me, this fantasy was shattered. This place was now tainted in my view; it was now Ejaculation Central for all of the unfortunate pricks like me reluctantly going on this formidable journey.

Finally, after three-quarters of an hour my nemesis emerged. I made sure to avoid eye contact as the last thing I wanted was to be able to visualise his face in future. Seconds later I was called by the nurse, led to the room, explained the procedure, then left to produce the goods. I grabbed a magazine for much needed inspiration and sat in the only chair. Immediately, I felt unexpected warmth from the seat as one does when they unknowingly choose a recently used toilet. This unpleasant sensation again triggered the unwelcome visions of my predecessor. In an instant my libido vanished. I was in real trouble. Even flicking through page after page of naked female flesh had no impact. It was as if I had been castrated. It was then that I seriously doubted whether I would be able to direct the blood flow to the relevant appendage to even start proceedings, let alone finish them.

I was now under unprecedented performance pressure. Ali was currently under the knife and relying on me to do my bit and I really didn't want to let her down. But the mind is in control and can be an almighty persuader.

After an extended period of unsuccessful agony I could fully appreciate the term 'flogging a dead horse'. This was not funny in the slightest. I desperately had to regain my composure and realised a change of tack was necessary. I discarded the pornography, closed my eyes and called upon salacious images from my own personal spank bank, reminiscing over the many memorable intimate encounters with my voluptuous wife. Arousal was achieved swiftly and things eventually came good—literally. I was beyond relieved on several levels.

Afterwards I was told by the receptionist that Ali was already in with one of the nurses going through the results of the surgery. I hurried to join her in one of the consultation rooms. I entered tentatively, momentarily interrupting the conversation between her and Doris.

'Where've you been?' Ali asked inquisitively. 'I thought your appointment was ages ago?'

'It was supposed to be', I replied, still a little flustered by the whole sordid affair.

'What happened?'

'It's a long story, I'll explain later', I replied hurriedly, not wanting to be interrogated any further.

'Well I'm glad you made it,' Doris chimed in from across the desk, 'I was just telling Alison that nine eggs were collected, which is an improvement on last time.'

'That's great', I said, settling into the chair nearest the door.

'I also mentioned that we have a new embryologist on staff named Marie. She has over 30 years experience and prefers to be a little more flexible about the timing of transfer and tailors it to the individual.' Then the door opened unexpectedly and in walked a lady in her fifties wearing tan-coloured medical scrubs. 'Speak of the devil, here she is. I was just talking about you.'

Marie introduced herself and spoke to Ali about when she would be contacted about the progress of the eggs and the possible timing of transfer. I was impressed by her down-to-earth, no-nonsense manner—clinical yet compassionate—traits that must be a conscious part of the clinic's recruiting strategy given all the staff had this refreshing bedside manner. Once she had finished explaining the details she wished us both well and made her way towards the exit, pausing in the doorway.

'By the way Matt, your sample was superb. You're a trooper!' she announced, patting me on the back as she left the room.

Finally I had received some feedback on my swimmers. Her comments were extremely gratifying considering that not so long ago my much maligned sperm were considered the culprit most likely responsible for our conception conundrum. Not anymore. To have a senior embryologist make special mention of the quality of my little battlers was priceless, particularly considering she must have seen bucketloads of baby batter in her time.

'Wow that's great darl!' Doris said jovially. 'We normally have a real problem with sperm around here', she whispered, giving me a subtle wink.

'Well I'm just glad to see my efforts have paid off. I've been drinking green tea non-stop for months and eating loads of berries and cooked tomatoes! Maybe I should consider donating some to the clinic', I replied with a smirk.

'We've been meaning to ask what the success rate with this method of IVF is?' Ali asked, bringing the discussion back to a more pressing topic.

'Most couples are successful after two attempts. Typically 40 per cent get pregnant with fresh eggs and around 60 per cent with frozen ones. The frozen ones tend to do better because they are transferred six weeks later, after all the hormone levels have settled down from the trauma of egg collection. Do you have any other questions dear?' Doris asked caringly.

'No, I think we're right', Ali replied.

'OK then sweetheart. Well, best of luck, I really hope all goes well this time. Try not to worry too much. Matt, make sure you take care of her, mister!' she insisted, looking me sternly in the eye as she gave Ali a spontaneous enveloping motherly hug. This impulsive gesture epitomised Doris's affectionate nature and nearly had us all in tears.

Once again Ali and I had to endure the excruciating 24-hour wait. Despite all the encouraging talk by Doris and Marie during our consultation, I refused to get my hopes up. I tried in vain to treat the next day like any other. But instead I just constantly checked my email and mobile for a message from Ali. When I hadn't heard any word by mid-afternoon I suspected the worst. I considered contacting Ali but didn't want to pester her unnecessarily. Then around 4:00 pm I got a call on my work phone. I instantly recognised the number as being from Ali's work. I knew we had agreed not to use the phone to discuss our fertility matters, so I immediately became worried. Why was Ali ringing me? Were the results a disaster? I answered the phone anxiously. 'Hello …'

'Hey doll, it's me. Do you need me to get any bread from the shops this arvo?'

'What …? What about the results?' I whispered, not wanting to be heard by my colleagues in the surrounding cubicles.

'Didn't you get my e? I sent it ages ago.'

'No … So how'd we go?' I asked, my voice trembling.

'I can't really say here, but it's good news. I'll text your mobile. OK?'

Within seconds my mobile beeped. I hurriedly grabbed it and opened the incoming message. It read: '7 have fertilised! YAY!! xxoo'

I stared at the screen for a while—dazed. *We were still in with a chance.* I promptly replied: 'Wow, that's fantastic!'

There was no denying that this was a vast improvement on our last IVF round. The following day we were told there had been no overnight attrition and that transfer was scheduled in three days time. Despite such encouraging progress I remained guarded. This tortuous quest had taught me the danger of optimism.

The evening before transfer, as we both lay in bed watching television, Ali asked a question that took me by surprise, even though I really should have seen it coming.

'Are you going to come?' she asked, rolling on her side towards me, the weight of this question evident in her eyes.

'I thought I already had?' I replied.

'Very funny', she said, playfully slapping me. 'I mean tomorrow, to the transfer?'

'Do you want me there this time?'

'Kind of …' she said, looking vulnerable.

'I'll be there', I said, leaning in slowly to give her a kiss.

The following morning Ali and I sat patiently in the waiting room of the fertility clinic aimlessly watching the morning news program, when a story came on reporting that Australia was in the midst of a huge baby boom, with current fertility rates at a 31-year high. Ali and I both looked at each other in disbelief, rolled our eyes and shook our heads.

'Maybe for some!' I spat vehemently at the television as if the talking heads were in some way capable of hearing me.

'How are you feeling babe?' I asked, trying to draw her attention away from the TV.

'Fine. This part's easy compared to the egg collection.'

'Look on the bright side, not everyone gets to see the baby go in, as well as come out.'

'Yeah, and I'm sure it will be a hell of a lot easier on the way in that's for sure!'

A while later Doris popped around the corner and asked us both to follow her. We were led into a room I hadn't ever been in before, with its complicated hospital bed, complete with various buttons and levers capable of numerous adjustable options, an ultrasound machine and a large plasma TV on the wall. Ali was asked to change into a medical gown and lie on the bed while her blood was taken. Afterwards Doris vacated the room, leaving the two of us alone in stunned silence for several minutes, expecting to again have company at any moment. As we waited, I glanced around the room at the various posters on display. One I found particularly fascinating showed enlarged photos of what the fertilised egg looked like at different stages. I marvelled at these pictures that captured the first few signs of life. Nicci, Marie and Doris entered and greeted us, then Marie leant towards Ali and asked her to verify that the details on the test tube matched hers.

'We don't really need Matthew here now do we … really', Marie commented with just a hint of sarcasm.

'Yeah … I've done my bit', I replied shyly, feeling embarrassingly superfluous.

'Well we don't really need men to make babies anymore', Marie quipped to reinforce my expendability. 'So that you don't feel too unnecessary, I'll give you a job to do. Here, you can hold this', she added, handing me an envelope. Inside was a photo of the one-in-a-million fertilised egg that was about to be transferred. 'You have four like this in the freezer, and this fresh one that is a splendid embryo. So hopefully you'll both be getting a special Christmas present this year', Marie said with a wink, looking over her black thick-rimmed glasses.

'Oh, no pressure—thanks', Nicci chimed in as she was about to start the process.

'You realise Matthew, that once Alison is pregnant you'll have to do all the housework', Doris added.

'I find it impossible to keep the house clean, the kids are always making a mess', moaned Nicci, seconds from commencing the procedure. 'Are you sure you want this?' she asked sarcastically, looking up from between Ali's legs. Everyone laughed, except me.

Watching this all unfold from a distance I was initially put off by the relaxed banter that was taking place. I had always been sceptical of the high jinks that were depicted in the operating theatres of the various American medical dramas. But it appeared I had it wrong, this sort of behaviour looked to be commonplace, which astounded me. This was serious business—for Ali and me the stakes were enormous. I wanted to see more focus demonstrated. But I needn't have worried because the entire mood in the room switched in an instant when Nicci started the transfer. She promptly had her game-face on, a look of undivided concentration where nothing could distract her.

Ali and I watched in amazement at the screen as she skilfully and gently deposited the embryo into the uterus using a fine plastic tube, giving running commentary as she went.

And just like that Ali was impregnated with me only holding her hand.

We were later told that the blood test to confirm implantation was due a few days before New Year's which created a bit of a problem for us because we had already planned a holiday to Newcastle with friends during this period. A vacation that was booked months in advance of us having any idea that we might be in the midst of another IVF round. The nurse, who had been through IVF herself, thought that waiting for the results until we returned from holidays would be excruciating. So instead she recommended that Ali do a home-pregnancy test while we were away, to put our minds at ease. She stressed, however, not to get too upset if the home test was negative because these results could sometimes be false.

Chapter 45
The ultimate Christmas gift

Not surprisingly Christmas held little significance that year, presents were graciously accepted but rapidly dismissed from mind. Ali and I both knew what we badly wanted from Santa. Similarly our holiday was enjoyable but no longer experienced with much excitement because our priority had shifted— all we could feel was anticipation.

The morning Ali was due to take the home-pregnancy test was bizarre. We both woke around 9 am in the two-bedroom serviced apartment we were staying in with our close friends. They were sleeping in the room next to ours and knew nothing about the significance of today, so Ali and I had to be as covert as possible. We both lay there quietly listening for noises to suggest our friends were up and about already. The apartment was silent.

'So are you going to pee on a stick or what?' I whispered.

'Yeah OK', Ali replied, her voice shaking with nerves.

'Good luck', I said, planting a kiss on her cheek before she slid out of bed and tiptoed out the bedroom door.

She returned moments later and placed the stick on the bedside table.

'So what are we looking for?' I asked sitting up, my heart pounding with promise.

'If we're pregnant, another line should appear on the stick.'

'How long does this one take?' I asked staring incessantly at the stick.

'Between two and five minutes, according to the instructions.'

I rolled over in bed leaving my back to Ali and the all-important indicator, unable to stand the tormenting wait.

'Is that a line?!?' Ali squeaked seconds later, thrusting the stick towards me for confirmation. 'I think that's a line!?' she shrilled.

'… that's a line', I confirmed in stunned disbelief, rubbing my early morning eyes as if they were deceiving me.

Ali hurriedly grabbed the instructions and re-read them softly.

'It says here that the line may appear lighter but it's still "positive"', she added as if looking for reasons to question the delightful early result.

'Well, that's definitely a line!'

'It is, isn't it!' she squealed, grinning like a Cheshire cat.

We hugged and kissed each other in relative silence, trying like mad to contain our elation so as not to alert our friends only metres away.

The following evening our New Year's Eve celebrations were relaxed and festive. After all, we were apparently pregnant—but definitely shell-shocked. Nevertheless, our attitude towards pregnancy had become so tainted by our sterility struggle that we both now perceived it to be one of the most improbable and challenging obstacles we had ever faced. So, Ali and I found it relatively easy to keep our revelation on the QT because neither of us was really convinced, as we had become so accustomed to lousy news throughout our infertility ordeal. Over the days that followed I casually asked Ali whether our 'friend' had arrived to spoil the party. But there was still no trace, which was a record absence.

By the time we returned home for the conclusive blood test neither of us knew what to expect. We were both still off work which meant I could accompany Ali on this potentially auspicious day. Entering the clinic Ali was set upon by several nurses, Doris included, eagerly asking whether her dreaded period had arrived. They looked more thrilled than Ali and me when told of the promising status. It was hard not to be sincerely moved by their truly empathetic and affectionate nature. All the nurses were emotionally invested in our struggle, yet you would half expect them to be the opposite— desensitised by the daily overexposure to countless couples like us. Instead they all wished us luck and you could tell they really meant it.

After the test we returned home and both pottered around the house trying to preoccupy ourselves with mundane chores, quietly hoping for some good karma. Around midday Ali's mobile rang as we both sat in the kitchen. My heart leapt. Ali answered it and I listened closely to her voice and studied her face intently for any early signal of success. Then I noticed the slightest raise in the corner of her luscious lips, which soon turned into a radiating smile, followed by a rapturous guffaw.

'Great thanks', she said, hanging up the phone.

'Did it stick? Are we pregnant?' I pleaded, on tenterhooks.

'Yes, but not just pregnant', Ali beamed. 'Very pregnant!—according to Nicci and my hormone levels.'

'That's fantastic my darling!' I hooted, drawing her in and giving her a full-bodied kiss. We were both elated and I was again struck by how a single moment in your life can make all the difference and cause such a monumental chain reaction. This was one of those moments— one sperm and one egg creating new life—but there had been many more throughout this journey to this memorable day: one wave to rejuvenate, one love to conquer all, one mistake to end a life. If only there had been one crucial conversation between brothers then this day might have been perfect.

Straightaway we decided to only tell people about this astonishing turn of events if they asked us directly—which meant we only expected those select friends and family who were aware of our infertility tribulations to probe.

Later that afternoon there was a knock at the front door. It was Mum. She explained she was in the neighbourhood and thought she would pop around to see how things were. *Subtle Mum, real subtle.* Not willing to spill the beans, I played coy, chatting aimlessly about relatively inconsequential banalities like our holiday and what I had been doing around the house that morning. Mum soon got fed up with my ploy and cut to the chase.

'So how did the IVF go … ?' she asked hesitantly.

'Good', I replied poker-faced, trying to savour the moment that I recently feared would never come.

'How do you mean "good", Matt?'

'Well, those hypotheticals you used to speak of so often might not be so hypothetical anymore. You might be a grandmother sooner than you think', I replied. 'Ali's pregnant!'

'That's wonderful! I'm so happy for you both', she gushed as we embraced. 'When's it due?'

'The day before my birthday.'

'Really … Father's Day? How fabulous—'

It truly hit home telling Mum and I was suddenly overcome by an unparallelled wave of euphoria and relief and found myself fighting back tears. It was surreal because not so long ago it looked like all hope was lost and we had come so perilously close to giving up—seemingly resigned to our infertile fate—until this miracle. We had been endeavouring to conceive for what felt like an eternity, I was almost deluded into thinking we had now finally reached the end of this arduous, soul-testing odyssey. But as most fertile couples take for granted, this was really only the beginning.

Epilogue
Loss and Love

After a positive 12-week ultrasound we thought that maybe we had finally shaken our infertility hoodoo but we weren't taking any chances. Again Ali became the model patient, purchasing all the leading pregnancy bibles and dutifully following their instructions on how to lay the perfect golden egg.

Over the many weeks that followed all signs suggested we had become members of the 'normal' pregnant couple club until, shockingly, Ali suffered a stillbirth at 22½ weeks. On Mother's Day no less. Forced to endure the induced delivery of poor lifeless baby Isobel in the maternity ward—surrounded by everything we so desperately craved. Later, the post-mortem revealed nothing about what may have caused her death. So we were left with the diagnosis of intrauterine Sudden Infant Death Syndrome (SIDS) —which only amplified our feelings of fertility failure given our tumultuous history.

Our sorrow threshold had been recalibrated after Steve's suicide. Nonetheless, we both took the loss of Isobel hard. Ali was particularly gutted—understandably. But my emotional handbrake on fatherhood was still very much on prior to losing Isobel, because I knew childbirth is never a done deal until the baby's safely in your arms. Yet for Ali I could see the experience was different—this baby had started transforming her—she had begun to feel its every move. Then nothing. Gone in an instant. All Ali was left with was the remnants of her partially changed body with the added burden of grief.

At the time I worried this painful and unexpected shock could trigger another bipolar episode. So I continued to really work at maintaining a healthy mental state to ensure I was capable of supporting Ali. I stayed committed to my daily exercise routines, ate and slept well, took my medication, refrained from alcohol and still pursued my passions of surfing and music—many of the things I had no time for when Steve died. And it worked—I avoided another mental meltdown—and I'm pleased to say it continues to work. But in no way do I believe I have beaten bipolar. This would be arrogant, naive and dangerous of me. However, I have now come to terms with my diagnosis and have gradually become more mentally resilient and adept at monitoring and adjusting my behaviour and emotional response to situations.

One positive was that the shared loss strengthened our relationship. We often spoke about Isobel and were both intent on never forgetting her. Celebrating her life, even though she never made it into the world. We sensed some of our family and friends may have considered our approach to remembrance to be unhealthy behaviour—as if we were wallowing in our own misfortune—which upset Ali and me. By law, losing baby Isobel was a death and we simply wanted to acknowledge her existence.

To that end, on the anniversary of her passing, we lit a white candle under the stars in our courtyard, atop a piece of metal artwork we commissioned in her memory that depicted sprouting seedlings, titled 'New growth'. I also recited a poem I had written:

A year had passed since you went away
Such shock and grief the saddest day

We never got to know you at all
To see you crawl, watch you grow tall

We know that you are safe and well
Exactly where it's hard to tell

When we look up at the stars at night
We will think of you sleeping tight

It breaks our heart you had to go
Isobel we love you so.

Despite the horrendous setback, Ali was as committed as ever to continuing with IVF as soon as she was physically able. How she summoned the fortitude to try again so soon astounded me. I suspect her burgeoning 'baby ache' may have been to blame.

Unfortunately, we had another two failed IVF attempts, with frozen eggs, in quick succession. At which point I announced that I was done. Over it. Finished with the fatherhood dream. Yet Ali was determined to keep trying. So we had another fresh egg implanted in early 2011. For us it seemed fresh was best and it stuck. We were pregnant again!

Ali was astonishingly calm as the weeks ticked slowly by. No doubt this was due to our exceptionally talented and nurturing obstetrician who gave us both tremendous reassurance—beyond the call of duty really—as she knew our history all too well having met us while delivering Isobel. In contrast, I was a pile of nerves. And the closer we got to D-Day the more I became hypersensitive to any possible threat to Ali's and the baby's health. Risk consumed me. I saw potential tripping hazards everywhere and was convinced Ali was on the cusp of losing all coordination given her unbalanced baby-bulging body. I wanted nothing more than to be her bodyguard—her constant shadow—to prevent any mishap. But I knew I mustn't smother, as this would be likely to heighten her anxiety.

It was an excruciating nine-month wait—torturous really. We were told to enjoy the experience but instead I found it agonising. I willingly attended everything and anything baby-related: antenatal classes, beer'n'bubs, infant first aid. The lot. All the while desperately hoping Mum and bump could hang on. I wanted this bub badly. Days from delivery our nursery was completely empty—a blank canvass. Neither of us could bear the torment of having to pack up and return baby paraphernalia if things weren't to end well.

But as it turned out we needn't have worried. Sure there were complications during labour but with the skilful work of our expert obstetrician and midwife (remarkably the same team who delivered Isobel) our beautiful bundle, Oliver Stephen Barwick, was born. He arrived precisely five years after we decided to start trying for a baby—to the day. And he has been worth the wait—our little miracle.

He is perfection. And I completely agree with the random woman we encountered at the supermarket who eagerly proclaimed, 'He's so gorgeous ... I could just eat him up!' My heart has doubled since his arrival and I was lucky I could take three months off work to rejoice in and be fascinated by every minute phase of his development—with my sole purpose to make him giggle and grin. Oh and to help Mum out, of course, who is phenomenal with him and constantly beaming in disbelief at finally having her divine bundle.

Interestingly, becoming a parent soon reminded me of what I had let slip from my memory many years ago: that my parents were once in this position and had enveloped me with the same care, affection and love. Something which is easily forgotten later in life, particularly at times when you feel your parents aren't even from the same planet, let alone related, because of your differing views on things. It is sometimes near impossible to comprehend you were ever conceived at all.

We both feel immeasurably blessed to have finally gained membership into what we consider an exclusive club. Yet I still have a fleeting fear that one day there will be a knock on the door, we will be told there has been an appalling mix-up and Ollie's not ours and he will be taken from us to be reunited with his rightful parents. I doubt this fear will last, because overwhelmingly I feel utterly content and fortunate—fortunate to be a father, fortunate to be alive, fortunate to be in love and fortunate to be given the opportunity to share my story and, in doing so, at last discover my 'calling'.

I now want for nothing, except my brother back. But this wish can't ever be granted, no matter how much I long for it. So instead I'm left to hope that sharing my story will in some way make a difference and help people. Help by encouraging others, particularly men, to confide in whomever they are most comfortable, about their concerns and problems, health-related or otherwise—because this whole experience has taught me that open and honest communication is the first vital step towards a brighter future.

Acknowledgements

Thanks to all my family and friends, many of whom are in the book; your love and support has helped immeasurably, particularly when my confidence wavered.

Heartfelt thanks also to Mum who taught me the value of a good read and who spent endless hours teaching me to write during school.

Thanks, too, to all the artists who crafted the inspiring songs mentioned throughout this book—if you ever read this rest assured your music makes a real difference to me and countless others. And to Sylvia and Jenny from the ACT Writers Centre for their insight and for giving me the courage to approach publishers.

My gratitude also to Diane and the talented team at Big Sky Publishing for enthusiastically getting behind my story from day one and for sharing the passion to have it told—and to Rosemary for editing my scribble so finely.

And to all the medical professionals who helped along the way: Nicci, for her refreshing bedside manner, and the entire Isis Fertility team for their expertise; the staff at the PSU who showed me nothing but care and Jyotica and Anne, the dynamic duo, who excelled in good times and in bad.

Thank you also to *beyondblue* for allowing us to publish the resource information that appears at the end of this book; the fantastic support they provide, along with many other similar organisations, is invaluable to people experiencing mental illness and their families.

Nicole deserves special mention, for her inspiring resilience and willingness to share this story.

Deepest thanks of all to my darling wife Ali without whom there would never have been a happy ending to this story.

What is Depression?

While we all feel sad, moody or low from time to time, some people experience these feelings intensely for long periods of time (weeks, months or even years) and sometimes without any apparent reason. Depression is more than just a low mood – it's a serious illness that has an impact on both physical and mental health. On average, one in six people – one in five women and one in eight men – will experience depression at some stage of their lives.

A person may be depressed if, for more than two weeks, he or she has felt sad, down or miserable most of the time or has lost interest or pleasure in most of his or her usual activities, and has also experienced several of the signs and symptoms across at least three of the categories below:

Behaviour
- Stopped going out
- Not getting things done at work/school
- Withdrawing from close family and friends
- Relying on alcohol and sedatives
- Stopped doing usual enjoyable activities
- Unable to concentrate

Thoughts
- "I'm a failure."
- "It's my fault."
- "Nothing good ever happens to me."
- "I'm worthless."
- "Life's not worth living."
- "People would be better off without me."

Feelings

- Overwhelmed
- Guilty
- Irritable
- Frustrated
- No confidence
- Unhappy
- Indecisive
- Disappointed
- Miserable
- Sad

Physical

- Tired all the time
- Sick and run down
- Headaches and muscle pains
- Churning gut
- Sleep problems
- Loss or change of appetite
- Significant weight loss or gain

What is Bipolar Disorder?

Bipolar disorder used to be known as 'manic depression' because the person experiences periods of depression but at other times periods of mania. In between, he or she has periods of normal mood. Mania is like the opposite of depression and can vary in intensity – symptoms including feeling great, having plenty of energy, racing thoughts and little need for sleep, talking fast, having difficulty focusing on tasks, and feeling frustrated and irritable.

This is not just a fleeting experience. Sometimes the person loses touch with reality and has episodes of psychosis. Experiencing psychosis involves seeing or hearing something that is not there (hallucinations), or having delusions (for example, the person believing he or she has superpowers).

Bipolar disorder seems to be most closely linked to family history. Stress and conflict can trigger episodes for people with this condition. It's not uncommon for bipolar disorder to be misdiagnosed as, for example, depression only, alcohol or drug abuse, Attention Deficit Hyperactivity Disorder (ADHD) or schizophrenia. Diagnosis depends on the person having had an episode of mania and unless observed, this can be hard to pick. It is not uncommon for people to go for years before receiving an accurate diagnosis of bipolar disorder. It can be helpful for the person to make it clear to the doctor or counsellor that he or she is experiencing highs and lows. Bipolar disorder affects approximately 2 per cent of the population.

Getting help

People with depression, anxiety disorders, or bipolar disorder can find it difficult to take the first step in seeking help. They may need to get help with the support of family members, friends and/or a health professional.

There is no one proven way that people recover. However, there is a range of effective treatments available and many health professionals who can give advice and assistance to help people on the road to recovery. There are also many things that people can do to help themselves recover and stay well. The important thing is finding the right treatment that works and a health professional with whom you feel comfortable.

The above excerpt from the beyondblue resource 'Depression and Anxiety: an information booklet', printed in January 2012, has been reproduced with the permission of beyondblue.

Beyondblue, the national depression and anxiety initiative, aims to raise awareness and understanding, and provide clear and comprehensive information about, depression, anxiety and related disorders, available treatments and where to get help. More information is available at the *beyondblue* website – www.beyondblue.org.au – or by calling the *beyondblue* info line on 1300 22 4636 or emailing infoline@beyondblue.org.au. You can call the info line for the cost of a local call from a landline or send an email.

National information, help and support lines

beyondblue	1300 22 4636
Lifeline	13 11 14
Suicide Call Back Service	1300 659 467
MensLine Australia	1300 78 99 78
Kids Helpline	1800 55 1800

About the Author

Matt Barwick was born and raised in Canberra and has worked for over a decade for the Australian government. He was motivated to share his unique story when he realised how few titles, from young, average Australian males, were available to help and inform those dealing with infertility, family suicide and mental illness diagnosis. Having lived through these experiences and written about them in his daily diary when his life started becoming memorable for all the wrong reasons, he shares his story from an emotive, less clinical, sufferer's perspective. Throughout his remarkable journey, he has constantly looked for positives and focused on what makes him most happy: music, surfing and the unconditional support and love of his wife and soul-mate, Ali.